The Global Educator

Leveraging Technology for Collaborative Learning & Teaching

Julie Lindsay

International Society for Technology in Education
EUGENE, OREGON • ARLINGTON, VA

The Global Educator

Leveraging Technology for Collaborative Learning & Teaching

Julie Lindsay

Editor: *Emily Reed*

Copy Editor: *Kristin Landon*

Proofreader: *Ann Skaugset*

Indexer: *Wendy Allex*

Book Design and Production: *Ryan Scheife*

Library of Congress Cataloging-in-Publication Data

Names: Lindsay, Julie, author.

Title: The global educator : leveraging technology for collaborative learning & teaching / Julie Lindsay.

Description: 1st ed. | Eugene, Oregon : International Society for Technology in Education, [2016] | Includes bibliographical references and index.

Identifiers: LCCN 2016007132 (print) | LCCN 2016014905 (ebook) | ISBN 9781564843722 (pbk.) | ISBN 9781564845740 (mobipocket) | ISBN 9781564845757 (epub) | ISBN 9781564845764 (pdf)

Subjects: LCSH: International education—Computer networks. | Group work in education—Computer networks. | Education and globalization. | Educational technology.

Classification: LCC LC1090 .L57 2016 (print) | LCC LC1090 (ebook) | DDC 370.116—dc23

LC record available at http://lccn.loc.gov/2016007132

First Edition

ISBN: 978-1-56484-372-2

Ebook version available.

Printed in the United States of America

ISTE® is a registered trademark of the International Society for Technology in Education.

ABOUT ISTE

The International Society for Technology in Education (ISTE) is the premier nonprofit organization serving educators and education leaders committed to empowering connected learners in a connected world. ISTE serves more than 100,000 education stakeholders throughout the world.

ISTE's innovative offerings include the ISTE Conference & Expo, one of the biggest, most comprehensive ed tech events in the world—as well as the widely adopted ISTE Standards for learning, teaching and leading in the digital age and a robust suite of professional learning resources, including webinars, online courses, consulting services for schools and districts, books, and peer reviewed journals and publications. Visit iste.org to learn more.

Also by Julie Lindsay

Flattening Classrooms, Engaging Minds: Move to Global Collaboration One Step at a Time, with Vicki A. Davis

Related ISTE Titles

Let's Get Social: The Educator's Guide to Edmodo, by Ginger Carlson & Raphael Raphael

Making Connections with Blogging, by Lisa Parisi & Brian Crosby

ABOUT THE AUTHOR

Julie Lindsay is a global collaboration consultant, teacherpreneur, innovator, leader and author. Originally from Melbourne, Australia, she worked in international schools for fifteen years as an educational technology leader across Asia, Africa and the Middle East. Her passion is for online global collaboration and with her unique approach to digital learning she designs and manages online projects for all K–12 levels and customizes learning experiences for educators including virtual courses and live events. She has presented keynotes and workshops at conferences around the world. Her first book, *Flattening Classrooms, Engaging Minds* was the first definitive text on how to embed global connections and collaborations for meaningful learning.

Julie is a Quality Learning and Teaching Leader (online) and Adjunct Lecturer at Charles Sturt University, Australia; Director of Learning Confluence Pty Ltd, Founder and CEO of Flat Connections. She is currently President of the ISTE Global Collaboration PLN, a former ISTE International Representative on the Board of Directors, and a member of the Horizon Report Advisory Board from 2008. Julie is recognized for her academic achievements, MA in Music (La Trobe University), MA in Education and Human Development specializing in Educational Technology Leadership (George Washington University) and is completing an EdD at the University of Southern Queensland with research focusing on online global collaborative educators' and pedagogical change.

Based back in Australia Julie lives in the idyllic seaside town of Ocean Shores, northern New South Wales. When not travelling she enjoys working virtually from home, walking the beach, and dabbling in her ongoing passion as a jazz pianist.

Find out more about Julie (http://flatconnections.com/about) and connect with Julie on Twitter (http://twitter.com/julielindsay). Read more about global education issues on her blog (www.julielindsay.net). Explore more resources to do with being a global educator on the website: http://theglobaleducator.net.

Acknowledgments

We wish to acknowledge the many global educators who willingly gave their time and shared stories and experiences to enrich this book. It is because of your ongoing efforts that this book is possible and through it you will now inspire even more educators and learners. A special thank you for all that you do everyday to connect learners and learning with the world.

Educators who contributed to this book, in alphabetical order:

Marzieh Abedi, Theresa Allen, Yvonne Marie Andres, Pedro Aparicio, Mike Bartlett, Chris Betcher, Sue Beveridge, Mali Bickley, Mulugeta Birhanu, Krista Brakhage, Madeleine Brookes, Eva Brown, Devon Caldwell, Corinne Campbell, Julie Carey, Adam Carter, Craig Chidgey, Andrew Churches, Rob Clarke, Kim Cofino, Kevin Cojanu, Katrina Conde, Roger Crider, Carly Damen, Sophie De La Paz, David Deeds, Wayne Demnar, Barbara Edwards, Jane Ellem, Michael Ellsworth, Matt Esterman, Holly Fairbrother, Brian Flannery, Anne Fox, Wesley Fryer, Michael Furdyk, Attilio Galimberti, Peggy George, Roland Gesthuizen, Terry Godwaldt, Michael Graffin, Ed Gragert, Jason Graham, Lucy Gray, Katie Grubb, Steve Hargadon,

Matt Harris, Danielle Hartman, Bonnie Hermawan, Suud Hibatullah, Maggie Hos-McGrane, Ruth Hou, Mike Hourahine, Lizzie Hudson, Adnan Iftekhar, Vicky Iglesias, Amy Jambor, Eunhee Jung, Craig Kemp, Emily Kibble, Tiina Korhonen, Jacqueline Liesch, Karen Lirenman, Rodd Lucier, Natasha Luxford, Janice Mak, Cameron Malcher, Marianne Malmstrom, Brian Mannix, Aaron Maurer, Simon May, Sharon McAdam, Emily McCarren, Barbara McFall, Matt McGuire, Brian McLaughlin, Ann Michaelsen, Felipe Mileo, Anne Mirtschin, Becky Morales, Vickie Morgado, Janice Newlin, Ben Newsome, Cindy Nickodam, Stefan Nielsen, Kate O'Connell, Judy O'Connell, Máire O'Keffe, Leah Obach, Toni Olivieri-Barton, Stephen Opanga, Mark Otter, Lisa Parisi, Cameron Paterson, Chuck Pawlick, Louisa Polos, Maria Ponce, Alan Preis, Edna Pythian, Amanda Rablin, Dane Ramshaw, Pernille Ripp, Kristina Rivers, Michael Roemer, Julio Rojas, Donna Román, Lara Ronalds, Ann Rooney, Emily Roth, Brett Salakas, Betsye Sargent, Larisa Schelkin, Tina Schmidt, Moliehi Sekese, Dianne Shapp, Mahmud Shihab, Parambir Singh Kathait, Marilyn Snider, Karen Stadler, Andrea Stringer, Robyn Thiessen, Silvia Tolisano, Nikki Turner, Jeff Utecht, Sonya van Schaijik, Katrina Viloria, Nancy Von Wahlde, Eric Walters, David Warlick, Tom Whitby, Jennifer Williams, Sheri Williams, Tracey Winey, Stephanie Wujcik, David Young, Perla Zamora, Jan Zanetis, Leigh Zeitz, Yong Zhao

CONTENTS

Contents

DEDICATION

*To John Lindsay for his tireless and unwavering support of my
global adventures and to Violet Rose Lindsay, my third culture
kid daughter, who understands what I do and why I do it.*

FOREWORD

I call myself a global educator. In fact I have proof! For over 30 years I worked in nine different schools in six countries across four continents and three education systems. Australia, Zambia, Kuwait, Bangladesh, Qatar, China—Australian system (in Victoria 1980s–1990s), British international curriculum, IGCSE, and also the International Baccalaureate PYP, MYP and DP. My husband is also an educator and together we have been able to craft these working, traveling and life experiences. At the end of 1997 we grabbed the opportunity to teach and travel as a couple, not realizing it would be almost 15 years before we came back to our home country, Australia, to live again. Our daughter having spent from the age of 3–18 across the five non-Australian countries grew up as a "third culture kid" attending school and gathering many global friends and experiences. As an adult third culture kid she now fluently connects with her global peers and many personal and family friends, with many of these connections being via Facebook.

> **Third culture kid** (TCK, 3CK) is a term used to refer to children who were raised in a culture outside of their parents' culture for a significant part of their development years.

There may be some tension between the terms "global" and "international". Although I have worked internationally does that really make me global in outlook and actions? There is some discussion about this in this book by other international educators. Alan, USA, now located in Shanghai tells us, "At one level, the terms "international educator" and "global educator" seem synonymous to me. Both are about a more worldwide view of education. At another level, though, perhaps "international" suggests familiarity with different countries and cultures, while "global" captures the idea of a broader, transcendent mindset. While "international" speaks to the understanding of different cultures, "global" evokes the idea of seeing these different cultures as part of a connected whole and of forging connections between them" (Alan Preis, @preis).

I believe my global approach and disposition started well before leaving Australia, even as far back as when I co-founded the Music Education and Technology Association in the early 1990s and supported global interaction through sharing student musical compositions; even in the mid 1990s when I signed up my school in Melbourne to the International Schools Cyberfair, at a time when we had no idea how to create web pages, and subsequently won an HM for our Environmental Awareness website; even when I attended the iEARN Conference in Melbourne in 1995 and became further intrigued and totally passionate about making global connections for my students. My curricular and extracurricular focus had already started to go beyond the immediate learning and usual set of learning resources and assessment modes. I had embraced a global outlook and curiosity about the world well before deciding to be an international educator.

The arrival of the internet in education supported and enhanced this need to look and connect beyond; we could now make real time connections and *see* for ourselves other lives, different landscapes and *hear* alternative sounds and opinions. Why would we *not* want to connect with the world when deeper understanding of the way it works is at our fingertips through telecommunications?

Today my work continues to be very globally focused and international as I travel to different parts of the world to work with schools, educators and students; design and deliver online global professional learning and global projects; and attend and run conferences and live events. I believe my disposition to learning and my intercultural understanding and empathy is global through the many and varied experiences I had before, during and around many global journeys, including my work in recent years with the innovative and unique THINK Global School. The reality is most people do not get this opportunity or do not want to work and travel at the same time across the world. Does that mean they can never be a global educator? No, it means they will never be an international educator but being a global educator can be seen as a behavior, an attitude, a disposition and a mindset. In fact international educators who are traveling and working across the world are sometimes not as global in their perspective or actions for learning as educators who remain in their home country. As global and international educator Maggie, UK, now located in India tells us, "Some international teachers tend to live in an expat bubble—a sort of hall of mirrors or echo chamber—and sadly many of them never take the opportunities to connect deeply with those in whose countries they are living" (Maggie Hos-McGrane, @mumbaimaggie).

So what is a global educator? Good question, and that is what this book aims to clarify. The role online technologies play in supporting global educators is a significant factor and an important focus of this book. It is through the use of emerging and established online technologies that global educators connect, communicate and collaborate. Enhanced learning experiences for all education leaders, educators and students—learners at all levels—are available every day in many ways. This book provides resources, real-life stories and case studies from educators, discussions about global learning and insights into how online technology supports a new learning paradigm—one that is global, ubiquitous and potentially very exciting for all learners.

Why Read This Book?

In the current world of online communication and social media that provides many of us with a multitude of ways to communicate the concept of a book seems juxtaposed with being a connected global educator and learner. However this book is a vital snapshot of a period in history when the world was shrinking and becoming more accessible; it is a collections of anecdotes, inspiring examples, methodologies for becoming global and implementing online global collaboration, and other vital resources to provide educators and education leaders new ideas and modes for connecting and collaborating with the world for meaningful learning.

This book is for ALL educators, at any level, in any country and across multiple digital learning environments. It features the "educator" in many iterations and locations. The stories shared are personal educator contributions, "warts and all". Some of the contributors are well known in the global collaboration education community, others are relatively unknown beyond a small network. Everyone in this book is important and all examples are relevant to helping us learn more about becoming a global educator. Apologies in advance to anyone or anything I may have left out that could or should have been included as a prime example or case study. I invite you to connect with me and consider contributing to the additional and ongoing online material being developed.

Along with this book, the companion ebook offers in-depth case studies from the contributors as well as links to resources and multimedia. It essentially brings the experience of global learning to life. As you learn from the contributors' stories you will have the opportunity to interact with them and form global connections of your own.

Learn more at **theglobaleducator.net**

#theglobaleducator

This work is independent of systems, although there is often reference via contributing educators to the education system they currently teach and/or lead within. It has been written with an underpinning philosophy of the need for a constructivist approach to learning and is presented very much from the educator and education leader perspective.

Introduction

The proposition of this book is that modern learning (or if you prefer, digital-age learning) has to be global for all learners, and therefore learning environments must be connected and "flat" to support this. The implication is a shift in pedagogy, a shift in mindset, and an essential purpose for the integration of digital and online technologies across the curriculum. In order to embrace global, connected, and flat learning, teachers, schools and leaders (and students!) are challenged to become connected and global through curriculum redesign and new approaches to digital learning infrastructure.

It is pertinent to mention here the work of David Warlick, who first told us, "Our classrooms are flat." David has been an inspiration to me for many years, and when I connected with him again while writing this book, he told me, "The idea [of the flat classroom] was initially a visual gimmick for provoking *shakabuku* [explained on his blog, 2¢ Worth, as "a swift, spiritual kick to the head that alters your reality forever]." David further related,

> Our notions of education continue to include a standing teacher, with knowledge to skillfully convey. We picture tall shelves of books, revered repositories of ageless ideas and ideals, and chalkboards, attached high on windowless walls, so that all seated students, trained to be open vessels, can passively accept an unquestioned education.

> It's easy. It works. Gravity drives the curriculum from high places to low places. But what use is gravity when reference books are replaced by information sources most children carry in their pockets? What use is gravity when students, in their adulthood, may need to relearn for new jobs every 4 1/2 years (Meister, 2012)? What use is gravity when children are more comfortable, knowledgeable, and literate than many of their teachers about technological innovations that are central to our society?

Classrooms are flat. How do we drive curriculum without gravity? What energy powers that learning engine?

A flat classroom recognizes that in a time of rapid change, learning becomes universal. It is no longer merely the result of instruction being imposed by trained teachers. Learning becomes the principal reason for being literate. What is learned can no longer be the prime objective of school. Learning, modeled by teachers, becomes the central essential skill developed and refined into a lifestyle by the school's graduates.

A flat classroom harnesses freely curious and self-directed learners, who are globally oriented to the future, with an intrinsic need to communicate and influence, and actively seeking to reconcile past with present, so that they can own their futures. In a flat classroom, learning becomes the energy that drives curriculum.

DAVID WARLICK, USA, @DWARLICK,
PERSONAL COMMUNICATION, FEBRUARY 4, 2015

The term "flat" has also been influenced by the writings of Tom Friedman in *The World Is Flat* (Friedman, 2007), where he discusses how digital technology has brought us closer together and we do not have to go "around" the world anymore; connections are flat; collaborations are flat. The original Flat Classroom Project of 2006 that I co-developed is described in this 2007 third edition of the book as "a learning initiative that brings the world to the classroom—flattens it!" (p. 502).

The aim of this book is to share ideas and practices to do with global connectivity and "flat" learning in order to encourage a deeper understanding of collaborative working modes so that these practices can be embedded into current curriculum objectives and beyond. The book content examines connected learning and learning communities; how teachers and leaders can foster networked professional development to support global objectives; online global learning opportunities; and managing change. It also includes pedagogical support for collaborative learning modes at all levels of education. Material in this book is narrative and includes many examples of global connections with a focus on curriculum design for successful collaborations for K–12 and above. Throughout, the voice of the educator is strong, while my voice weaves stories together and provides other pertinent material for consideration of new ideas and pedagogical approaches.

Some questions to consider before you read this book:

- What is global learning?
- What is a global education?
- What is a global educator?
- What is a global education leader?
- How is becoming global supported across the country? Across the world?
- What technology infrastructure is needed for global connections and collaborations?
- What are the best examples of educators and leaders who are implementing global learning for students?
- What is online global collaboration? How do you do it?
- Where can you get help to go global?

In the emerging learning landscape supported by online technologies, different modes of interacting and sharing provide a multitude of opportunities for educators, education leaders, and students. Learning has never been as fluid as now. A mobile device in conjunction with ubiquitous wireless network access literally means we can learn anywhere, anytime, from anyone. Not only is this fact a catalyst for true analysis and subsequent changes in what we perceive as necessary schooling, it ultimately means each individual can shape their learning pathway in such a unique way that no two learners need ever have exactly the same experience. It also means that those of us who do have technology access are now in the age of true "personalized lifelong learning."

It's time to connect the world for intercultural understanding, collaborations that lead to action, co-created curriculum outcomes, and global competency. The digital revolution has provided myriad opportunities that will continue to change schools and support learning connections and collaborations. Are teachers and school leaders ready to be connected and model best-practice global approaches? Are school communities able to go beyond the fear of using technology and embrace a balanced, learner-centered approach that will benefit all? Those who are will move forward and provide alternative approaches to learning while encouraging global attitudes, understandings, and competencies. These alternatives must include flat, connected learning modes.

Who is doing this? How? What can we learn from them? How do we navigate these new waters of networked learning that takes the local to global? What model can be developed for technology-infused, globally connected learning that will support classroom teachers, education leaders, and higher education? This book shares numerous current global examples of educators who are already taking those first steps, as well as examples of those who are now running ahead.

Why is "going global" an important objective? My response is that learning does not and should not happen in isolation. One teacher with 25 students is an outdated model that is limited in concept and practice. Technology allows for teachers, students, parents, experts, and other knowledgeable people and resources to join the learning community virtually when needed—both locally and globally. Growth can be exponential, especially with enlightened leadership modes in place. Communities can and should be planning professional learning opportunities in order to flatten the experience of learning for all. There is more discussion about this throughout the book.

Getting Started

This book is presented in four parts:

Part One: The Global Educator

Part Two: Leadership for Global Education

Part Three: Online Global Collaboration

Part Four: Take Learning Global

The logic of this progression is that we explore distinct global educators, their attributes, and their activities first. We then explore global education leaders and emerging pedagogy. This leads to online global collaboration as a curriculum priority, including how to design and implement collaborations, once again with lots of rich examples. The final part explores pathways to becoming global, including where to find inspiration, partnerships, and professional learning.

Each part features examples of global learning and education from educators and organizations around the world. For further reading and to connect with these resources, I have indicated where related case studies can be found in the ebook.

Part One

The Global Educator

P art One of this book looks specifically at "the global educator." In Chapter 1 the characteristics of a global educator are defined, including attributes and associated activities. In Chapter 2 the technologies used are explored, and global connected learning is described. Chapter 3 extends the material in Chapter 1 to take a deeper look at global connected learning, while Chapter 4 explores the impact on learning of going global as well as challenges and enablers to becoming global. Authentic examples from global educators and their classrooms are shared in the ebook to further support understanding. The focus throughout this section of the book is on educators, in terms of what they do and how they do it as they push the boundaries of learning while being digital, online, and global.

Attributes of a Global Educator

How do we define the global educator? Is it a qualification? Is it a self-declaration? Can it be proven through disposition, curriculum design, workflow, pedagogical approach, use of digital technology, or an ability to adapt and be flexible in learning? Is it all of these? As soon as the word "global" is used, we need to think about "global competency"—are educators ready themselves to prepare students for adopting understandings that are global? Consider the concept of "international mindedness," a pillar of International Baccalaureate (IB) programs where multilingualism, intercultural understanding, and global engagement are key qualities—are these prerequisites for embarking on global education? Are they in fact essential qualities of a global educator?

As a brief diversion at this point, I draw your attention to the research done by the Western Academy of Beijing (WAB), a K–12 IB World School. As part of an accreditation process, they surveyed, discussed, and workshopped the term "international mindedness" in order to try and come up with an inclusive definition. There were many nuances of understanding through this experience, and participants were challenged to come up with one definition that could support the school as a community to understand and apply to teaching and learning. Part of what they created is classroom indicators of application, including the following.

Teachers and students will . . .

1. Take action as responsible global citizens
2. Demonstrate sensitivity to multiple cultural perspectives
3. Be open to change their ideas about cultures when presented with new information or experiences

4. Demonstrate behaviors that focus on ways in which people are similar rather than different
5. Develop deep knowledge of other cultural groups
6. Use learning resources that are culturally diverse
7. Engage in external intercultural engagement activities

So, coming back to the focus of this chapter, how does an educator start to think and act globally? In today's digitally rich world, being a global educator means adopting practices that include technology-infused and networked workflow habits to connect learners with the world and connect learning approaches from local to global. Table 1.1 shares a summary of the attributes or characteristics of a global educator (LH column) and what activities align with them (RH column).

Table 1.1: The Attributes of a Global Educator

ATTRIBUTES	ACTIVITIES
You know you are a global educator when you...	**A global educator...**
connect and share	• makes connections for themselves and others and is able to leverage these connections when needed
	• has an understanding of "connectivism" and networked learning
	• connects the past, present, and future
	• uses social media to connect and collaborate
	• builds a viable personal learning network
	• finds and joins purposeful professional learning communities
	• establishes a strong global personal brand
	• contributes online globally daily as part of established workflow
	• is willing to share, mentor, lead, and be led as part of the learning landscape

(continued on next page)

Table 1.1: The Attributes of a Global Educator *(continued)*

ATTRIBUTES	ACTIVITIES
You know you are a global educator when you...	**A global educator...**
"flatten" the learning	• learns about the world, with the world • understands learning in a digital world means working with others at a distance and online • adopts new pedagogies for "flat" learning • understands how the learning space walls are brought down or "flattened" to bring the world in • is able to sustain connections and collaborations • is fluent in three essential actions to flatten learning: connection, citizenship, collaboration

encourage and model global citizenship	• fosters global competency through global context
	• has empathy learning with other cultures and by doing so:
	  • is comfortable learning with and from others in other parts of the world, and aims to get to know learning partners virtually
	  • is confident working with other cultures
	  • is someone who understands varied perspectives, and empathizes with others in an effort to resolve global issues
	  • is adept at encouraging empathy that leads to positive action through global connections
	• adopts and encourages multiple perspectives
	• is knowledgeable about current events to stimulate authentic communication, shared understanding, and appreciation of different perspectives

ATTRIBUTES	ACTIVITIES
You know you are a global educator when you...	**A global educator...**

collaborate anywhere, anytime	• collaborates with anyone, anywhere, anytime, in any way possible
	• understands the degrees of global collaboration as distinct from cooperation for deep learning
	• is adept at teacher-sourcing
	• builds online global communities to:
	  • create an interconnectedness of communities
	  • address values of equity, social justice, and sustainability
	  • foster relationships for learning
	• knows how to learn synchronously and asynchronously

use online technologies	• is able to use both synchronous and asynchronous online technologies to bring learners together • knows how to use Web 2.0 to publish global experiences • is digitally fluent across devices and software • encourages student interaction and collaboration that leads to action
design futuristic learning environments to connect with the world	• is able to design learning in order to develop students' global competencies • is conversant with design thinking • understands the importance of collaboration as a global learning objective and important practice

Let's look at the characteristics of a global educator more closely with contributions gathered from many global educators across the world based largely on their practices. The following sections unpack each attribute and characterize what good global educators do.

Global Educators Connect and Share

Connected learning is the ability to connect, communicate, and collaborate with educators and students in all and any parts of the world using common online tools. Connected learning includes pathways and frameworks for communication, inter-generation, location, and information. A digital-age educator or modern learner is connected, communicates in a reliable and responsible way, and "flattens" the walls of their classroom in appropriate ways to enhance the educational learning experience of all by using internet-driven media. Therefore, every topic, every unit of work, every opportunity needs to be reviewed in terms of how it can be made relevant through external contact and collaboration with peers and co-learners—through connecting with authentic sources of information in order to build new knowledge.

In a highly connected and information-rich world it may seem odd that we need to examine what being connected is and what it means to develop connected learning modes in a global context. Being connected through the use of digital technology does not automatically mean you are a connected learner. We are still at the brink of discovering and utilizing true connected learning habits and strategies in education. Using certain tools, being somewhat fluent with social media, integrating blogging into the curriculum—these are all parts of being connected, but they do not in themselves provide the infrastructure and essential learning pathways for connected learning.

"Working with educators and education stakeholders outside of my immediate community is a part of my regular week. We may co-teach, share ideas and resources or work together on professional development" (Leah Obach, Canada, @Leah077).

To hear more about collaborative global learning from Leah's experience, see Case Study 3.3 in the ebook.

Connectivism

Through the use of new technology tools, connected learning focuses on the building of networks and the development of personal learning resources through interaction with personal learning networks and professional learning communities (Siemens, 2005). The social nature of learning and in fact the development of a "Community of Practice" or CoP, (a group of people who share a craft and/or a profession) is also part of what is recognized as connected learning (Wenger, 2000).

A **Community of Practice (CoP)** is a group of people who share a concern or a passion for something they do, and learn how to do it better as they interact regularly. This definition reflects the fundamentally social nature of human learning.

"**Connectivism**…. describes a form of knowledge and a pedagogy based on the idea that knowledge is distributed across a network of connections and that learning consists of the ability to construct and traverse those networks" (Downes, 2008, p. 2).

Connected learning is influenced by the need for pedagogies that are more personal, social, and participatory, with special reference to Web 2.0 tools (McLoughlin & Lee, 2010), and provides infrastructure for global collaboration as a pedagogical approach that includes the use of technology. It relates to and is heavily influenced by connectivism theory (Downes, 2005, 2006; Siemens, 2005, 2006). Connectivism is often described as the learning theory for the digital age and is based on the use of networks and nodes to create connections and develop a personal learning network. This therefore implies diverse, autonomous, open, and connected networking (Downes, 2008) that informs community building as a prerequisite to learning; collaboration that leads to co-creation with other learners who are not in the same time and space; and pedagogical independence and leadership within a school/institution. According to Siemens (2005), connectivism principles include that learning and knowledge are contextual and new information is constantly being acquired that users prioritize to feed into decision-making, and also where the end user constructs knowledge through contribution and involvement within the network (Siemens, 2006).

Establish and Develop PLNs and PLCs

A global educator knows that connected learning is about not working in isolation, but learning with and from others. It is through networking and interacting with others that a personal learning network (PLN) can be established. Online communication is the key to PLN proliferation, with tools such as Twitter, Facebook, and other social and educational networks providing a means for frequent and meaningful exchanges. A PLN needs to be nurtured over months and years. Understanding what a PLN is and does ensures quick growth. In fact, it can become exponential, depending on the tools being used and the user's ability to respond and share online. Each learner, with the use of online tools, is responsible for developing

A **personal learning network (PLN)** is an informal **learning network** that consists of the people a learner interacts with and derives knowledge from in a **personal learning** environment (Wikipedia).

their own personal connection strategy that includes building a viable PLN. This goes beyond the immediate and usual school and work interactions. A strong PLN can provide uncountable resources and support across cultures, across countries, and across generations.

In addition to a PLN, learners can find and join purposeful learning communities. These learning communities, often called professional learning communities (PLCs), are made up of collections of people often already in the learner's PLN who come together for a purpose. This purpose may be ongoing, such as the "iPads in education users group," or may be for a short period of time, such as a professional development course, a 10th grade History class, or a conference or event. These PLCs are important, because they provide access to ideas and resources that go beyond what we have traditionally considered authentic and viable learning modes and tools (such as books, articles, lectures, videos, or face-to-face discussions) to include webinars, tweetchats, TeachMeets, and more.

"Becoming a globally connected educator has been the best professional development of my career—and the fact that my learning can happen anytime anyplace also makes it the most flexible and relevant to me. No matter how much time I have available to spend online on any given day, being connected means I am always learning something new, relevant and engaging—just for me, thanks to my Personal Learning Network!" (Kim Cofino, Thailand, @mscofino)

Read more about Kim's global journey in Case Study 1.2.

In order to function, a PLC builds trust among its members and is usually quick to self-moderate and filter what is not appropriate or necessary. A PLC extends the boundaries of learning beyond the immediate circle of interest and encourages involvement from the wider community through online practices including tweeting, discussions, blogging and sharing multimedia. The sociability of online learning and PLC development is what builds a strong and viable learning community both locally and globally.

> A **professional learning community (PLC)** is an extended **learning** opportunity to foster collaborative **learning** among colleagues within a particular work environment or field. It is often used in schools as a way to organize teachers into working groups (Wikipedia).

Degrees of Connectedness

In an attempt to make sense of the wide range of relationships educators are building with online colleagues, Rodd Lucier, Canada, @thecleversheep created an interesting and relevant framework introducing the concept of a PLN, "Seven Degrees of Connectedness." What is relevant here is that this is not a taxonomy—there is no ideal place to be at any point in time—and as a global and connected educator each stage will be relevant. As Rodd states, "The thing is—I see myself in different stages with different people and groups. I'm wondering, where you see yourself in the different relationships you've developed? Each stage of connectedness has impacted my learning in different ways. Have you had similar experiences? Explicit actions lead from one stage to another, but maybe the stages are not sequential" (Lucier, 2012).

Silvia Tolisano, USA, @langwitches created an infographic to support this that clearly outlines the seven degrees or stages of being a connected learner (Tolisano, 2012a):

Stage 1—Lurker

Stage 5—Collaborator

Stage 2—Novice

Stage 6—Friend

Stage 3—Insider

Stage 7—Confidant

Stage 4—Colleague

For descriptions of each of the stages and to see the infographic (Tolisano, 2012b), visit http://tinyurl.com/jv4cp6c.

Use Social Media and Personal Branding

Social media—or, a better description for our purposes, "educational media"—is the bridge to connected learning and to building those vibrant relationships with others that are so important to supporting new online and global learning modes. To be a global educator, you must use appropriate social media and be accessible. There is nothing more frustrating today than not being able to connect with someone online.

Despite all the tools and methods available, many educators often fail to understand the difference between having privacy and cutting themselves off from the world. Yes, we all want privacy, and the degree to which we achieve this is a personal choice—but a global educator does not close the door on social media. Essential tools include Twitter, LinkedIn, Slideshare, YouTube, Diigo, Google+, and, even more often now, Facebook. There are also networked communities that gather like-minded educators together, such as the Global Education Conference network (read more about this conference in the case study ebook).

Social media is the collective of online communications channels dedicated to community-based input, interaction, content sharing, and collaboration. Websites and applications dedicated to forums, microblogging, social networking, social bookmarking, social curation, and wikis are among the different types of social media (Whatis.com, http://whatis.techtarget.com/definition/social-media).

As a professional educator, you are under no compulsion to share any of your private life online. However, there is a compulsion for you to share your professional thoughts and activities. Some, or a lot, or all—it is your choice once again. It is also polite and forward-thinking to make sure people can contact you and, more importantly, interact with you. Although you may not want direct email contact, consider being accessible via a comment on your blog, or via a Twitter interaction, or via an online form for others to ask for further contact details. All of these approaches you can control and filter according to your preference.

In terms of personal branding (or you may prefer, as I do, to think of it as "professional branding"), a global educator thoughtfully crafts an online presence that represents the global and connected learning that is taking place. Images, tweets, blog posts, online portfolio material, and interactions with others combine to be part of the "brand of me" in an online and global context.

Personal branding is the practice of people marketing themselves and their careers as brands. Whereas previous self-help management techniques were about self-improvement, the personal-branding concept suggests instead that success comes from self-packaging (Wikipedia).

Be a Contributor and a Sharer

A global educator understands that sharing online is not an addition to the work of being an educator—it *is* the work! The development and extension of a global PLN and PLCs means it is obviously impossible and just downright ridiculous to contribute to every network and every online space all the time—both physically and emotionally. The 1% rule, also called the 90-9-1 principle, of internet culture tells us that in a collaborative learning environment 90% view or lurk, 9% edit content, and 1% actively create new content (Arthur, 2006). Regardless of these statistics, it is essential that, as a global educator, your workflow allows you to contribute some-where every day. This could be through sharing a resource, blogging about an activity or event, starting a discussion, commenting on a discussion or other online contribution, uploading multimedia, "liking," and sharing forward; through social bookmarking, curating resources, or through other social media to announce and respond such as Twitter.

"Sharing new learning is my main way to continue to be 'global'" (Rob Clarke, New Zealand, @robclarke).

According to Brown (1999), the essence of social learning and lifelong learning—a web-enabled learning ecology—is a shift from using technology to support the individual to using technology to support relationships. Our students are networking like this in their social lives with Facebook and other tools. They reach out across the world already; therefore, the expectation is that their classrooms (real and virtual) will allow and encourage the same practices. Develop a culture of sharing for both you and your students that paints a picture of learning and aligns with the sociability of learning being experienced by contributing users of social media.

A global contributor works hard at keeping posts, messages, and announcements as culturally neutral as possible unless they are specifically about a local commu-nity. A global contributor does not alienate their audience by using language that is colloquial or by using terms and references pertinent to a local situation without further explanation and sharing of hyperlinks to provide a global context. He/she is also willing to share, mentor, lead, and be led as part of the emerging global learning landscape.

Pay it Forward

The goal of being a global connected learner is not to merely gather information, but to respond and share it forward *and* to create personal information and artifacts for others to gather and respond to.

Global Educators "Flatten" the Learning

"Flat" and connected learning is a multimodal approach to learning with and from others in a global capacity. There is no hierarchy of learning as such, because all voices are equal, and there is no one dominant group delivering the information to another group. All learners, through access to online technologies including the use of Web 2.0 and, more often now, mobile computing, develop an external network, bring the world into their everyday teaching and learning, and learn about the world, with the world. It has distinct parallels with Warlick's "flat classroom" (see Introduction) where "learning becomes the energy that drives curriculum." More importantly, flat learning is about being able to work with others at a distance as well as in person. This much-needed modern learning skill hones in on effective connection, communication, and collaboration so that ideas can grow and bridges can be built for us all to walk over to reach new pathways of knowledge construction.

Web 2.0 is the second stage of development of the World Wide Web, characterized especially by the change from static web pages to dynamic or user-generated content and the growth of social media for people to collaborate and share information online.

Flat Learning Pedagogy

Flat learning is part of a pedagogical approach enabled by online technologies and has parallels with connected learning, but in many ways it goes beyond just connecting. It is about global citizenship, and it is about breaking through stereotypes to accept others as equal learning partners. Flat learning can change the world as we know it—both locally and globally. More importantly flat learning dictates active rather than passive learning, as it assumes a responsibility on the part of the learner to connect through their PLN and PLC networks and to understand the consequences of those connections (cultural, social, political). It assumes that a responsible, active learner will be a reliable contributor and collaborator and give to others as well as receive. Student-centered and personalized learning is a natural outcome of flat learning.

"Developing partnerships across the world develops deeper learning. Textbook questions are the quick learning, but the process of global collaboration promotes deeper learning. Inspirational!" (Terry Godwaldt, Canada, @tgodwaldt)

Flat learning means partnerships and new global learning opportunities are a lot closer through the use of emerging technologies than before the world was flattened. Figure 1.1 shows "Flat, Connected Learning" as a superset of other approaches to learning—in other words, you cannot implement "blended" or "flipped" learning, for example, without being flat and connected! The pillars that make this work are Web 2.0, learning design, leadership, and new approaches to pedagogy.

Flat connected learning is part of a pedagogical approach enabled by online technologies and has parallels with connected learning, but in many ways it goes beyond just connecting. It uses digital technologies to forge connections and support everyday workflow, communication, and collaboration.

Actions to Flatten the Learning

A global educator understands that contained learning environments, closed learning management systems, and text-book based curricula do not support the goal of "flat" learning. Learning in a digital world is personalized and uses Web 2.0 and social media tools to connect, communicate, collaborate, and co-create. Student agency and autonomy through digital literacy and knowledge management can make the teacher irrelevant to learning in a global context. However, an astute global educator understands this and uses multiple opportunities to connect themselves and their students to the world. An astute global educator is not the barrier to learning but becomes the bridge to many and varied global journeys such that flat learning becomes the norm and "unflat" learning stifling and constrictive.

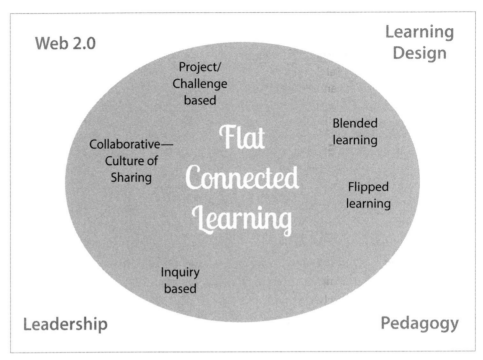

Figure 1.1: Flat Connected Learning (Julie Lindsay, 2014)

Pay it Forward

For the global educator flat connected learning means bringing the world into the learning space and putting you and your students out to the world for meaningful collaborations, co-creations, and knowledge sharing.

"For me [connected learning] means to open my classroom to the world—bringing down the walls—and look back into other classrooms as well. It means to collaborate with anyone, anywhere, anytime, in any way possible!" (Stefan Nielsen, Denmark)

There are *three* essential actions to flatten the learning:

1. Connect the learning
2. Build global citizenship practices
3. Collaborate for shared outcomes and solutions

Pay it Forward

An astute global educator is not the barrier to learning but becomes the bridge to many and varied global journeys such that flat learning becomes the norm and "unflat" learning stifling and constrictive.

Global Educators Encourage and Model Global Citizenship

Much discussion has taken place regarding the terminology of digital citizenship and global digital citizenship. To cut a long story short, the suggested way forward is to discuss "global citizenship" as an all-encompassing attribute that includes global competencies, empathy with other cultures, and knowledge of historical as well as current events while assuming that digital literacies will be the bridge to these attributes. Global citizenship is about conversations, connections, and sharing that will help students (and teachers) develop global competency. Why do we want to develop globally competent students and adults? Global competition for jobs means that today's students must not only be well-educated, creative problem solvers but they must also be equipped to collaborate globally and work with others at a distance as active "socialpreneurs" or "social entrepreneurs."

Social entrepreneurs are individuals with innovative solutions to society's most pressing social problems. They are ambitious and persistent, tackling major social issues and offering new ideas for wide-scale change (www.ashoka.org/social_entrepreneur).

Global educators are better able to empower digital/global citizenship and help students form educated opinions and behaviors for online learning when they are informed and confident with the technologies themselves. This involves monitoring and modeling online collaboration to foster engaged learning that is both safe and legal. Ann, Australia, @AnnRooney6 states, "Global digital collaboration goes beyond research. We found out more through the learning experience of meeting and sharing knowledge" (Rooney, 2014). Do not wait for students to "learn" about digital citizenship before jumping into a global collaboration. It is through the hands-on digital experience, as Rooney tells us, that students learn.

"It's important for us to teach our students about being responsible digital citizens. That they respect the creative talents of others and that they use or modify only those media for which there are creative commons rights" (Maggie Hos-McGrane, India, @mumbaimaggie)

Foster Global Competency through Global Context

Context is king when discussing global competence and citizenship. All learners need to be aware of safety, privacy, and legal issues to do with connecting online. They also need to be aware of and develop technical, social, cultural, and global awareness.

A global educator is familiar with current thinking and models for approaching global citizenship for both local and online globally collaborative experiences. These models can be freely shared with global partners and discussed with students and teachers across the project or collaboration in order to come to a common agreement about online behavior, habits, attitudes, and actions.

In his book *Digital Citizenship in Schools: Nine Elements All Students Should Know* (2015), Mike Ribble shares the "Nine Elements of Digital Citizenship." These include "digital access," "digital literacy," "digital etiquette," and "digital rights and responsibilities." Ribble believes young people's ability to practice digital citizenship ought to include their developing awareness of social and political issues as well as their online participation in public life.

Digital citizenship in a global context is a focus of the "Enlightened Digital Citizenship Model" created by Lindsay and Davis (2012). As shown in Figure 1.2, enlightened digital citizenship provides lenses for being better global citizens through "areas of awareness," including:

Individual awareness, which means being aware of one's values and goals and having the self-confidence to advocate for oneself online and speak out when issues arise.

Social awareness that allows the digital citizen to interpret situations and retain interpersonal skills with face-to-face and online friends and colleagues. Social awareness helps a person understand the norms of

Learn more about the Nine Elements of Digital Citizenship: **Digital Citizenship in Schools: Nine Elements All Students Should Know**, (Ribble, 2015) **http://digitalcitizenship.net/.** (Mike Ribble, USA, @digcitizen)

behavior in social and vocational spaces. This must apply to learners and technology users of all ages, cultures, genders, and situations.

Cultural awareness, which means being aware that cultural differences exist and being able to understand deeply the nuances of cultural differences, is a vital awareness for effective online collaboration and citizenship. It means understanding that the world is diverse and that other cultures have different religions, holidays, and school practices—and that it is important to find commonalities rather than always focus on differences.

Global awareness is understanding the regional nuances of other places in the world and causes the digital citizen to ask such questions as: What are the impacts of technology use and access in other countries and cultures? How can I connect and communicate with someone on the other side of the world? Understanding geography, politics, and local bandwidth concerns and the fact that one should understand these areas leads to a global awareness that makes one an effective digital citizen.

Sonya, New Zealand, @vanschaijik analyzes these areas of awareness, taking them to the next level, and concludes, "I think the term lends itself better to just being citizenship—to ask how do we act with others in ways that enhance the common good online and offline? Yes the technologies certainly make our task of collaboration transparent and easier to coordinate but ultimately it is about people. It is about building relationships for the common good and we do this by making connections online and offline and in the between" (Van Schaijik, 2014a).

In the National Youth Paper on Global Citizenship (TakingITGlobal, 2015), produced in partnership between the Centre for Global Citizenship Education, The Centre for Global Education and TakingITGlobal, and a "town hall" virtual coming together of young people across Canada, a statement about the importance of global citizenship education in transforming schools locally and globally includes, "To become global citizens we must empower youth by facilitating explorations into various perspectives and encourage collaboration with global entities" and "Discussions amongst

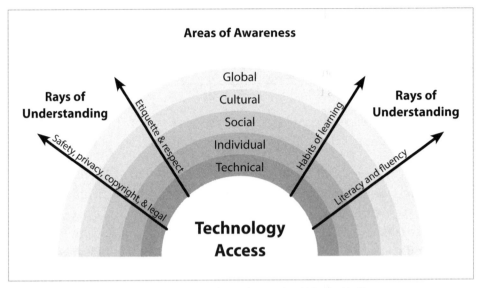

Areas of Awareness

Rays of Understanding

Rays of Understanding

Global

Cultural

Social

Individual

Technical

Etiquette & respect

Safety, privacy, copyright & legal

Habits of learning

Literacy and fluency

Technology Access

Figure 1.2: Enlightened Digital Citizenship (Julie Lindsay and Vicki Davis, 2012)

Global Digital Citizen Foundation **http://globaldigitalcitizen.org/**

youth of different cultures should be facilitated; technology can be used for youths in varying geographic areas to communicate with each other, thereby connecting the global community."

The "global digital citizen" model from the Global Digital Citizen Foundation (2015), developed by Lee Crockett and Andrew Churches, includes the tenets personal responsibility, global citizenship, digital citizenship, altruistic service and environmental stewardship. Global citizenship encourages people to understand we are no longer isolated, we are all global citizens and technology has eliminated many of the boundaries by enabling communication, collaboration and dialogue. Digital citizenship focuses on going beyond the acceptable use policy and shifting accountability for appropriate behaviors in an online world to the student thereby fostering independence and personal responsibility.

Global Citizenship Construct

Flat learning supports global citizenship and global competency because it allows students to frame an understanding of the world through connected experiences that go beyond the textbook and beyond the limitations of face-to-face interactions, whether local or global. A refreshed model of global digital citizenship is suggested here that integrates ideas and influences from many of the resources shared already. The Global Citizenship Construct (shown in Figure 1.3), already assumes the use of digital/online technologies to support global connections and flat learning. Therefore all global (and digital) citizens have awareness of and accountability for "Individual", "Social" and "Cultural" attitudes and behaviors while connecting online.

Individual: purposefully relate to the world as an independent learner, personal branding and ethical use of online technologies

Social: sociability of online learning within parameters that are legal and safe, and use of social technologies to connect, communicate, collaborate, co-design and co-create

Cultural: positive attitudes and adaptive habits for learning with others from beyond, understanding of differences and similarities to find commonalities

Global Citizenship Construct = 'Individual + Social + Cultural' when 'Global' = GISC

This is a refreshed model of global digital citizenship that encourages individual, social and cultural framing of the world through connected and global learning.

The model becomes powerful when all three areas of the construct, individual, social, and cultural, overlap to form "Individual + Social + Cultural" when "Global" = GISC. This is when the learner (educator, or student) becomes able to connect and learn comfortably and confidently with others, anywhere.

Have Empathy Learning with Other Cultures

A global educator is comfortable learning with and from others in other parts of the world, and knows them well virtually. It is important to be open-minded and understand varied perspectives, and empathize with others in an effort to resolve global issues. Global educators are adept at encouraging empathy and are able to adopt and encourage multiple perspectives that lead to positive action through global connections.

Figure 1.3: Global Citizenship Construct

 "Around the world, our geopolitical and intercultural misunderstandings are profound and we are often inept at understanding other people's perspectives. Educating for global citizenship has become a pressing need and empathy may well be the key skill for the 21st century" (Cameron Paterson, Australia, @cpaterso).

Chris, from Australia, shared that while working on one particular global project with a group of students, they developed strong working relationships that required lots of patience and understanding to deal with the cultural nuances. "My students remarked that one of the most important skills they learned was how to "disagree without being disagreeable." That idea of respecting the viewpoints of others, trying to understand their perspectives, see the world from a different angle, is price-less" (Chris Betcher, @chrisbetcher). Stephanie, from the USA, @StephWuj45, has the goal of inspiring and training students to engage in their world as informed, empathetic global citizens. To do this, her students must understand the value and necessity of multiple perspectives and learn to analyze the predispositions within these perspectives. As a result, Stephanie shares that students learn to realize that a firm grasp of varied perspectives leads to a stronger understanding of one's identity and a better comprehension of our changing world.

The Australian National Curriculum "Intercultural Understanding" capability suggests that students learn more about their own culture and the variable nature of culture (languages, beliefs, customs) and thereby develop intercultural understanding. As stated in the curriculum's introduction, "The capability involves students in learning about and engaging with diverse cultures in ways that recognise commonalities and differences, create connections with others and cultivate mutual respect" and "Intercultural understanding is an essential part of living with others in the diverse world of the twenty first century. It assists young people to become responsible local and global citizens, equipped through their education for living and working together in an interconnected world." The curriculum framework includes these three organizing elements:

1. Recognizing culture and developing respect
2. Interacting and empathizing with others
3. Reflecting on intercultural experiences and taking responsibility

Read more about the Australian National Curriculum and "intercultural understanding"

**www.australiancurriculum.edu.au/generalcapabilities/intercultural
-understanding/introduction/introduction**

After 12 years working outside the USA, David is finally mastering the practice he calls the "Here-There Check." When he has something that needs to be taken care of, such as technical problem, there are different ways to handle this compared to the "home" country, and little things make a big difference. He tells us, "In Latin America, for instance, you don't just walk up to a technician and say "My computer's broken!" No, you exchange greetings, including shaking hands . . . and then say that! 30 seconds . . . the definition between failure and success regarding work relationships" (David Deeds, China, @dwdeeds).

Pay it Forward

A global educator knows how to foster intercultural learning experiences that go beyond merely "connecting and waving" across the world. Making connections for deeper discussions and co-creations is vital in order to fully address the directive for intercultural understanding in an ever-changing world.

Know about Global Current Events

A global educator knows how to find different perspectives on current events, often through direct contact and communication with global partners (flat learning once again!). The ability to curate information is a vital skill here and is the key to knowing and sharing current events. Stephanie, USA, regularly mines news sources and saves compelling articles or resources in Evernote folders because she believes, "global education necessitates a firm grasp of contemporary issues, stemming from self-education and civic engagement. My global ed course is constantly in flux as a result of changing resources, but this practice makes the course incredibly relevant and dynamic" (Stephanie Wujcik, @StephWuj45). Sophie, also from the USA, reads local and international news sources in the classroom, examining issues in specific countries and how these affect others around the world. She says, "We teach our students to look at the situation through multiple perspectives and have them play devil's advocate—often seeking to understand the actions of others and work collaboratively with people around the world to gain a deeper understanding of what we are doing. For example, when we read *I Am Malala* we connected with a school in Pakistan to get their point of view on Malala's story. We discovered that in Pakistan the general consensus about Malala and her family are far different from ours in the US. It was very eye opening for our students" (Sophie De La Paz, @gpsteach).

Global Educators Collaborate Anywhere, Anytime

A global educator is able to collaborate with anyone, anywhere, anytime, in any way possible. Don't forget: the room is the school is the community is the country is the world. It's that simple! Once learning is connected, the walls do come down and learning becomes flat. The hierarchy of learning is flattened, and the flow of information and creation of knowledge is changed so that in effect Weinberger (2011) is correct when he says, "the smartest person in the room is the room." The "room" (school, ….world) becomes the smartest as learners work together, collaborate together, and create new meaning together. "Global" in this context is defined as being beyond your own walls—it could be the teacher with a class up the street, across town, the next state, or another country. The strategies and understandings for collaboration remain the same. The reality is that new connections you make are not the same people as you or those you meet in person each day, and most likely not in the same time zone as you, and most likely of a different culture than you—therefore the opportunity is open for enhanced cultural and global understanding.

Build Online Global Communities

A global educator knows how to build global communities using online technologies and is able to create an interconnectedness of these communities to establish new relationships for learning. An important feature of this is understanding how to learn both synchronously and asynchronously in a blended mode. Blended learning is an evolving pedagogy that includes some face-to-face and some virtual learning. In a global context it means establishing a workflow that is observant of time zone differences and includes developed asynchronous online learning skills to foster communication to support ongoing collaboration.

Blended learning is a formal education program in which a student learns at least in part through delivery of content and instruction via digital and online media with some element of student control over time, place, path, or pace.

At the classroom level Theresa, technology integration teacher from the USA, supports students in preschool through eigth grade to be immersed in some type of global connection or project. "Whether it's a quick mystery Skype or trimester-long project, students learn the basics of how to communicate virtually" (Theresa Allen, @tdallen5). One example, the Flat Connections Global Project for high school students, supports blended learning through synchronous online meetings for teachers and student leaders as well as online asynchronous spaces for interacting, sharing, and co-creating.

Global Educators Use Online Technologies

The global educator has a level of digital fluency that affords essential connections, communications, and collaborations for themselves and their students. They know how to manage different learning platforms. They understand the difference between a more restrictive school or institution learning management system (LMS) and other, usually Web 2.0, tools that provide freedom to interact and exchange with learners beyond their everyday experience. They are willing to experiment and try new tools and work hard to gain access to educational learning experiences that may need unblocking. There is a lot more to be said here, but case studies and further sections of this book will support this extreme need for fluency and innovation with online tools.

Use Web 2.0 to Publish Global Experiences

Global educators know that online publishing (a form of sharing) using Web 2.0 tools is essential in order to connect with peers and experts across the globe. Invisibility is a serious condition that cuts short communication and causes global confusion. It is important for learners to share their work (some of it, at least) in public spaces in order to seek feedback from the global community and in order to fully collaborate and co-create new products. Remember the term "public" of course can refer to visibility to members of a particular collaboration or community and does not necessarily mean open to the world. Global learners decide the level of access to their work and, after consultation with learning partners, to their students' work.

Global Educators Design Futuristic Learning Environments to Connect with the World

The global educator understands that the future of learning is not textbook driven, it is learner driven. Although this is a conceptual shift for many educators, it is an important shift that needs to be made in order to become a global educator. As digital technologies become even more ubiquitous, it is the power of people and of relationships that will influence the changes we want to see in education for the future. At all levels, educators are rethinking and redesigning learning to accommodate connected and collaborative modes.

In Egypt, Adam, an international teacher from the USA, created an entire class at his international school called "CONNECT." This is a multidisciplinary team-taught course for a mixed-grade (6–8) class. The focus is on instilling global citizenship and using all sorts of service learning activities, global collaboration tools, and multi-media content to help educate students about the issues and let them find their voice in making a difference and inspiring them to seek solutions. Adam tells us, "Mind. Heart. Action. This is the mantra of our new CONNECT class. Use your Mind to understand the issue and seek solutions. Follow your Heart to empathize with those in need and then take Action to create a positive change" (Adam Carter, @SocialActionCol).

In the USA, Janice, a teacher educator, connected her pre-service students to Flat Connections global projects in a number of ways, such as having them become "Expert Advisors" for a high school project in order to influence and support students as they research and develop original content and responses to issues and trends in emerging technology. "At the end of the semester, the students are assigned the task of developing their own Global Project Plan, which is later shared with the Flat Connections Ning community" (Janice Newlin, @janicenewlin). You can read more about Janice and her experience in Case Study 1.4 in the ebook.

Eric, from the USA, shares that in his Atmospheric Science class (which is project based), he always seeks to include a global communication component. If students are creating virtual flyers on the California drought, for example, he makes sure that these flyers are promoted publicly. The students know this (and it ups their game!). He says, "Moreover, I am a big proponent of students presenting their work at conferences—of educators. It's another way for them to connect globally. They have presented locally here at Maker Faire, and at the Global Education Conference, at OzELive, and at Leadership 2.0" (Eric Walters).

> **Maker Faire** refers to an event originally created by *Make* magazine to "celebrate arts, crafts, engineering, science projects and the do-it-yourself mindset."
>
> A **makerspace** is an area where people gather to make and create.

What Does Being a Global Educator Mean to You?

The following global educators are inspiring in their convictions about the importance of being a global educator. Being able to share their thoughts and motivations in this book is inspirational to us all. These vignettes of global learning share attributes of what it means to be a global educator.

Becky, USA, addresses the concern educators, parents, and businesses around the world have preparing today's youth for the challenges they will face tomorrow in our interconnected world and tells us, "Global educators encourage communication across cultures and collaboration throughout the digital world; educating global citizens also means incorporating lessons in empathy and service learning" (Becky Morales, @kidworldcitizen). In line with this, Perla, a teacher in Mexico, believes being a global educator "is to accept challenges, confront fears and get out of your comfort zone and that being a teacher means being a learner forever. It also means embracing the idea that our students are part of a new generation, they are wise in technology usage by nature, and they will be our teachers, at times, but that is fine also" (Perla Zamora, @pzamoraats).

Stefan, from Denmark, says it means to open the classroom to the world and to collaborate with anyone, anywhere, anytime, in any way possible! Jason, an international teacher in Indonesia, states that it is not just connecting your class, but modeling your own connections and contributions to the global community: "To help our learners become connected learners, educators must know the power of the connections themselves" (Jason Graham, @jasongraham99). Lara, an Australian educator in China, talks about the privilege of being a global educator and leader and being able to make connections for others. She says, "The world is as small as it is large and working with teachers, students and people from other cultures allows a richness and understanding that can be lost if the doors, walls and bandwidth are not opened up" (Lara Ronalds, @LaraRonalds). Jane, another Australian teacher currently in Indonesia, knows that being a global educator enables us to address values of equity, social justice, and sustainability in order to provide a "differentiated,

"There are two main areas or parts to [becoming a global educator]. Firstly, developing a personal network, seeking out and participating in a global community of practice has been a catalyst for his practice. Peers who inspire and mentor him literally come from all over the world and share, often ubiquitously, through social media creating a constant input of diverse global perspectives. Secondly, the other side to this is personal global practice and adopting the concepts of global competency and global citizenship" (Michael Furdyk, Canada, @mfurdyk).

Read more about Michael's practice in Case Study 2.7 in the ebook.

change focused and inquiry based classroom" (Jane Ellem, @janeellem). Julio from Venezuela, shares a global educator is someone who looks to the future and who believes that ideas without borders, without limits is capable of creating freedom.

Global Vision

Stephen, a teacher in Kenya, believes a global educator must have a worldwide or global vision and a multifaceted and eclectic approach to emerging issues; should appreciate the diversity of cultures, languages, opinions, and attitudes on the global landscape; and needs to be a strong team player and facilitator who allows every voice to be heard.

Matt, from Australia, shares that a global educator "is not restricted solely to the parameters of localised expectations. It means going beyond the curriculum documents, the experiences and the opportunities provided in the local community (though these can be important) and making a strong attempt to connect students with people, places and experiences outside their day-to-day lives. The role of the global educator is to be connected to a world of peers and ideas through social media, formal professional networks and learning, inspiring other educators to do the same" (Matt Esterman, @mesterman).

You Do Not Need to Leave Home to Be a Global Educator!

As Maggie, from India, tells us, "When people ask me to say something about myself I often use the words "international teacher". Yet what I've been coming to see more and more over the past few years, especially as a result of the connections I've made on Twitter with teachers who have only ever taught in their home countries, is that being an international teacher is not the same as being a global educator. It's possible to be a global educator without ever leaving your home, as a result of reaching out and connecting with other educators worldwide who often have many different perspectives. Global educator refers to the whole world, however international teacher can be something that is much more narrow" (Maggie Hos-McGrane, @ mumbaimaggie).

Three Things?

Ann, Australia, shares the three aspects of education that she is currently passionate about that supports her being a global educator: first, the design thinking model as a structure for research; second, emerging technologies; and third, current events to stimulate authentic communication. Edna, USA, also shares three things that being a global educator means: "Being connected myself and leveraging those connections where needed; being aware and equipped to design work that aims to develop students' global competencies; and working with others to build capacity for this to happen for and by others at all age levels" (Edna Pythian).

Pushing the Boundaries

Emily, USA, tells us it means bringing multiple perspectives into the classroom, and pushing the boundaries of what "classroom" means. Chris, Australia, picks up on this theme when he shares, "It means having a constant awareness that the extent of our classroom does not stop at the classroom door. It means understanding that there are always other perspectives on issues, that there is a wider world out there that does not live in the same time zone, the same climate, and have the same worldview. It means thinking of ourselves as belonging together not just with people who live in the same geographical boundary but with people who live on the same planet" (Chris Betcher, @chrisbetcher).

Making a Difference

Felipe, education leader in Brazil, talks about making a difference as a global educator in terms of spreading the knowledge and using it, or at least trying, to change people's mindset regarding 21st-century education. He says, "Our world has changed, and so have our students. Our schools have to move on in the same direction" (Felipe Mileo). Parambir, a teacher in India, knows that a global educator is "someone who learns from the global community and transforms classroom strategies and at the same time shares his/her innovative practices with the global community to enhance teaching learning practices" (Parambir Singh Kathait).

Pay it Forward

As a global education educator, Mahmud, from Lebanon, exposes students to world issues and helps them research solutions beyond what's available in their country and community. "I make students feel they are living in a global village rather than just their own country. We make them care about global issues and not just our own issues" (Mahmud Shihab, @mahmudshihab).

Tracey, USA, creates opportunities for students on both sides of the camera to learn, interact, and understand one another. She also helps facilitate other teachers to do it. Andrew, New Zealand, supports experiential learning of alternative viewpoints beyond the immediate classroom, school, or community and "prepares students for the world they are going to inherit, a world where collaboration is critical, where global understanding is vital; a world where there are no borders to virtual communication and collaboration" (Andrew Churches, @achurches).

Digital Technologies to Support Global Learning

With so many digital options for learning, the global educator survives and flourishes by having a "generic toolbox" approach to adopting new tools. In this toolbox there are specific tools in each generic category that can be used all the time, with alternatives available for variety or for different reasons, such as when collaborating with someone else who does not have access to the usual tool you use. Connecting with China can often be problematic, given that many Web 2.0 tools are blocked. However, connecting within and beyond other global classrooms (such as with Australia and the USA) also poses some challenges, given internet filters and government and/or organization policies to block Web 2.0 technologies and social media.

Pay it Forward

There is always a way to connect and then to collaborate with other learners. Technology is not the real barrier; it just takes further understanding of what tools are available for educational use and then maybe a little more effort to implement.

Digital Tools for Effective Global Learning

We will focus on connected learning that revolves around social and educational media, especially with Web 2.0 tools. It is *not* possible to create viable global connections and collaborations using a school LMS, or a school-based, closed Google Apps implementation, or even a school Moodle. These tools are designed specifically for internal users and support a "walled garden" digital learning environment not usually conducive to accommodating external partnerships or modes of global collaboration. Trapped in a walled garden, new global educators can become confused and disappointed—but take heart! Although learning about new technologies is always a challenge, the benefits of being able to connect with interesting partners and provide rich learning experiences for students is the end goal.

The **digital learning environment (DLE)** refers to the tools, skills, standards, attitudes and habits for learning while using technology and accessing digital and online resources.

The **digital learning ecology** includes online communities of practice, social networks or collegial groups in which learners can share and explore and form new relationships for learning.

The Global Educator's Generic Toolbox

This book is not specifically focused on tools; other books do a much better job. However, it is important to provide an overview of what tools are needed for global learning and collaboration. This generic approach includes some specific examples of currently available tools. It is the responsibility of the global educator to be aware of new trends and emerging tools that will support generic needs (another reason why a vibrant PLN and PLC is so important!).

Communication tools foster communication between teachers and students, among students and among teachers. Community tools can help build learning spaces for gatherings and developing communities for learning. Scheduling, calendar and workflow tools offer practical assistance and time-saving solutions for scheduling meetings, collaborating on projects and taking notes. Collaboration and co-creation tools offer synchronous as well as asynchronous possibilities and co-creation opportunities. Celebration tools facilitate sharing and showcasing process and outcomes.

Table 2.1: Global Educator's Toolbox

Category	Communication	Community & Social Media	Workflow & Scheduling	Collaboration & Co-Creation	Celebration
Uses	Instant messaging, online meetings, chat	Sharing blog posts, discussions and multimedia	Meeting organization, scheduling, sharing	Collaborative learning spaces	Sharing outcomes
Tools	Skype (skype.com)	Ning (ning.com)	Evernote	Wikispaces	Wikispaces
	WeChat (wechat.com)	Edmodo (eedmodo.com)	Google Apps/Docs	Padlet	Pinterest
	Today's Meet (todaysmeet.com)	Blogger.com, Edublogs, WordPress	Timebridge	VoiceThread	Symbaloo
	WhatsApp (whatsapp.com)	Google+	Time and Date (timeanddate.com)	Google Apps	Blogger.com
	Remind (remind.com)	LinkedIn	Buffer (bufferapp.com)	OneNote	Storify
	Google Hangout	Twitter		Google Draw	VoiceThread
	Fuze (fuze.com)	Scoop.it		Mindmeister	Google Presentations
	Blackboard Collaborate	Pinterest		WeVideo	
	Adobe Connect				

Workflow and Digital Tools

These are the tools that are common to your digital learning ecology, but not necessarily common to all learners. Today's learning is about personalization and customization of workspaces and workflow—there is never a one-size-fits-all anymore. There is, however, a need for every global educator and learner to have a workflow that supports and enhances global connections and collaborations. This includes the use of mobile technologies and cloud computing.

At the time of writing, this is my digital workflow, offered as a brief example of how one global educator connects with and makes sense of the ongoing communication and information coming across my desk daily.

Julie's Digital Toolbox

On reflection, I am quite email-centric, more so than in the past when I used more specific RSS syndication and aggregation tools (such as the now-defunct Google Reader). Although I always advise others to "communicate beyond email!" I find email a good personal way to contain communication, and I have a number of different email addresses feeding through my Gmail account. For Flat Connections global projects and teacher groups, I use Google Groups as a way of simplifying emails and containing specific groupings. I use Evernote for *everything*, almost—notes, web clippings, daily to-do lists, anything I need to remember and keep a record of such as consultancy and travel arrangements and all global connections. My long-standing blog is on blogger.com, and I use this to share what is happening in my global life across different areas. My websites use WordPress and Weebly, and I spend time each week attempting to keep these current.

My personal and professional branding uses LinkedIn and about.me for biography material, and Google+, Facebook, and Twitter for connecting with myriad communities and followers. My personal Facebook account is used for professional communication as well as personal—the former more so these days, and I also have Facebook groups and pages to maintain for global activities and connections.

I use Buffer (https://bufferapp.com/) in conjunction with my Twitter, LinkedIn, Google+, and Facebook accounts to schedule tweets across the week. I use social bookmarking *always* to store and share resources (both Diigo.com and delicious.com) personally and with the many groups I run and belong to, and scoop.it as a curation tool.

Google Apps play a major role in my daily, connected life through sharing docs, spreadsheets, and presentations and creating online forms to capture and share information. Google sites have become more important to me as content builders and collaborative environments, although I continue to use Wikispaces for much global collaboration, as it is generally more accessible across the world than Google. I am starting to explore the new version of OneNote as a collaboration tool.

For global community building I use Ning and Edmodo—both of these are excellent tools for different purposes and age groups. For online meetings I use Skype and Fuze, and sometimes Blackboard Collaborate. Some communications require Adobe Connect, Zoom, and RingCentral. I also use YouTube and Slideshare to upload artifacts, Flickr to store photos . . . and among the many Web 2.0 tools right now, my favorites are Padlet and VoiceThread! In addition I use WeChat app to connect with China, and VoiceThread as an essential tool to connect learners.

Global Educators Share Their Digital Workflow Toolboxes

Let's start this section with classroom teacher and instructional coach Janice Mak, USA, (@jmakaz), who shares a specific list of tools with learning objectives.

In her toolbox, Janice uses:

1. Cisco TelePresence to present real-time at a global e-learning conference (Phoenix, AZ, to Slovakia)
2. Skype to connect to teachers and students in other countries
3. Google Hangout to connect with students and teachers in other countries
4. Email to maintain communication with global partners
5. QQ to maintain communication with global partner in China
6. Google Forms to conduct student surveys
7. Google Docs shared with teachers who I mentored so that we could all edit the global learning plan at the same time and all provide feedback

At Jane Ellem's (@janeellem) international school in Indonesia, every tech opportunity is mapped and structured to support the ongoing teaching program with the focus on ISTE Standards, TPACK, and SAMR, ensuring that technology is used well and effectively for learning opportunities. The tools used include:

1. iPads: images of our learning used for creation ... incorporating literacy and numeracy and voice to demonstrate their learning and share their ideas in the early years.
2. Creation apps: DoodleBuddy, Book Creator, Explain Everything, Puppet Pals, Toontastic, Story Robe, VoiceThread
3. Subject apps that offer an interactive/creative element: Human Body, Sphero, iMovie
4. Google Apps for Education (they are a GAFE school)
5. Global Classrooms through Skype
6. PLN development: Twitter–Facebook, Google+
7. MOOCs (Massive Open Online Courses): study—and furthering high achievers
8. Others: Code.org, Scratch, Khan Academy, YouTube, CAD, Microsoft and Adobe platforms

Stefan is in Denmark and uses a large range of blogs including class blogs, school blogs (Danish and English), and student blogs in some classes. Skype is often used for interaction and mystery Skype; Facebook and Twitter for networking; cell phones for sound and picture taking. See the work of Stefan at Vonsild School via the class blog (http://www.vonsildskole11.blogspot.dk/).

An example of workflow using digital tools is shared by Stephanie, USA, whose students have a digital "course pack"—readings and resources housed on the course website. They use technology to conduct real-time research, to read news features or articles, and to implement creative activities. She shares, "Students make digital brochures, websites, digital narratives and timelines, etc. to show their understanding of course content. These mechanisms are constantly changing, which makes the course exciting for them and for me" (Stephanie Wujcik, @StephWuj45).

Chris, Australia, shares that the internet is obviously the core technology to support being able to share, communicate, and work together online. His students also use communication tools (email, messaging, videoconferencing, etc.) to brainstorm, share and develop project ideas, and collaborative tools (Google Apps, blogs, wikis, and more) as shared working environments. Interestingly, he thinks it's also important to build in some element of physicality to global connections, too—it's exciting to receive a package in the mail with things from your global partners. Holly, middle and high school international teacher in Qatar, uses Twitter, Blogger, GAFE, Edmodo, VoiceThread, SlideShare, WordPress, Pinterest, Weebly, SoundCloud, Picasa, PowToons, iBooks, iPads, and more!

ISTE Standards—The ISTE Standards for Students, Teachers, Administrators, Coaches, and Computer Science Educators, describe the skills needed for work, life and citizenship in a digital age global economy. Learn more at **http://www.iste.org/standards**

TPACK—Technological Pedagogical Content Knowledge (TPACK) is a framework that identifies the knowledge teachers need to teach effectively with technology—Content (CK), Pedagogy (PK), and Technology (TK). **http://www.tpack.org**

SAMR—(Substitution, Augmentation, Modification, Redefinition) is a model designed to help educators infuse technology into teaching and learning. Developed by Dr. Ruben Puentedura, the model supports and enables teachers to design, develop, and infuse digital learning experiences that utilize technology. (Puentedura, 2013)

GAFE—Google Apps for Education is a core suite of productivity applications that Google offers to schools and educational institutions for FREE. **http://edtechteacher.org/gafe/**

What Is Global Connected Learning?

So far we have talked about global learning, connected learning, and flat learning; explored digital technologies; and enlisted the help of educators globally to share their practice. In this chapter, "global connected learning" is defined and described with examples shared from global educators themselves.

> "Before being connected I had no idea what I didn't know. Now that I'm a globally connected educator I realize there is so much I don't know" (Karen Lirenman, Canada, @KLirenman).

When global educators were asked what their definition of "global connected learning" is, this is what they shared.

Learning That Goes beyond the Classroom

Lara, teaching in China, shares that "global connected learning is the way in which we connect and learn together over and beyond our own classroom. It begins with the school community, then to the local community, the country, the nation, the region, the world and the solar system" (Lara Ronalds, @LaraRonalds). Whereas Jane in Indonesia states, "Global connected learning is learning that encompasses connectedness, sustainability, relationships, cultural understandings, innovation and equity along with development" (Jane Ellem, @janeellem). Sonya, New Zealand, adamantly shares that "Global connected learning is about making a difference. It is about ensuring that all voices are heard. It is about empathy and curiosity. It is about tracking the impact of the connection and continually reflecting on how to contribute and share in a better respectful way" (Sonya van Schaijik, @vanschaijik). In addition, Maggie, a Brit teaching in India: "I would say it is learning with others from around the world (as opposed to learning from others)" (Maggie Hos-McGrane, @mumbaimaggie). Chris, Australia, states, "Learning and teaching that ignores the limits of geopolitical boundaries (which are usually man made and artificial in many cases anyway" (Chris Betcher, @chrisbetcher).

Breaking Down Barriers to Learning

Perla from Mexico shares, "From my personal point of view, global connected learning means to take advantage of technologies to break limitations like time zone, distance, language and age to share learning experiences" (Perla Zamora, @pzamoraats). Jason, Indonesia, tells us, "Creating and fostering an environment of learning, and collaborating and sharing with those from other places in the world breaks down barriers" (Jason Graham, @jasongraham99).

"My students would come in the classroom and not say 'what are we doing today' but instead say 'who are we talking to today'" (Mali Bickley, Canada, @dreamteam51).

According to Marzieh, a global teacher in Iran, "Global connected learning means educators are from different countries and learners as well. It means we can have one class and learn new things through updated educators using new technologies. It means international classes and teachers get the newest information very soon" (Marzieh Abedi). Mike, in Australia, states, "I would need to think more on this, however in essence it is about cross-cultural collaborative learning which provides mutual benefits including perspective, motivation and encouragement towards global citizenship" (Mike Bartlett) and Kristina, Australia, defines it as, "A meaningful experience or relationship that fosters growth and is developed between individuals from different contexts" (Kristina Rivers, @kristinastoney).

Sharing Ideas and Perspectives

Stephanie, USA, says, "Global connected learning means to reach out and engage with individuals and groups that hold perspectives or live in places that are different than one's own viewpoint or home. This engagement enables a sharing of ideas that enriches global understanding, fosters empathy, and allows for comfortable conversations about our world's leading issues" (Stephanie Wujcik @StephWuj45). Adam, Egypt, shares that "Global connected learning is when students understand that their connection to other people in the world goes much deeper than a simple handshake activity" (Adam Carter, @SocialActionCol).

In Lesotho, Moliehi shares, "According to my understanding global connected learning is a type of learning that integrates personal interest, peer relationships and achievement in academics. This can be achieved by not working in isolation but rather connecting with other educators around the world" (Moliehi Sekese, @moliehi4sekese). Brian in the USA believes "Global connected learning utilizes technology to share stories, insights, perspectives, and knowledge with one another in order to round out the sometimes one dimensional perspectives we may have as students if the walls of connection are limited to a single school" (Brian Mannix, USA, @mannixlab).

Learning about Real World Issues

According to Ann, Australia, "Global connected learning is learning about real world issues through authentic communication that creates empathy and builds relationships using online tools" (Ann Rooney, @AnnRooney6), whereas Rob, New Zealand, believes it is about learning from/with others in other locales *as well as* learning about issues and events that transcend culture and locality. Emily, USA, shares that it is learning in which teachers and students don't hesitate to tap into a global network to get things done.

"Global connected learning is an active, collaborative, constructive, authentic, and goal-directed way of learning with others no matter where they are" (Theresa Allen, USA, @tdallen5).

Taking Global Connected Learning Further

Working in higher education in the USA, Leigh shares, "I think that I would phrase it as "Globally-Connected Learning" because it is learning that is connected throughout the world. Learning is an interesting thing to define. At the most traditional level, it involves students completing assignments that were assigned by the teacher. In a global learning situation, they might have students from various locations completing the tasks. On a more collaborative level, students from various locations will join together to create solutions for these assignments. On an inquiry-based collaborative level, teachers will assign problems that need to be solved and then these multi-located students will work in groups to develop creative solutions. On the highest level of learning, students will contact students to work out problems on their own" (Leigh Zeitz, PhD, USA, @zeitz). Read more from Leigh in Case Study 4.7 in the ebook.

Felipe, from Brazil, states "It's a small world, and day by day it becomes even smaller, and connected in different ways. That concept also works with education. We know we're tired of saying/hearing that "we've got to bring down the school walls" but as long as we don't do it (or convince—in a good way—people that this is something which is absolutely needed in today's schooling society, in order to keep up with the Society) this jargon will be carried on and on. We cannot keep our students in 50-minute lessons in which before we get to the fifth minute they're not even paying attention to the teacher anymore. We cannot keep our students in a one-way class-room, only listening and not creating content and knowledge. The world is small and connected by itself and definition nowadays. Our students and schools must follow the same way" (Felipe Mileo).

Why Is Global Connected Learning Important?

If we are to pursue global connected learning as an ideal approach, or perhaps a new pedagogy, then why is this important? Lara, China, tells us it is essential to ensure that authentic engagement, curiosity, and connections are nurtured and developed for and by the students. Sophie, USA, shares, "A globally connected learning environment transcends the walls of its building. It creates a learning reciprocity where the world becomes the classroom and its people, the teachers. Students and teachers learn alongside one another and share ideas with others: locally, nationally, and internationally" (Sophie de la Paz). Aaron Maurer, USA, believes global connected learning involves students learning to manage the synchronous and asynchronous communication in a way that allows for students to develop a solution to a problem.

According to Eric, USA, global connected learning is more than just setting up a Skype or a Twitter. It needs to be a personal (or schoolwide) culture of connecting, conversing, observing, and action and that "Global connected learning for students is more than just signing up for an online course with global participants. The connection needs to be made between collaboration and action. Let's use these global connections to effect change for both our students and ourselves as educators" (Eric Walters).

Global Connected Learning in Practice

The daily or regular activities of global educators provide anthropological insight into how an educator supports and sustains not just a global persona, but also a new paradigm for teaching and learning. So, what does a global educator do each day or on a regular basis? How do they manage workflow to include connections and collaborations? Many of these activities happen outside the normal school day. A global educator knows and understands that connected and flat learning is 24/7 and also understands the need to craft a schedule that also includes "unplugged" or "off the grid" time each week. It goes without saying that health issues and educator burnout are concerns if a sensible approach is not taken.

"If you want something done, ask a busy person."

—Benjamin Franklin

Flatblogging

This next blog post is written by Kate O'Connell, @innovatecreater; Dianne Shapp, @dshapp; and Louisa Polos, @MSPolos as part of the Flat Connections Global Educator course in the first half of 2015. "FlatBlogging" means to co-write a significant blog post asynchronously.

Typical Activities of Global Educators

The following are typical things that global educators do, often on a daily basis.

Visit other locations via the internet—blogs, Google Earth, online maps
Use social media to:
- keep in touch with other PLN educators
- establish online relationships for learning
- find out what is happening in education around the world
- share ideas, thoughts, and knowledge
- read other educators' ideas

Maintain a class blog and invite comments
Write a personal blog and share via Twitter
Implement mystery Skype connections
Skype with partner classrooms to support inquiry and literacy
Join global projects
Join and/or initiate a tweet chat session
Check and read global news online
Interact with PLCs
Create new learning designs for global understanding
Share resources via social bookmarking—for example, Diigo
Incorporate Web 2.0 tools into teaching
Find suitable apps to create handshake introductions
Facilitate conversations about global learning and design
Collaborate online (synchronously and asynchronously) with other educators to:
- Plan
- Team teach
- Teacher-source

Connect directly with other learners to understand an outside perspective
Interact online with authors
Video conference a live debate, with an expert or with an author
Attend online conferences and webinars
Link educators and projects together
Create interactive live streaming events for students
Work in a paper-free environment
Follow conversations on Twitter via hashtags (#) to expand the international PLN
Observe cultural expectations
Share resources, concepts, and ideas and ask questions or seek clarification and
    support using social media

Connected Learning—A Blog Post

Among the most fulfilling aspects of being a teacher in 2015 are the many diverse resources and experiences available that facilitate our efforts, as teachers, to be a lifelong learners. Our students teach us, we teach ourselves, and other teachers and learners across the globe offer exciting new lessons for each other and us!

Connected Learning Provides Access to Inspiration

Connected learning affords teachers the opportunity to see, hear, and learn about a myriad of educational experiences that can be replicated, tweaked, played with, and amplified. When a teacher has a question today, numerous answers are just a tweet away.

With weekly educational Twitter chats covering topics like "Bring your own device questions" and teacher blogs that usually end with a question like, "How do you manage your literacy block?" . . . the connected teachers and learners of today will never need to experience seclusion and isolation. And that is a great thing.

Connected educators share not only their questions . . . they exchange ideas, resources, visuals, lesson plans, frustrations, joys, and the lessons they have learned along the way. And we are all better teachers as a result.

In addition to connecting with other teaching professionals, educators can easily connect with other types of professionals. For example, educators can follow authors on social networks such as Twitter. These connections will enrich the learning experience for both the educator and their students. Authors will often post about new books coming out or other titles they are reading. In addition, authors love to hear about students' reading experiences. They will often agree to Skype or visit classes in person! These types of interactions are not only memorable for students but are truly opportunities for authentic learning. What a great way to flatten the English classroom!

Changing the Way "Learning" Happens with Students and Teachers

As educators we are very aware that the way learning happens is changing every single minute! Students must be aware of the vast resources at their fingertips and how to use them productively. Educators must model how to use digital resources by integrating them into curriculum in meaningful ways.

Pay it Forward

If we assign projects that allow students to connect with others and create projects with others beyond the walls of our classrooms, students will be well on their way to understanding how fast the world is changing. They will be exposed to new learning practices and therefore be engaged in the conversation through the many digital resources that allow them to keep up with the constantly evolving landscape of education.

Therefore, connected learning changes education in *how* we teach and learn, as well as *why* we teach and learn. No longer must we live independent of each other, defined by our immediate surroundings and limited to the social norms of our physical community. Now, in this information age, not only is connecting possible—it is our obligation to learn beyond our walls, to become involved in world issues, and to teach the next generation that they matter and that they can effect positive change in their world. Being a connected learner helps educators feel part of the bigger world.

In this digital world, you can learn from anyone, anytime, anywhere! Just as important, an educator has the freedom and access to *interact* with this vast network of professionals. This changes the playing field about what learning "looks like." For example, as we read *Marty McGuire* during Global Read Aloud last year, we were able to ask the author, Kate Messner, why she chose a certain character or plot. How powerful is that?! When the author mentioned my student by name, that child felt like she mattered and she was heard!

An important question recently asked: "How do we create students who 'need to know'?" I believe that when students are engaged and connected through authentic learning experiences, they will naturally need to know more. They will dig deeper and think more thoughtfully about assignments. They will know there are resources to tap and experts who will respond when asked. This is possible with the increase in technology resources. We must help students become connected to the world outside their classrooms because we all must step out of isolation and into all the partnerships that are possible through online connectivity. In order to do this, we teachers must model connecting with others outside of our schools for them!

The Impact of Global Learning

This chapter examines the impact of global educators and global education leaders on schools/institutions, students and the community. It also explores goals, barriers and enablers to global connected learning. Some of the responses from global educators share impacts that are obvious, and others are more subtle—but they all add up to establishing a learning environment that expects and supports global competence and global understanding.

Global Learning's Impact on the Educator

Apart from the possible extra work developing skills to be a global educator, it is interesting to consider the positive impact of taking a global approach on the educator as a teacher and a learner. According to Brian, USA, "The ironic thing is that anyone who so chooses can be a "Global Educator". It merely involves a simple decision to commit. You make a decision to commit to continuously asking and continuously connecting to those outside of your current vision. As soon as the commitment is made to take the leap, that is when the real leadership begins and that is also the moment where responsibility, purpose and integrity show you for who you are" (Brian Mannix, @mannixlab). Interestingly, Mulugeta, high school teacher in Ethiopia, shares a slightly different perspective and one that in fact could be applied to *all* global educators: "I am expected to teach, to solve problems related to education and I am considered as exemplary in every aspect by my junior staffs and students as well as outsiders" (Mulugeta Birhanu).

"Time, space and language are not viewed as barriers to the global educator. They are viewed as opportunities to create authentic learning experiences and develop the intercommunication skills needed in today's world. A global educator is someone who looks beyond the four walls of a classroom to create bridges between learners, the community, business, and different cultures to find mutually beneficial solutions to real world issues. Technology fast becomes a best friend and an essential tool for learning and interacting with a global professional network. It means you have moved beyond consuming content to being an active contributor and are passing this way of being on to your students. It means you are not afraid to be seen, learn from your mistakes, and never give up because you are always connected to the bigger picture and understand the power of sharing ideas to create positive futures" (Katie Grubb, Australia, @katiegrubby).

Personal Awareness of "Being Global"

A major impact of becoming and being global for an educator is enhanced personal awareness of what it is and what is possible. This personal or individual awareness affects us all, sometimes dramatically, regardless of whether we live in a large city or a small rural community.

Stephanie, USA, tells us that being a global educator is inspiring, but takes work. "In order to effectively model and teach global engagement, the educator must first be deeply well engaged. This process takes time and effort to identify resources, especially given the frequency of change, in order to prepare and execute lessons" (Stephanie Wujcik, @StephWuj45). Edna, also from the USA, says, "The biggest impact thus far has been how these conversations, trainings, and support have given teachers permission to dream and take risks when designing work for kids. The students see this effort by their teachers and appreciate it. The kids love having the opportunity to get to know others around the world. They get so excited!" (Edna Pythian).

Matt Harris, from the USA, now working in Indonesia, is influenced by the term "cosmopolitanism" as it applies to being a global citizen and being able to take a global perspective and work and live beyond the home country. Read more about Matt in Case Study 2.9 in the ebook.

Cosmopolitanism is the ideology that all human ethnic groups belong to a single community based on a shared morality. A person who adheres to the idea of cosmopolitanism in any of its forms is called a cosmopolitan or cosmopolite.

In the context of this book, the Latin roots are "citizen of the world," referring to the idea of international students and teachers being citizens of a society greater than their country of origin and being part of a true global community.

Enhanced Collegiality and Role Modeling

Global educators benefit from enhanced opportunities for networking and community building and enhanced collegiality with other educators within and beyond their immediate environment.

Moliehi, a head teacher in a local school in Lesotho who, through Microsoft opportunities and global connections, has traveled the world to learn more and bring new ideas back to her school, says, "Many teachers have used the opportunity to learn from me and to improve their teaching and learning" (Moliehi Sekese, @moliehi4sekese). Matt, Australia, tells us, "I am able to draw on a huge well of critical support for my ideas and gather [further] ideas, practices and possibilities from a global network of educators and non-educators. I can then work with others to translate this into our school context and see what works for us" (Matt Esterman, @mesterman). Suud, from Nigeria, says, "I gain ideas which I will refer to as international ideas because these ideas come from different foreign regions or locations. I use these ideas to expose my students to the wider world" (Suud Hibatullah).

Global educators also become role models within their networks—mentoring and supporting others. The work of the global educator also helps to raise the profile of the school by sharing and exposing new experiences and showcasing extended connections. Although sometimes appreciated by school administrators as merely a marketing advantage, global educators know and understand the real meaning of global learning and spend time and hard work making collaborations work—sometimes to the detriment of other more rigid programs. Jason, Indonesia, tells us, "I am in touch with my PLN constantly mainly via Twitter. If I have a question, wondering, or challenge my first stop is my great network of almost 4,000 educators around the globe. I also share my ideas, thoughts, and knowledge whenever I can. It's all about helping each other become the best educators and learners we can be. In the case of

#pypchat it is sometimes hectic, and so many great ideas and resources being discussed. It is definitely a reflective process" (Jason Graham, @jasongraham99).

Pay it Forward

Although not always understood, often "outlier" in nature, being a well-connected and often well-known global educator provides a license to try out new learning experiences for both students and other educators.

Maggie, now teaching in India, relates "I think one of the impacts I have, as a global educator who has lived and worked in seven different countries, is that I have many connections in those countries for both the teachers and the students. I think our students in India also have very authentic connections with "real life" in India through our CSR programme" (Maggie Hos-McGrane, @mumbaimaggie). Dianne, USA, shares, "Being a global educator has provided me opportunities to learn about our sister community in Shaar HaNegev, Israel, and connect our students to bridge our two communities. The students have been thinking "outside the box," learning about other cultures, comparing their lives to those abroad and asking meaningful questions. My students are growing up to be problem solvers and critical thinkers" (Dianne Shapp, @dshapp).

Transformation of Learning

The realization that learning can happen anytime and anywhere (using online technologies as a catalyst) has a major impact on an educator. Understanding the importance of living in a globalized world and working toward building a foundation for future global citizens of the world is important and transformative work being done right now by global educators.

Carly, Australia, shares, "[The impact of being a global educator] is making me more aware of how I construct lessons and materials so that they are not only relevant and

"My goals as a global educator and leader are to facilitate transformative, unforgettable learning experiences and human connections between people of diverse backgrounds to show that it is absolutely possible to collaborate, communicate and co-innovate together" (Janice Mak, USA, @jmakaz).

useful for the students in my classroom but also of use to individuals accessing them beyond my classroom" (Carly Damen, @CarlyDamen). Wayne, also in Australia, tells us, "I will be modeling what it means to be a connected, global learner and in doing so create the climate where others might follow" (Wayne Demnar, @wdemnar).

Global Learning's Impact on the Student

For students, "going global" can become an expectation and a learning habit—a good learning habit! "The impact of being a global educator is that we are providing a foundation for the future global citizens of the world, the well travelled, the active citizens, the artistic, scientific, the nurturers. . . . Being part of the development through education is a privilege" (Jane Ellem, @janeellem). Marzieh in Iran shares, "My students are more interested in my classes and listen to my words more than other teachers that do not have global view" (Marzieh Abedi).

> "The change from a local student to a global learner is one I see played out annually and it is always my favourite global adventure" (Andrew Churches, New Zealand, @achurches).

Excitement and Engagement

Bringing the world into the learning environment *is* exciting and engaging—for teachers and students. While learning to be teachers, educators are often briefed on the "rabbit out of the hat" method for an engaged learning experience—and haven't we all chased new rabbit and hat opportunities? I laugh to remember as a music educator (before the internet!) my two best "rabbit and hat" tricks were to take apart an acoustic piano to see hammers hit the strings and observe the inner design, or to bring a full drum kit into class for students to take turns learning basic beat (great for coordination, and such fun to take turns). Engagement with these activities in that era for the average middle school student was palpable, and now in a global technology-supported scenario excitement and engagement come from the impact of using digital-technology synchronous communication (such as a live Skype call with video) as well as carefully planned and implemented asynchronous communication (such as sharing class videos and discussing common interests in an online forum). Students love to see what others are doing beyond their classroom. As Karen Lirenman from Vancouver shared with me, when their partner global classroom was not available one day to do one-on-one Skype with her students to read aloud, they insisted on Skyping each other from opposite sides of the room. Fun and skill building, but more importantly the students had the global advantage— they expected a read-aloud activity to be different from the norm. Read more about Karen's global classroom in Case Study 1.5.

Vicki, from Canada, tells us, "They learn from others around the world and not just myself but we also teach others about ourselves, country, world. You cannot get that experience from any text or website" (Vicki Morgado, @vickiemorgado1). In conjunction with this, Craig, USA, educator in Singapore, says, "Better ideas, more engaged and better opportunities. Student confidence is the most noticeable outcome" (Craig Kemp, @mrkempnz). Mahmud, IT leader in Lebanon, shares, "Students love it [global connections], this is one big relief from the daily stress in our society. They learn and share with other cultures. They think out of the box, they enjoy interacting with other cultures. It is widely known that students compete to make friends with kids from other countries. They love to learn more about them" (Mahmud Shihab, @mahmudshihab).

Open-Mindedness and Breakthrough of Stereotypical Understandings

For a student, of any age, participation in global activities and collaborations fosters open-mindedness as they learn to respect the opinions and customs of others. It has been shown that, by doing this, students are able to break through certain stereotypical attitudes and via personal interactions with others gain a deeper understanding of how the world works.

Sophie, USA, tells us that her students "often exhibit an understanding of "big picture concepts" or "big ideas." They have shown an increased in tolerance and understanding towards others that are of different backgrounds and have learned that the information we receive is often culturally biased. They seek information from multiple sources and question more deeply" (Sophie De La Paz). Stephen in Kenya says, "The learners' minds are opened up to unlimited possibilities. They also begin to view themselves as global citizens irrespective of any prejudices or barriers, physical or imagined. They begin to emerge from their self -imposed or other-imposed cocoons and express themselves freely for the benefit of all. This results in a more peaceful and loving school environment. There is environmental sustainability because he/she cares about posterity" (Stephen Opanga).

Change Makers

Learning about the world fosters understanding among students of what might be possible to help change the world.

According to Stephanie, USA, students are more aware of what's occurring in the world around them and more committed to making change. Adam, Egypt, supports students becoming more vocal about issues, and understands that when kids see the big picture and they realize they can actually make a difference, it empowers them. Barbara, USA, reiterates this with, "Global education allows me to impact the future in a positive way. It allows the students to take a leadership role in their communities and realize that they, too, can have a positive impact—even at the young age of ten or twelve!" (Barbara Edwards, @jane_edwardsbjh).

> "A student once said to me that he thought all schools should have to work together with students from other parts of the world. When I asked why he said that, his response was that it would lead to less wars. His reasoning was that he had made many overseas friends during the project, and why would anyone want to go to war with their friends?" (Chris Betcher, Australia, @chrisbetcher).

Authentic Learning, with Real-World Partners

Students who learn in a global classroom expect to have different (and real) learning partners of all ages. They also expect to have an authentic audience for their products and produce artifacts that include blog posts, videos, images, and more. This is beyond textbook learning—the students become the textbook! What will provide more up-to-date information about a global occurrence, a historical event, or a current issue? A textbook—or interaction and collaboration with others involved in and related to the information being sought?

During the Flat Connections "A Week in the Life" project from February to June 2015 (upper elementary global issues project), a major earthquake hit Nepal. The Kathmandu school in the project, Lincoln School, was naturally affected, and both students and teachers in the project learned by direct contact and conversations about this impact on life and school for that community. This experiential and global learning is profound in many ways.

Pay it Forward

Students who learn in a global classroom expect to have different (and real) learning partners of all ages. They also expect to have an authentic audience for their products and produce artifacts that include blog posts, videos, images, and more. This is beyond textbook learning—the students become the textbook!

Kim, Thailand, tells us, "My students have an authentic audience of other students around the world for their work. They regularly share their thinking with other students in other parts of the world, get feedback on their work and offer feedback on theirs" (Kim Cofino, @mscofino). Tracey, USA says, "A more connected world. Kids work harder when their assignment is meaningful and authentic. I hope kids on both sides of the collaboration learn from one another. I hope the students take charge of their own learning and I merely facilitate" (Tracey Winey, @premediawine). Marianne, USA, also tells us, "My current leadership demonstrates they have little value for my international connections. My students, however, are very cognizant that I am connected with lots of interesting educators and that their work has an international audience. They are extremely excited that a game they developed was played in an Australian classroom. Occasionally, my students present via virtual worlds to international audiences; it's a huge thrill for them to have their work see that kind of reach" (Marianne Malmstrom, @knowclue).

Ann's students in Norway learn about social entrepreneurship and how to best help and solve global problems through making vital connections with a school in Lesotho. After devoting a day in Norway to raise funds to help rebuild the African school, seeds of understanding were sown among the students about the rest of world. The reality is that one day of work for a Norwegian can provide a one-year education scholarship for a Lesotho student. The new buildings, including technology, will be done by 2016. Read more about this in Case Study 2.5.

Future Employment

Julio from Venezuela says, "My students begin to discover a world of opportunities. For many of these, school is their only hope. Thanks to our project called Global School, we managed to win at least their hearts so that they can begin to believe that they can have a future" (Julio Rojas). Kevin, USA, states, "Preparing them for the future of work—that should ultimately be a global experience" (Kevin Cojanu).

Interest in Travel and International Study

"Many students become interested in travelling and leaving Lebanon when they see the better options in higher education and work opportunities," says Mahmud Shihab in Lebanon, while Tina, in the USA, says, "Our connections with other countries have made that country come alive for my students instead of it being just a spot on the map that they read about" (Tina Schmidt, @MrsSchmidtB4).

Technological Savvy

Digital tools and the fluency needed to implement and manage them provide the bridge for students to learn about the frustrations and excitement of communicating and co-creating with people who are different and far away.

Ann, Australia, tells us, "For my students they have been impacted by communicating with people from overseas using technology. They learnt about the frustrations and the excitement of communication and co-creating with people who were new and different, and also discovered similarities in online conferences using Fuze.com" (Ann Rooney, @annrooney6). Felipe tells us, "The company I work for looks after nearly 400K students in Brazil. Being a global mind-set educator enables you to have some interesting insights and to benefit from them too. Recently, through our partnership with Intel Education, we managed to pilot an initiative with Intel tablets powered with a classroom management system of another partner, and it was a huge success. This is one example of the impact you can make in the life of students, we've got many others!" (Felipe Mileo).

Global Learning's Impact on the Community

Attilio, teacher and teacher trainer in Italy, tells us global collaboration "broadens their [students'] perspectives, and provides a means for them to connect with learning within and beyond the classroom. Students and their families understand the importance of living in a globalized world and how the new learning technologies can help them connect to other schools in the world" (Attilio Galimberti). Theresa, USA, says, "Today we had our Open House where potential families come and visit our school. The hosts who walk the parents around visit my room and compliment on the great things we do in the lab and classrooms. They love hearing about how we connected with a school from Germany or they shared what their daily lives are like at their schools. Parents see the value and tell other parents about the things that are done in our school" (Theresa Allen, @tdallen5).

Goals, Challenges, and Enablers to Global Learning

When asked about goals and then related challenges and enablers, global educators shared a diverse range of ideas and influences.

Michael Roemer, USA, Director of Trinity Valley School, Global Initiatives Program, is challenged by the aim to create a culture of dignity and empathy through virtual and in-person exchanges, curricular enhancements with a multinational focus, and faculty development and training. The motto for the program is: OUR WORLD: Think about it, Talk about it, Do something.

Making Connections, PLN Development, and Shared Expectations

For Lara, China, some challenges include staying up to date; time constraints; shared understandings; and awareness of possibilities. Sonya and Andrew, both in New Zealand, also have time zone challenges, being on the far end of the date line! Andrew says, "Timezones, technology and teacher reluctance are the key challenges. In an isolated country like New Zealand our nearest neighbors are two hours different from us. This challenges the strictures of the teaching day from 9 a.m. to 3 p.m." (Andrew Churches, @achurches).

Maggie, India, tells us, "It's important to have really strong links with the teachers you are collaborating with *before* the students start to connect. I think it's important that all the teachers and students feel they are getting something out of it and that they are invested in it—not just that they are sharing information that only one of the classes wants" (Maggie Hos McGrane, @mumbaimaggie). Toni, USA, says, "It is also important to find other teachers who understand and are dedicated to the importance of being globally connected" (Toni Olivieri-Barton, @toniobarton). Aaron, USA, shares that the main challenge for him is "working with people with different calendars, time zones, and expectations. The most frustrating piece is the follow through. So many times people drop the ball and after investing a lot of time and effort it falls flat" (Aaron Maurer, @coffeechugbooks).

Marianne, USA, shares that her goals are to learn from others from their personal practice to national policies and share how education is moving forward (or not) around the world. Whereas Marilyn, Australia, says, "I'd like to see all schools in Australia become global learning hubs—places where the process of learning is connected, collaborative and communicated in as many ways as possible, to many interested learners in local, national and global communities, through the use of tools for social learning. Here we are challenged by the availability of reliable connectivity for all global communities, available education hubs for all learners and the proficiency of teachers to enable global and connected learning to take place in their schools. Changes to the traditional thinking behind the delivery of education— the buildings, rooms, the blended learning model, the flattening of classrooms, the pedagogies involved—these are all part of providing a conducive environment for global learning" (Marilyn Snider, @malmade1).

Support and Guide Other Teachers

As the technology coach in an international school in Indonesia, Jane's goal is to provide learning opportunities that enable students to connect with their environment and global issues and to provide support and guidance for teachers to do this while using technology and maintaining the momentum. Perla, Mexico, says, "Changing minds is not easy, sometimes we [teachers] say that we would like to try global learning but we don't want to "waste time" learning something new. It is hard to accept that time will be a limited factor always, but being a global learner and risk taker brings a bigger reward" (Perla Zamora, @pzamoraats). Ann, Australia, states, "I also aim to support other teachers to use online learning systems and to connect globally. I am currently supporting a teacher in Nepal and this means limited internet but even limited connectivity helps build relationships so we can empathise with others" (Ann Rooney, @annrooney6).

Wayne Demnar, international school leader, shares, "I love the notion of sharing professional development with an international cohort—there is nothing more stimulating than learning with a coalition of the willing—it is inspiring to share your stories with people beyond your national borders." Parambir, in India, shares that her challenge is that a global educator or global education leader has to learn from people living at a distance who are teaching and learning in specific conditions and environments. They then have to make innovations to adapt practices to their own infrastructure, environment, and needs. She states, "Presently, I have to motivate and inspire the teacher community of my region for the use of technology in education. Technology has become cheap enough to be adopted by the teacher community but lack of infrastructure at school level is a challenge. I have to make the teacher community learn to use technology to enhance their own competency, learn from the global community, and adopt/innovate classroom practices as per availability of resources at school level" (Parambir Singh Kathait).

For Judy, higher education lecturer in Australia, the goal is to change/nurture as many educators as she can to become global educators themselves! Theresa, USA, says, "I want to be in a position where I can share my experiences and knowledge with other teachers—a much larger group than just my school and Diocese. I want to reach others and show them the importance of global education and how fun it really is!" Her challenge is "being flexible and knowing the outcome may not go as planned. To be structured is to be fractured. You will lose learning time on the little things. If things don't work out, have a plan B and move on. Get back to it another time" (Theresa Allen, @tdallen5). Moliehi in Lesotho aims to make teachers aware of the importance of integrating technology in the classroom and to help teachers as well as learners in their teaching and learning in all the schools around the country. She states, "The limitation of resources is a serious challenge in my case. I am working day and night to get information that will help teachers and learners to perform their work better" (Moliehi Sekese).

Make a Difference and Effect Change

In New Zealand Sonya shared that her goal is to make a difference, "It is all very well sharing and curating what I do, but my current aim is to make a difference in the lives of the current generation of children. That together we can make changes to policies and laws that affect our daily lives" (Sonya Van Schaijik, @vanschaijik). Emily, USA, says her goals are: "To change the world for the better. To change the education system to be more inclusive and equitable. To make things better for those who struggle in a system that is not often fair" (Emily McCarren, @emilymccarren), while Kevin, USA, wants to, "prepare every student I touch to be a global leader and someone who shares experiences—pays it forward! The challenge is boundaries that prevent sharing and human growth in every economic level" (Kevin Cojanu).

Felipe, Brazil, wants to give students chances of being better human beings and make their lives better, and shares, "I reckon the biggest challenge is to keep up to date with all initiatives and innovations within the market, and also change the mindset of people, or at least make them start thinking about changing their mindset, toward 21st century education" (Felipe Mileo). Larisa, USA, is challenged by leading change and transforming education and wants to "increase participation in STEM disciplines by all students to meet the needs of an innovation-driven globally competitive workforce ... to enable the next generation ... to be effective in and with other countries/cultures in solving the problems urgently confronting the world's populations and working successfully across global cultural differences" (Larisa Schelkin, @Larisa_Schelkin).

In Iran, Marzieh, an iEARN educator, tells us, "I like to make differences. I want to make people think deeply and have peace in their minds and respect to all people with different views. I want to make problems be solved and if every country or school or student have problems and need help and advice I could do something and make good connections among all teachers and students. Iran is challenged by being updated and trying to get new methods and solutions to issues including online access with good speeds, and learner motivation" (Marzieh Abedi).

Technology Issues

So, now we get to some of the issues specifically related to availability, access and maintenance of the much-needed technology. It is interesting to note at this point that a multiple case study research design employed by Ertmer and colleagues (Ertmer, Ottenbreit-Leftwich, Sadik, Sendurur, & Sendurer, 2012) examined similarities and differences among pedagogical beliefs and technology practices of educators using emerging technologies. Results suggest that knowledge and skills as well as attitudes and beliefs (described as second-order barriers), not hardware, software, and networking issues (known as first-order barriers), are the gatekeepers to better use of technology for learning.

Julio shares, "In our country, Venezuela, we face great difficulties, one of which is precisely the technology gap. My society still sees with skepticism the use of technology. My challenge is to demonstrate that technology can open up large and very important experiences" (Julio Rojas). Vickie, Canada, says her challenges are with technology not always working and goes on to list, "Technology not always enough for what I want to accomplish and people being fearful of what I am trying to accomplish due to a lack of knowledge or ignorance" (Vickie Morgado, @VickieMorgado1). In Australia, Sue Beveridge, @BeveridgeSue, is challenged by "interoperability of technology," and Mike Bartlett, also in Australia, by "funding, technological barriers and the pace of technological change, teacher willingness and capacity to engage with collaborative technologies, ensuring equity of access and opportunity for local students."

Community Engagement—Closing the Gap

Another major challenge for global educators is fostering positive community engagement. There continue to be stories of communities blocking teachers and schools from connecting with the outside world, for a variety of reasons, including social, political, and religious. One challenge is to engage the learning community in positive global engagement that is customized to their needs so everyone feels comfortable and can be proactive in their support. This is very doable! One size does not fit all circumstances, and we know enough about building learning communities to understand the important role the education leader—the global education leader—plays in this.

Pay it Forward

One challenge a global educator and leader has is to engage the learning community in positive global engagement that is customized to their needs so everyone feels comfortable and can be proactive in their support.

Stephanie shares, "I think the primary challenge is explaining the importance of global education within the context of a traditional history curriculum. I am often in the position of describing to parents or families the rationale for my global education course, as they expect a chronological, historically rooted course underpinned by a textbook. Because my course is so far from that (we do not have a textbook and instead, use contemporary news sources to develop context for global issues), parents sometimes share discomfort, confusion, or distaste for the method of teaching" (Stephanie Wujcik, @StephWuj45). Suud, from Nigeria, states, "Well. I feel I still need more international experience. My goal is to be an educator that helps my nation in closing the gap between my nation and the civilized nation" (Suud Hibatullah), and Jason, in Indonesia, is challenged by getting buy-in from parents, administrators, and staff members through being able to "Convince new parents and admin and maybe other teachers as to the benefits of global connections and why we need to model responsible digital citizenship" (Jason Graham, @jasongraham99).

Finding Global Partners

There is a lot to say about how and where to find global partners, and this is covered later in this book. However, Michael in the USA is challenged by "finding schools to partner with in different regions of the globe; convincing teachers of the value of a global education; creating exchanges that work with current curricula and do not add much to the teacher's (already) full plate" (Michael Roemer).

Curriculum Development and Change

Global educators need to push the boundaries of global learning and pedagogy and build new learning experiences in meaningful ways.

Sophie, USA, says, "There is no test to "prove" the students are learning something. This type of learning cannot be measured by state standardized tests and therefore it is often used as a secondary curriculum when it could be the main aspect of the learning environment. Schools could implement entire units of study and utilize a PBL approach to reach CCS in various subject areas whilst working on globally themed projects. Unfortunately, these types of projects are often regulated to a computer class project and are not given the importance they merit" (Sophie de La Paz).

Challenges to curriculum development and change shared by global educators include:

1. To design projects that excite other teachers
2. Getting people to understand that it's not "one more thing," but that it is how you achieve the many things desired for students. It takes upfront work (planning) and maintenance throughout exchanges that take time—and time is what people don't have
3. Every school is different. Great ideas in one place don't always work in other places. This makes it hard to apply things from one place to another
4. To move beyond just simple activities like mystery Skype or letter exchanges and develop something more long term and deep

Sue, Australia, tells us, "The goal is to build the capacity of teachers to use technology to take their students beyond the walls of the classroom, to embed in their learning programs a regular opportunity for students to collaborate and connect with people and students from other cultures and fields of knowledge. The challenge is curriculum alignment and space within the workday and curriculum demands of teachers to complete complex projects" (Sue Beveridge, @BeveridgeSue). Emily, USA, shares, "My goal as a global educator is to teach children in Mexico and Colombia and Venezuela to be bilingual at an early age and to have the media and materials available to learn. I feel like people that went and got their four-year degree in the United States will talk about Thoreau or Emerson as great novelists, because they are important to Americans. But that doesn't mean they are necessarily important to people in other countries. My other goal is to be more informed with different writers and novelists in these countries, not just musicians, athletes and actors" (Emily Kibble).

Andrew in New Zealand says, "Teachers are often reluctant to change and adapt their teaching programmes. Most schools are assessment driven and with this restriction struggle to change and seize the teachable moment. Technology can provide barriers and challenges, access to sites and tools blocked by local administrators or national policy; reliability and connection speed all provide obstacles, but like all obstacles they can be overcome and the outcome far outweighs these challenges" (Andrew Churches, @achurches). Matt Esterman, Australia, aims to "test and adopt great ideas that will be of benefit to my students. To connect my students with experiences that they could not otherwise get (or might not think to engage with)" and tells us he is challenged by time to organize and maintain globally focused projects as well as curriculum restrictions.

Inspire Students

Kristina, Australian edupreneur, says she always aims to connect educators and students to social and environmental sustainability with the intention of fostering solution development and is challenged by making the time in structured timetables. Dianne, USA primary-level teacher, says, "I would like to inspire my students to change the world or to at least make a positive difference. They need to be able to interact safely and responsibly online and with each other. The challenge is time to collaborate and invest in these connections PLUS time zone issues" (Dianne Shapp, @dshapp). In Lebanon, Mahmud tells us, "Our main goal at International College is to prepare global leaders. We strive to do that. We are investing in encouraging social entrepreneurship to prepare our students to create sustainable solutions to our world problems. Sometimes we forget our own traditions and we focus more on the others'. This is a main challenge. It is important to preserve our own values and traditions and present them to others while learning the best from others" (Mahmud Shihab, @mahmudshihab).

"Our goal is to widen the horizons of the young and the young at heart. To ensure social integration, peaceful coexistence amongst diverse cultures and racial or ethnic backgrounds. To cause and enhance environmental care and sustainability for posterity. In many places you are ahead of your time, so you will be misunderstood, but so was Plato and Einstein." Stephen Opanga, Kenya

Further encouragement for global educators comes from Maggie Hos McGrane at the American School in Bombay, India.

Global Connected Learning in Action in India

The International Baccalaureate (IB) mission statement refers to international mindedness as understanding that "other people, with their differences, can also be right." As a global educator I try to actively model respect, acceptance and tolerance for others' viewpoints and to open up students to these too.

At ASB we are constantly asking, "What are the purposes of education?" Traditionally we say that education should prepare students for the future. Our Superintendent, Craig Johnson, recently asked "What future?" Are we preparing students for their future here at ASB? For their future in another school, as our students' families are highly mobile? For their future at university? For their life?

When asked this question, John Dewey's response was that a teacher should provoke "a continuous interest in learning throughout a student's life." In today's world, we see many national curriculums with narrow standards and high-stake tests that mean that what is important to learn has been whittled down to the things that are easily testable. The impact of this is that many key, creative, subjects such as music and art as well as foreign languages, science, social studies and PE are getting less and less time. I would say that another of my goals as a global educator is to question this and to ensure that there is a broader focus in the schools where I work.

I'm hoping that our students will come to see the power of technology for creating virtual classrooms and learning communities with other students whom they have never met offline and that this will lay good foundations for them becoming responsible digital citizens and being able to create their own networks and learning communities in the future.

Global Educator Case Studies

As a culmination to Part One: The Global Educator, seven global educators tell their personal stories of the 'how and why' of being a global educator. These educators span primary, middle and high school as well as teacher-educator levels of learning. More importantly these educators share how taking a global pathway has shaped their learning environments and impacted their students and how, despite some obstacles, it is a pathway they take every day with renewed determination. The full case studies can be found in the Global Educator ebook.

Case Study 1.1 Anne Mirtschin: The World is My Classroom

Anne Mirtschin is an award-winning teacher from Victoria, Australia whose most recent major awards are ICT in Education Victoria Educator of the Year and Australian Computer Educator of the Year 2012. She teaches information and communication technology (ICT) from Grade 3 through Year 12 at Hawkesdale P12 College, a small rural prep to year 12 school and is passionate about rural and global education, immersing technology in the classroom. Anne loves collaborating, teaching and learning online; is the Australasian Coordinator for the Global Education Conference, an active member of Flat Connections Projects and live events, a lead teacher for the Global Classroom projects, and has presented locally, nationally and globally.

Background

Anne is what I call a 'teacherpreneur' in that she finds and designs opportunities for her students and fellow teachers and brings rich learning activities to the classroom. Anne and I connected online in the early Web 2.0 days through like-minded approaches to global collaboration in the classroom. In 2009 she intrepidly brought students to the first Flat Classroom Conference held in Doha, Qatar. Although at that time other schools from Australia were not allowed to travel to the Middle East, Anne was not daunted.

What immediately becomes obvious with Anne is her facility and skill with the technology—making it usually do what she needs when she needs it, and her absolute love of connecting with the world. Seeing the world through her student's eyes and facilitating, or rather, in the words of John Hattie, 'activating' learning connections and collaborations is what Anne does best through her passion for global learning. She is an ongoing inspiration to many other global educators!

Connect with Anne Mirtschin

Twitter: **@murcha**

Blog: **www.murcha.wordpress.com/**

In this case study find out Anne's strategies for connecting with the world, the challenges she faces to global collaboration in the classroom, and how she prepares for and scaffolds global collaboration across the school curriculum. Most interesting is the Anne talks about how global collaboration has changed the learning ecology of her school, and how it has impacted positively on her students.

Case Study 1.2 Kim Cofino: A Globally Connected Educator

Kim Cofino, international educator from the USA, is an experienced, enthusiastic and innovative globally minded educator. She is passionate about empowering teachers to become learning leaders, as well as building strong collaborative teams among teacher leaders. Kim is a COETAIL co-founder (www.coetail.com), and an Eduro Learning Founding Partner (http://edurolearning.com), as well as a regular presenter and keynote speaker at conferences and professional development sessions worldwide.

I first came to know Kim online, as I get to know most colleagues in my network, and then in 2008 brought Kim into my school, Qatar Academy in Doha, Qatar to lead a 2-day workshop for the Primary Years Programme (PYP) teachers focusing on the use of technology to build new learning experiences, including global connections. Subsequent to that successful experience Kim and I worked together occasionally leading teacher and student workshops and we joined forces to bring the Flat Connections Conference to Yokohama International School (YIS), Japan, in 2013.

If any one educator could be designated to encapsulate the words 'global' as well as 'international' it is Kim. In conjunction with her meticulous and methodical approach to embedding new technologies into effectively-designed curriculum Kim has a unique perspective on what it takes to move an international school forward, and shares her story of having led new connected and global teaching and learning approaches at international schools.

Connect with Kim Cofino

Twitter: **@mscofino**

Blog: **http://kimcofino.com/**

In this case study Kim shares her many experiences as an international educator in roles where student and teacher use of digital technology is a focus.

Case Study 1.3 Michael Graffin: Leading The Global Classroom Project An Australian Teacher's Story

Michael Graffin is a K–6 ICT Teacher and Integrator at Iona Presentation Primary School (http://ionaps.com) in Perth, Western Australia. He is a relatively new global educator whose passion for alternative approaches to learning globally led him to co-found The Global Classroom Project. Although not an extensive global traveller himself yet, Michael has a unique determination to bring global learning to his students and shares his pathway of doing this.

I first met Michael in person at the iEARN Conference in Qatar, 2013, and then in the following year he took the trek from the west coast of Australia over to Sydney to join the Flat Connections Conference in 2014. In 2015, Michael received international recognition for his work at Iona PS, and with The Global Classroom Project. He won an Emerging Leader Award from the International Society for Technology in Education, and our project came Runner Up in the inaugural ISTE Innovation in Global Collaboration PLN Award 2015—and he trekked to Philadelphia to claim it!

In this case study Michael shares his journey, ambitions and vision as a young global educator. He shares the challenges of global collaboration and the message that we are not alone—technology brings us together—and together we can help to change the world.

Connect with Michael Graffin

Twitter: **@mgraffin**

Blog: **http://blog.mgraffin.com**

Case Study 1.4 Janice Newlin: Taking Teacher Education Global

Janice Newlin is an adjunct instructor who teaches Educational Technology courses for two universities, Athens State University in Athens, Alabama and Auburn University Montgomery in Montgomery, Alabama, USA. She also serves as an Intern Supervisor for Athens. She has over 17 years classroom experience most of which she has integrated technology in her curriculum. She also has experience training pre-service and in-service teachers on how to integrate technology into their own curriculum as well. She believes technology is a tool for students to become the creator of their learning and to engage in deep and higher level thinking.

Janice is one of the teacher-educators featured in this book. Through careful curriculum redesign Janice has mapped out a pathway for her students to connect, communicate, and collaborate with others beyond their usual boundaries, often to their amazement! Her resolve that global learning is imperative is encouraging for all educators and inspiring to other teacher educators perhaps working in systems that need overhaul and change to produce the teachers we need to see in schools and new learning environments today.

Connect with Janice Newlin

Twitter: **@janicenewlin**

LinkedIn: **www.linkedin.com/pub/janice-newlin/41/456/aab**

Case Study 1.5 Karen Lirenman: Early Years Students Go Global

Karen Lirenman, an early years educator in Vancouver, Canada, is an award winning primary school teacher who is transforming education by connecting her students with the world using Twitter, blogs, and video conferencing. Her students have choice in how to learn, show, and share their knowledge. In 2013 Karen was awarded ISTE's Kay L Bitter Vision Award for excellence in technology-based PK-2 education.

Karen's mission as a teacher is to change the world one six year old at a time (or through their teachers).

When talking with Karen I was struck by her flexibility to not just integrate technology but to also embed technology-infused learning into everyday classroom experiences where in fact 'flat' learning has become the norm and the expectation of her students. In this case study Karen shares the foundation of her 'flat' classroom and how being a global educator means everything to her!

Connect with Karen Lirenman

Twitter: **@klirenman**

Professional Blog: **http://learningandsharingwithmsl.blogspot.ca/**

Class Blog: **www.mslirenmansroom.blogspot.com**

Case Study 1.6 Lizzie Hudson: Being an International Educator

Originally from the USA, Lizzie and her husband have taught overseas for more than 10 years and between them have taught in Korea, Hong Kong, Honduras, Thailand and Colombia. She now works in Malaysia at IGB International School and continues to push the limits of digital technologies.

Lizzie came onto my horizon when writing this book and her bubbly enthusiasm inspired me to share her unique global journey of international teaching.

Connect with Lizzie Hudson

Twitter: **@hudson_ea**

Coetail Blog: **http://www.coetail.com/hudsonea/**

Case Study 1.7 Julie Carey: Write Our World

Julie Carey is a Flat Connections Global Educator who is following a passion for helping kids share their stories. She wrote to me recently, "I have just founded an international nonprofit called Write Our World, an online library of ebooks created by kids for kids. We work with children everywhere to publish bilingual ebooks about their cultures, using their native languages. We also reach out to schools to build our library patronage and provide teachers with guidance about how to use it. Our work is inspired by the emergence of collaborative online educational innovations that connect students from all over the world."

This case study is her inspirational story from being an international language educator to a creator of global books!

Connect with Julie Carey

Twitter: **julieswords1**

Website: **http://writeourworld.org/**

Part 2

Leadership for Global Education

Who are our global education leaders? Where are they located, and what impact are they having? You may find they are already in every school, not always in traditional decision-making positions, but determined to positively move learning into the global realm.

Part Two examines the role of leadership in implementing global learning experiences at all levels. Chapter 5 is about the evolution of global leadership in education. It explores the profile of a global education leader and observes different ways leadership is emerging in a networked, flat and connected learning landscape. Alternative terms are defined such as "teacherpreneur" and "outlier," "learning concierge" and "parallel leadership," and the importance of effective leadership to foster global perspectives and actions. Chapter 6 explores how to lead for global citizenship and effect pedagogical change and suggests a new approach to pedagogy, "cosmogogy," for learning while connected to the world. Chapter 7 brings together a number of examples of global leaders from Australia to Mexico to New Zealand and the USA who focus on what they do to lead change. Finally, Chapter 8 shares many examples of leadership through existing communities of practice and how these are bringing together global educators for different types of learning and sharing.

The Global Education Leader

Before we move into the complexities of this chapter, I want to share my quest to become a global education leader. It is not necessarily a unique quest, as many have walked this pathway before and continue to do so today. But it does share some of the struggles, many of which I believe were compounded by working in different cultures and situations while implementing online technologies for new learning modes. To me, global education leadership is about having empathy with the learning situation while striving to be innovative and orchestrating new opportunities for learners. A global education leader is also flexible and adept at working with diversity, at the same time insisting on better pathways and *never* willingly taking no for an answer!

It is important to mention here the global education leaders with whom I have worked and learned over the years—those in positions of power who, instead of crushing new ideas, provided support through time release from the classroom, who provided funds for digital resources, and who listened with some understanding to my vision of the way things could be. The culture of the workplace (school) is determined often by the willingness of leaders to listen, delegate, distribute, empower, and step out of the way of the learning. In my school in Bangladesh (2003–2007), new ideas and innovations were rife. It was a time for trying out new ways of integrating technology, and I was fully supported and encouraged in this respect. As Head of Technology and Director of E-Learning at International School Dhaka (ISD), I was able to think outside the box. I regularly shared many 21st-century learning objectives and ideals with teachers as I encouraged mobile and ubiquitous teaching and learning to support our 1:1 laptop program for Grade 9 and above. In addition, we implemented a mobile device program using Palms for all Grade 6–8 students—

at a time when the actual device was not even available to purchase in Bangladesh! I remember our intrepid CEO (Head of School) bringing back a suitcase full of Palms for teachers to experiment with and telling us he sweated all the way through customs. At the time, influenced greatly by the work of Elliot Soloway of GoKnow Inc. (who developed a suite of tools/apps called Mobile Learning Environment), I was adamant that personalized devices were essential for learning. At ISD we provided a wireless network for Grades 6–12, and we worked hard to provide enough bandwidth in the days before fiber-optic cable reached Dhaka. We diligently supported teachers with new pedagogical approaches to using emerging technologies for learning, and we smoothed over ruffles when technical issues and digital citizenship issues clouded the primary goal—which was to be digital, online, and global while learning.

It was in Bangladesh in 2006 that the original, and soon to be award-winning, online global collaborative project the Flat Classroom Project was developed. My largely Bangladeshi students joined virtually with students in the USA and worked collaboratively on wiki authoring and multimedia creation. The advent of Web 2.0 made this type of collaboration and learning with the world possible technically. It also became a reality due to my "outlier" disposition, risk-taking approach, and ability to network with other educators beyond my immediate environment and imagine new possibilities. The Flat Classroom Project was interdisciplinary; however, at the time it became a major unit in my Grade 10 Middle Years Programme (MYP) Technology class. I did not specifically ask permission to do this—my leadership style is more about asking forgiveness afterward (if needed!). This project was made possible through creative curriculum redesign, alignment with overarching needs of the school and the MYP framework and student assessment, and careful guidelines for student online use (behavior and learning). Leadership in conjunction with the culture of acceptance of change within the school at the time supported this.

When I worked in Qatar as Head of Information Technology and E-Learning at Qatar Academy (QA), a K–12 IB World School, the challenge in 2007–2009 was to prepare for mobile and blended learning. A robust wireless network was available, and senior students had started to bring mobile devices, but a plan for moving from desktop to laptop had to be formulated with clear parameters for what this would look like in a conservative, Muslim environment. Many discussions about 21st-century learning and curriculum integration for 1:1 took place, with opportunities for teachers to learn from guest leaders such as Kim Cofino and Gary Stager. One turning point was when a team of leaders from QA traveled to Mumbai for the inaugural ASB Unplugged conference in 2008 at the American School of Bombay. At that time this event was team-based and designed to support conversations and provide planning time for school teams to discuss necessary actions to embed digital technologies.

Another challenge at QA was changing the outdated, outsourced model of IT support into a school-based model to support what teachers and students needed. At this time the Qatar Foundation was working more with a business model for IT support that involved logging calls, then systematically attending and troubleshooting through an off-site team. If something went down in the classroom, the learning opportunity was lost if it took 24 hours to or more to get IT attention. It was an exciting day when we finally opened an on-site tech support office with three working and active IT specialists who serviced the full K–12 school of more than 1000 students and teachers with a drop-in desk and in-class support. When I left Qatar Academy, I remember distinctly my colleague who offered the farewell speech saying, "Julie just never took "no" for an answer!"

During my time in Beijing as E-Learning and Technology Coordinator at Beijing BISS International School (2009–2012), it was a similar challenge—building strategies for student mobile learning and supporting educator skills for technology integration and new pedagogies. For me, by then, it was also a major focus on how to take learning global across the school, not just within my own classes. One of the steps for doing this was systematically supporting online and virtual (also called blended) learning. With support from other leaders in the school, we implemented different systems for taking learning online. We even tried a "Virtual BISS Day," where all students and teachers stayed at home and lessons were taught virtually in real time via video conferencing and through the school learning management system (Lindsay, 2009). It was hugely successful and led the way in 2009 for online learning that could take the local into the global. It was also an important landmark in the evolution of an international school where sometimes political, geographic, or social circumstances cause the school to close (temporarily) on short notice. Knowing we could potentially still connect and learn as a community online was a big step.

In all of these examples, it is important to remember that teamwork supported the vision for new learning. Through a shared vision, and many discussions and collaborations, positive change can be effected in a school. This is an important message for a global education leader.

"We have so much to learn from jazz bandleaders, for jazz, like leadership, combines the unpredictability of the future with the gifts of individuals."

From *Leadership Jazz,* by Max De Pree

Gaining a Global Perspective

In education, terms such as, "global mindedness," "global perspective," "global literacy," "global learning," and "global competency" imply an awareness of aspects of learning that include communities and information beyond the local. A global leader must have a global perspective that aligns with the needs of learners as they connect with many different partners. Long before the internet was available in schools, Hanvey (1982) wrote about the "attainable global perspective" and came up with five dimensions of a global perspective:

1. **Perspective consciousness:** awareness on the part of the individual that their view of the world is not universally shared and others views may be profoundly different
2. **"State of the planet" awareness:** an awareness of prevailing world conditions and development, including emergent conditions and trends
3. **Cross-cultural awareness:** awareness of the diversity of ideas and practices to be found in human societies from around the world and how one's own society may be viewed from other vantage points
4. **Knowledge of global dynamics:** comprehension of key trails and mechanisms of the world system that may increase intelligent consciousness of global change
5. **Awareness of human choices:** awareness of the problem of choice confronting individuals, nations and the human species as consciousness and knowledge of the global system expands

Any one person does not necessarily have all of these dimensions, but Hanvey (1982) states, "The educational goal broadly seen may be to socialize significant collectivities of people so that the important elements of a global perspective are represented in the group." He also concludes that this is not a definitive list; rather, it is subjective and open to interpretation. It serves as a starting point as the next three chapters explore leadership for global education.

As Marilyn Snider, Senior Global Consultant, Australia, shares with us, "As a global education leader I promote open-mindedness leading to new thinking about the world and a predisposition to take action for change. Taking responsibility for their actions, learners come to respect and value diversity, and see themselves as global citizens who can contribute to a more peaceful, just and sustainable world. Enabling young people to participate in a better-shared future for all is at the heart of global education. In terms of impact, my perspectives of the world infuse my thoughts and ideas on a daily basis. I am more perceptive, more analytical, more understanding. I can see many angles to a story. My input is thoughtfully constructed with attention to identity, cultural diversity, human rights, social justice, and peace with its counter side, conflict resolution."

In the context of this book, global perspective implies an ability to understand how to connect beyond your own immediate learning environment using digital technologies. Being a connected and global education leader means you know how to advocate for global understandings, you know how to use the tools to forge connections between teachers and students, and you know how to not only interact but work and learn with others at a distance, and ultimately you know how to redesign your school's curriculum based on emerging pedagogies to "bring the world in." According to Fullan, Langworthy, and Barber (2014), new pedagogies thrive in a new culture of leadership that practices collaboration and builds social capital.

Profile of a Global Education Leader

Global education leaders have many guises. They are in the classroom; they are in administrative positions; they work in their home country, or they could be working now or have worked in the past in other countries beyond their home base; and they could be at any level of education, anywhere. In many respects, they are the same as global educators; however, distinctions are being made here in order to highlight and feature certain leadership characteristics that are a catalyst for new learning and initiatives.

"All mankind is divided into three groups: those that are immovable, those that are movable and those that move."

Benjamin Franklin

Teacherpreneur

The term "teacherpreneur" is a portmanteau of "teacher" and "entrepreneur." A typical teacherpreneur leader is a champion for change and realizer of the vision; is able to introduce new methods of publication and sharing; is adept at building and facilitating communities; is a researcher; innovates from within; has curriculum flexibility and autonomy; is able to work within and beyond the school culture; and takes on the roles of manager, director, mentor, and guide as needed. Teacherpreneurs want to see students engaged and learning and, in the quest for profitable learning experiences, can be considered disruptive leaders as they innovate and move ahead to forge global partnerships.

Teacherpreneur: a leader who "takes all the best practices in education and latest advances in technology and uses them to blaze new trails in teaching and learning that focus on connection and collaboration" (Caples, Casey, Cherian, & Espejo-Vadillo, n.d.).

A teacherpreneur can also be referred to as an "edupreneur" or even an "outlier," although for our purposes here, "outlier" is given separate status. The first step toward being a teacherpreneur is to be a connected and collaborative educator and education leader using online technologies. The next steps include leading curriculum reform, leading online and offline discussions, leading new approaches to professional learning, and working to connect students and teachers with the world for meaningful learning. It is this "leading by example" method, not a "do as I say" leadership approach, that ensures success.

"Most global educators start out as lone wolves, yet by connecting and collaborating with like–minded educators around the world, they can become leaders of change. We are teachers, collaborators, advocates, innovators, and pioneers who learn from the experiences and stories of those who have gone before. Together, we are exploring new ways to enable our students to learn with the world, not just about it" (Michael Graffin, Australia, @mgraffin).

Read more about Michael and the Global Classroom Project in Case Study 1.3 in the ebook.

Pay it Forward

Teacherpreneurs want to see students engaged and learning and, in the quest for "profitable" learning experiences, can be considered disruptive leaders as they innovate and move ahead to forge global partnerships.

The Center for Teaching Quality (CTQ), led by Barnett Berry, shares a more localized or national (USA-based) definition of the teacherpreneur. On the CTQ website, teacherpreneurs are described as "expert teachers whose work weeks are divided between teaching students and designing systems-level solutions for public education." Berry's co-authored book, *Teacherpreneurs: Innovative Teachers Who Lead but Don't Leave* (Berry, Byrd, & Wieder, 2013), in conjunction with numerous online articles, he has authored, shares a great deal of information about the importance of supporting innovative teachers through alternative approaches to school structures. This includes encouraging new blended learning modes using technology for community outreach. Highlighting teacherpreneurs and the global education marketplace, Berry (2010) states, "With emerging technologies, by 2030 teachers will have numerous options for entrepreneurial activity and participating in the global trade in pedagogy. Most of us know Wikipedia and Ning. They are powerful tools, but they are the technologies of 2010, not 2030. With advances in communications hardware and software, by 2030 master teachers will be engaged in a system of global trade, where they lead students through increasingly individualized learning experiences. The value they bring is not a series of prepackaged multimedia or online-delivered products, but teachers' special abilities to identify the needs of their students and facilitate learning in physical and virtual environments." (pp. 21–22).

Learn more about the Center for Teaching Quality and teacherpreneurship through this website: **www.teachingquality.org/teacherpreneurs** and video: **https://youtu.be/9Dhin1YmGuo**

Although Berry refers more specifically to teachers in public schools across the USA, his ideals of a hybrid role for teachers (partly in the classroom, partly working across classrooms to support and lead others) is relevant to the development of global education leaders anywhere in the world. We could ask, therefore, are all teacherpreneurs potentially global educators? How do we support one and the other to blend/merge so they become stronger with this dual or hybrid role?

Outlier

The term "outlier" came into vogue in 2008 with Malcolm Gladwell's book *Outliers: The Story of Success*. We need to examine this phenomenon as it applies to recent experiences of teacherpreneurs in terms of, first, education leaders who may be identified as outliers, and, second, education leaders who need to be able to identify outliers in their schools in order to positively support them. This has implications for recruitment within a learning institution to ensure that outliers are included and that innovation in global learning is being supported from within.

Outlier: a person or thing differing from all other members of a particular group or set.

Outlier teacher: An outlier teacher is a K–12 educator who is self-directed to create and develop an innovative pedagogy using emerged or emerging digital social media through collaborative and global open networking (Arteaga, 2012, p. 14).

Traits of an Outlier Educator

Wagner (2012), in *Creating Innovators: The Making of Young People Who Will Change the World*, shares five fundamental constants of the outlier educator. These are paraphrased here (Martin, 2011):

1. They presided over a classroom culture not of individual achievement, but instead collaboration.
2. Their teaching practice was one not of specialization but instead entirely multidisciplinary—that is the norm of teachers who cultivate innovative mindsets among our students.
3. They asked of their students, and practiced with them not risk avoidance but trial and error—try something, fail, try something different.
4. They promoted the value not of consuming, but creating.
5. They employed not extrinsic, but intrinsic motivation with their students.

Our Global Friendships (OGF—a small global group of educators who have built a community of practice around online global collaboration—see Case Study 4.5) is a formidable group in what they are doing by joining together globally to change the world, including meeting any and all days of the week and often at odd hours. As global educators, do their peers consider them crazy?

Robyn, a member of OGF, says "We are a group of outliers who have found each other and support each other and have conversations that we can't always have with other people because they are not where we are right now'" (Robyn Thiessen, Canada, @robynthiessen).

Characteristics of an Outlier Global Education Leader

Let's take this a few steps further and examine the research done by Arteaga (2012) on the outlier global educator as a leader in new digital pedagogies. The findings of her PhD research suggested that "a grassroots movement headed by outlier teachers' digital *collaborative and global* practices is impacting education in the early 21st century. The research revealed outlier teachers used social media in practical ways to create learning environments that are flexible and extend learning beyond traditional classroom walls, used social media as the vehicle to collaborative and global learning, had a strong sense of mission, a need to transform the system, to contribute to the global village, and to mentor and be mentored. Outlier teachers self-directed and engaged the global community in collaborative experiential learning. Where local support was tenuous, they went global and found support through virtual connections" (p. 163).

Aligned with Wagner (2012), Arteaga (2012) concludes that collaborative and global practice and the forging of new pedagogies, along with the use of social media and digital technologies, engaged the global community in a new learning ecology. Global education leadership needs to either emulate or be able to recognize this within an education setting and support this as a vehicle for purposeful professional action leading to ubiquitous learning.

Learning Concierge

One of the roles of a global education leader (and any teacher, for that matter) is to be a concierge for students. This is not just a label, but also an attitude and a habitual approach to teaching and learning that includes facilitation of learning through personal and professional online connections, 24/7. An early adopter of "learning concierge" is Curtis Bonk (2007), who advocates a freer approach to instruction and a nonhierarchical approach to knowledge construction.

Learning concierge: An educator who supports knowledge construction in a nonhierarchical approach to learning globally. Teachers must be true facilitators of learning, acting as a learning architect, learning concierge, modeler, network navigator, connected learning incubator, synthesizer, and, most importantly, a change agent and learning guide.

Digital Technology and Leadership for Global Learning

Engagement with digital tools is an essential requirement of a teacherpreneur and outlier education leader. Likewise, global collaboration today obtains greater validity in conjunction with digital, specifically "online" tools to support online connections, communication, and co-creation (see more in Part Three of this book, "Online Global Collaboration").

A global education leader knows that digital technology is part of the solution in meeting the needs of today's learners. This same digital technology also supports individual sharing of the vision and empowers learners through alternative and virtual networking capabilities, using both synchronous and asynchronous communication techniques. According to Papa (2011), technology leadership is more about pedagogy and human relations and less about the technology itself. Therefore, leadership to support technology is more about designing and implementing new strategies to help teachers and students recognize, understand, and integrate technology in various learning spaces. The context of technology does not alter the fact that it is a leadership challenge (not a technology challenge) to develop a culture of cooperation and collaboration. If this is not already in place, the introduction of new

Pay it Forward

A global education leader knows that digital technology is part of the solution in meeting the needs of today's learners. This same digital technology also supports individual sharing of the vision and empowers learners through alternative and virtual networking capabilities, using both synchronous and asynchronous communication techniques.

technologies is not going to change that culture and make it cooperative or collaborative. People need to develop the ability as well as the willingness to share knowledge by using technology, and they must be willing to form new relationships that are not face-to-face. This takes time.

Leadership to Support Flat, Connected Learning

The use of technology promotes transparency and accessibility. For example the principal or "Head of School" is now more accessible; teachers are branding their professional lives within and beyond the local community; and many other changes have taken place in a typical learning environment as to how people interact and with whom they interact on a daily basis. A new paradigm for educational leadership is emerging to support place-based learning, connectivism, and global outreach. A learning environment can aspire to have a certain flexibility so that all participants consolidate as well as innovate within the community, and to be able to break out of the bubble that constrains true global independence and collaborative learning.

One goal of a global education leader is to move away from strategic leadership (where only leaders are encouraged to look beyond the organization for information and new knowledge) and move to a more flattened leadership environment. A flat, connected learning environment has less hierarchy of command and encourages every educator to be looking out for critical information to support learning.

Pay it Forward

A flat, connected learning environment has less hierarchy of command, is more agile in approach, and encourages every educator to be looking out for critical information to support learning.

It is easy to say that "visionary" leadership is required to support flat and connected learning. In fact, global standards such as ISTE's Standards for Administrators include, "a shared vision for comprehensive integration of technology to promote excellence and support transformation throughout the organization." In terms of implementing the vision, however, we need to ask what is the best way to support students and teachers (all learners) to find their own voice and take charge of their own learning. How do we promote a culture of sharing and collaboration and the

Resource

ISTE Standards for Administrators

- Visionary leadership
- Digital age learning culture
- Excellence in professional practice
- Systemic improvement
- Digital citizenship

Learn more at **iste.org/standards**

mindset needed for flat learning that views change and the change process as normal? How do we redefine the role of the teacher *and* the role of the student to embrace active as opposed to passive participation in learning?

There is now a new paradigm of educational leadership that is addressing school revitalization in a digital world. Online learning communities and the ability to connect globally are leveling the playing field to advantage learners, while global education leaders are starting to recognize teacherpreneurs and outliers as providers of new forms of leadership.

Leadership actions to support Teacherpreneurs include:

- Encourage customization of learning experiences to local standards while being flexible to embrace connection
- Embrace innovation and encourage pedagogical excellence
- Implement an agile curriculum
- Equip teachers to investigate new global relationships and design solutions
- Create opportunities from perceived difficulties
- Build a culture of success

Suzie Boss rightly questions whether the teacherpreneur movement will lead to a long-term system change (Boss, 2015). However, I believe there is what could be described as a leadership imperative to acknowledge and support connected, flat, and global learning and teacherpreneurs as innovators for change. The power of networked learning is pervasive. Global education leaders must understand how this translates into networked leadership as well.

One new form of leadership that aligns with these needs is "parallel leadership," a form of distributed leadership (Crowther, Ferguson, & Hann, 2009). In this model,

Parallel leadership: a process whereby teacher **leaders** and their principal engage in collective action to build school capacity. It embodies three distinct qualities—mutual trust, shared purpose, and allowance for individual expression.

Read more: **http://eprints.usq.edu.au/5737/**

For a real-world example, watch the interview with Showk Badat, Principal at Essa Academy, UK: **http://vimeo.com/62035949**

teacher leaders and school principals engage in collective action to build capacity through mutual trust, shared purpose, and allowance for individual expression. For successful parallel leadership, a professional learning community must be accepted as integral to organizational development with the core purpose of creating and sustaining new knowledge (Crowther, 2010).

The Importance of Effective Leadership

Connecting learners and connected learning that lead to collaborative learning is a mindset and relates to the school culture. Global education leadership that will affect this involves a shared responsibility, including collaborative planning as a school community to take advantage of global learning. Support must come from within the school for educators who want to take risks and try new techniques and ideas. Otherwise, serious and lasting change cannot be sustained. Connected learning promotes ownership of the learning pathway, and all stakeholders rely on effective leadership to not stifle creativity and collaboration.

"Research has shown that schools where global interaction and collaboration is taking place using technology is where there is strong administrative support. There is encouragement and acknowledgement and recognition as well as appreciation and parental involvement. There is an almost unanimous response that the benefits for students and teachers are positive when involved in global projects but if there is resistance or non-support from administrators then they often do not continue. It becomes too much of a struggle and becomes too frustrating for them."

Yvonne Marie Andres, USA, @YvonneMarieA

Connected Learning Leadership Framework

In a global, connected, and flat learning environment, and one that uses mobile and ubiquitous tools, a more integrated leadership framework is needed. This includes the three main stakeholders—global education leaders, global educators, and students as leaders (global students). Instead of tension between all three groups, for global, connected, and collaborative learning the playing field can be leveled, with shared understandings and shared motivation to improve learning outcomes.

Stakeholder Roles

The following roles are from a "Connected Learning for All" document I co-created with THINK Global School. Read more about the unique THINK Global School and their global approach to connected learning in Case Study 4.3 in the ebook.

Connected Learning for All

The role of the Head of School (and other designated leaders on-site and off-site) is to navigate a pathway from consolidation to innovation as a cyclical approach. They must blur the lines between physical and virtual learning and connected approaches using digital technology through the learning concierge approach and model best practice connection, communication, and collaboration with the world. Above all, this leadership framework relies on a flattened hierarchical approach to leadership and promotes a parallel approach for sustained capacity, and a scenario where in fact leaders "get out of the way of the learning" by fostering technology-supported and engaged rather than passive learning modes.

The role of the global "school" as such (all stakeholders working together) is to provide motivation, encouragement, and accountability in the learning process; to provide the technology infrastructure for connected learning; and to create support for the most ideal conditions for learning possible, thereby limiting the friction and barriers to learning.

The role of the global student is to be the main driving force behind their own learning and to be a reliable and responsible communicator, contributor, and collaborator in online and face-to-face modes. As well as having a clear and ethical approach to using technology as a global citizen, they must learn how to work collaboratively while maintaining individualism and be able to create and co-create content and share this through their network.

> The role of the global teacher has the same objectives as for the student but also includes being a learning architect by creatively reshaping curriculum and opportunities to take advantage of multiple connections and modes of learning. The teacher must be able to find rich global learning opportunities and share them with their students while striving to become a change maker and teacherpreneur.

Consolidation–Innovation Cycle

The "Consolidation–Innovation Cycle" model (Figure 5.1) is proposed as a leadership strategy to encourage innovation and development of growth within an organization. It also accounts for building a culture of learning through clear organization strategies such as building global networks enabled by technology (Limerick, Cunnington, & Crowther, 2002) and creating professional collaborative communities and collaborative working environments (Kruse, Louis, & Bryk, 1994).

The aim of this approach is to create a culture of leadership to produce change (Kotter, 1992). The innovation comes about through fostering teachers as independent leaders (Crowther et al., 2009), also referred to in this model as "teacherpreneurs," who strive to bring opportunities for learners into the school and share the learning from within the school with the world. The model generated here aligns with the "founding, consolidation, renewal" (Limerick et al., 2002) approach of metastrategic leadership. This will also support building a professional learning community, with the objective of ensuring an online as well as offline workflow with reliable contributions and collaborations and allowing the school to move forward in connected learning.

With this model for leadership, stakeholders within the school have certain roles that move a shared vision to become an enabled vision; organization-wide strategies to support a connected culture of learning; parallel leadership mode to support collaborative individualism and the teacherpreneur expectation; and school improvement strategies to support a sustained capacity where teachers become knowledge workers. It is the understanding of these roles and how they mesh that is crucial to the success of the model.

Through cycles of consolidation and discontinuity (innovation) that entrench a distributed/parallel leadership approach, the movement from simple school improvement to sustained capacity can take place in conjunction with teacher and student confidence and ability to become connected and collaborative learners and leaders.

Teachers need to be encouraged to be collaborative individuals. They need to operate autonomously when out in the field and make the important connections with externals, yet bring back information that can build on a central resource.

Consolidation

Shared vision

Organization-wide strategies

Parallel leadership
- teachers
- students

School improvement

Innovation

Enabling vision

Culture of learning
- connected

Collaborative individualism
- teacherpreneur

Sustained capacity
- teachers as knowledge workers

Figure 5.1: The Consolidation—Innovation Cycle Approach to Leadership for Connected Learning (Lindsay, 2014)

Collaborative individualism: The dominant culture of network organizations stresses the need for individuals to work together with others toward a common vision and mission. It also stresses their emancipation—their freedom from groups, organizations, and social institutions.

Information technology is the catalyst that enabled a more atomistic structure of isolated individuals to become a proactive system of collaborative individuals who are:

- autonomous
- proactive
- empathetic

- intuitive and creative
- transforming

- politically skilled
- networking
- mature

(Limerick & Cunningham, 1993)

How to Lead for Global Citizenship

A global education leader must understand online citizenship modes and behaviors and also model and promote a positive mindset for global connections. Being online as a leader with other learners is an essential requirement here and yes, often there are a myriad of other priorities on the learning landscape vying for time, however leadership = digital = online = citizenship for learning....it's that simple! Individualistic approaches to internet use often produce ethical blindspots and "disconnects." The Global Citizenship Construct, introduced in Chapter 1, encourages a more holistic approach that considers individual, social and cultural aspects of online global learning. Leadership in a global context means additional responsibilities to foster knowledge and adoption of all elements of the Global Citizenship Construct (shown in Figure 6.1). Typical challenges for global education leaders include how to:

- foster real forms of communication and go beyond the artificial "behind the screen" communications typical across existing learning environments
- break down the walls and openly model and freely discuss ethical and moral issues to do with online learning, global collaboration, sharing and co-creating addressing individual, social and cultural issues
- communicate with local community members (students, parents, the wider community) about the added value of learning while global as well as cultivating "conscientious connectivity" (Carrie & Jenkins, 2014)
- foster "learner agency" and consideration of the value of online activities so that positive online social or civic deeds are encouraged as part of the greater good of global learning

Table 6.1: Leadership Using the Global Citizenship Construct

Areas	Actions
Individual + Social Social Individual	• Develop social approaches to online privacy that are built on respect. • Move beyond "stranger danger," protecting privacy and not posting something that will affect school and/or work life and effectively embrace an open learning approach based on "conscientious connectivity." • Build online communities and foster individual ethical and moral dispositions.
Cultural + Individual Individual Cultural	• Manipulate the distance between "us" and "others" and moderate a discussion forum or share information in ways that is sensitive to the safety of others across the world to avoid individual bullying, cheating, or disrespecting others. • Foster global decision making while learning and working online that takes into account the needs and situations of others. • Discourage anonymity of digital technology and appropriation of other people's content vs respecting others property/creative work.
Social + Cultural Cultural Social	• Raise awareness that people in other countries must follow their laws and that certain online behaviour, although legal for one person, may cause problems for another. • Build empathy through open connectivity and collaborative activities while ensuring communication is clear and devoid of misunderstandings. • Encourage social responsibility and working together for a better world.

It is interesting that research by Carrie and Jenkins (2014) found that young people were more likely to adopt an ethically sensitive mindset through participation in online communities - such as those focused on an activity like blogging, content creation, or gaming. This does not mean that an online community based around a racist or sexist theme is ethically sensitive, however the sense of community and "together we can learn and change the world" is real in a global context when learners are joined together.

A global education leader understands the imperative of networked, community-driven learning and how to support global digital citizenship objectives because they are active online learners themselves. When asked, "What do schools need for online global connections and collaborations?" the answer from Ed Gragert, USA (@ egragert), was:

More! Give teachers resources and professional development and then let teachers decide for themselves. It may seem like heresy, but leaders should get out of the way and let teachers do what works in their classrooms. Give teachers sanction for their global work and for enabling their students to engage with the world. Leaders need to give permission to do this knowing the learning outcome is better than if they do not do it. Sometimes it is hard to find concrete evidence—research is important—and leaders need to see this.

How to Build Virtual and Real Learning Communities

A global education leader has to know how to build virtual and real learning communities—and then blend them! Maybe the "real" (synchronous and face-to-face) is taken for granted…but its definition needs expounding here. It is one thing to build a working learning community that is internal to the school or organization—but another to then broaden this to include "significant others." As a generalization, one thing educators traditionally have not been good at is sharing, and once the words "community" and "collaboration" are used, it often sends them scuttling back to the classroom. Leadership is paramount in this scenario for building communities online, and watering them to see them grow and expand.

Pay it Forward

A global education leader has to know how to build virtual and real learning communities - and then blend them!

When I was working at Qatar Academy (QA) (2007–2009), Ning technology (http://ning.com) was in its early days and free to use. After a discussion with colleagues, we started a community for the school and across Doha where there was a mixture of expat and Arabic teachers, from K–12 and higher education. This was one of my first experiences learning that "build it and they will *not* come." Most of the 150 teachers at QA did not see the point of a virtual community, of sharing ideas and resources online, or even of blogging. However, it was pleasantly surprising how many did join and started contributing. It was also pleasantly surprising to have members join from across the world, having found our community via my tweets and networks. For some it was their first experience connecting virtually, and they were excited about sharing ideas and questions.

Around this time I also used Ning in my high school classes (and still do use it across high school and teacher education!), as it supported virtual communication and multimedia sharing for global collaboration. However, an incident regarding online advertising almost pulled down my program, until Ning finally came to the rescue. Read about this on my blog, "The straw, the camel and the Ning" (Lindsay, 2007). So, as leaders we walk a tightrope sometimes, ready to move, respond, and make quick decisions to avoid falling. As global education leaders, we must always connect with the world and design learning to be responsive to global situations and events.

While I was working in Beijing, a small group of leaders in 2011 started the Future Learning @ Beijing (FL@B) association (http://futurelearningbeijing.wikispaces.com). This was the message we distributed at the time: "The vision for FL@B was to create an association of education leaders who plan to improve teaching and learning through the appropriate use of emerging technologies and global collaborative pedagogy. All schools in Beijing, and surrounds, are invited to send representatives from cross-school curriculum areas, e-learning, information technology management and other areas where discussion centers around adopting new or improved practices." The group met a number of times and practiced innovative strategies, including one time where students also joined us and, in mixed groups, we discussed the most recent Horizon Report (on emerging technologies for K–12)—a good opportunity for cross-fertilization of ideas and flat learning.

In these examples, an online portal and opportunity for virtual exchanges supported the real-time meetings. Today, of course, with the rise of Twitter and other more popular tools, this has become even more pervasive, and teacher gatherings, such as TeachMeets, with supporting web portals are changing the way educators learn and share (see Chapter 8 for more on TeachMeets).

How to Lead Pedagogical Change

A global education leader understands the concept of "critical digital pedagogy" as an approach to teaching and learning predicated on fostering agency and empowering learners with practice centered on community and collaboration, openness to diversity and international voices, and emphasis on critical thinking about tools and technology (Stommel, 2014). Emerging practices with technology that support collaboration such as sharing, dialogue, and participation are not new, but the emergence of Web 2.0 organizes the learning around the user as a node in the network, rather than around the educator. Leaders must demonstrate and model collaborative practices to support pedagogical change. According to McLoughlin and Lee (2010), pedagogical change requires knowledge of appropriate teaching methods and awareness of the learner experience while using Web 2.0 technologies and social media. Fullan and colleagues discuss "new pedagogies" arising from the new learning partnership between and among students and educators when using digital technologies for deeper learning across the globe. Pedagogical capacity, an educator's repertoire of teaching strategies and partnerships for learning, has changed and will continue to change as technology becomes more pervasive to include content delivery and consumption as well as collaboration and creation of new knowledge and a focus on the process of learning (Fullan et al., 2014).

This changing culture of leadership leading to a new framework means that "Leadership becomes the expectation and the norm at every layer of the system, with students, teachers and leaders all leading their own learning.... This cascading model of learning through partnership extends through students, teachers and leaders—all learning with and from each other... not leadership from the top, but leadership and learning from within" (Fullan et al., 2014, p. 52).

From Pedagogy to Cosmogogy

The discussion about leading pedagogical change in the context of our digital and online world would perhaps benefit from an infusion of new terms to help align with the goals of global, connected, and flat learning. In his book *Open*, David Price discusses the shift from pedagogy (to lead the child, or "instructional learning"), to androgogy (to lead the man/adult, or "self-directed learning"), to heutagogy (to lead to find, or "self-determined learning"). Heutagogy has been applied to adult education, as described by originators Hase and Kenyon (2000). It "recognizes the need to be flexible in the learning where the teacher provides resources....As teachers we should concern ourselves with developing the learner's capability not just embedding discipline based skills and knowledge. We should relinquish any power we deem ourselves to have" (p. 6). I tend to agree with Price when he states that heutagogy is as applicable to children as it is to adults. It's defined by approach, not age (Price, 2013).

Another concept that supports knowledge building among learners in a community of practice (CoP) is that of "peeragogy." The work of Corneli and Danoff (2011) on Paragogy, a theory of peer learning using online environments to support freely available peer production of content (Wheeler, 2012a) inspired Howard Rheingold (2012) to start the Peeragogy Project. Peeragogy, an open learning environment and a new way of seeing and collaborating and learning, is often unstructured in practice, and learning is collaborative, not just cooperative or contributory. Increased accessibility to online networks enables the development of collaborative learning, which in turn builds skills and competencies needed in a learning community. "Peer learning and peer production are probably as old as humanity itself, but they take on new importance in the digital age" (Rheingold, 2014).

Pay it Forward

Peeragogy, an open learning environment and a new way of seeing and collaborating and learning, is often unstructured in practice, and learning is collaborative, not just cooperative or contributory.

Not only attitudes and skills, but also tools are important to support peeragogical practices. These include places to work simultaneously (synchronously) and at individual times (asynchronously), and of course some tools provide facility for both needs.

Cosmogogy

In this book I am suggesting a new "-gogy,": that of "cosmogogy," coming from the word "cosmo" which means "of or relating to the universe." A cosmogogical approach to teaching and learning applies to having a global or a world approach. It applies to being comfortable and familiar learning with others in different places through the use of online technologies. It puts the learner at the center of the "universe," a node on the network, with the capability of reaching out and connecting to anything and anyone in order to find information, in order to collaborate and to co-create with anyone, anywhere, anytime. It also means learners approach problems and solutions from a more openly networked and in fact global perspective to the point that "unflat" learning feels strange and closed in. Cosmogogical leadership pertains to understanding how to foster and support approaches to learning while connected to others in any part of the world. It is about how to support individualized and personalized learning that is less teacher and school directed, more self-determined as with heutagogy; aligned with developing a culture of collaboration as with peeragogy; and with a focus on student/learner autonomy.

Cosmogogy: The method and practice of learning while connected to the world using digital technologies whereby the context of learning is "with" rather than "about." It is not location based and considers whom you learn with and what you construct together most important.

(Lindsay, 2016)

The Global Education
Leader in Action

A major challenge for global education leaders is encouraging connected and collaborative learning within their schools, organizations, and networks. For some educators, a change in teaching approaches (including understanding and embracing the cosmos!) is very slow to come. In a recent online conversation with global leader Craig Kemp, international educator in Singapore, he shared how it takes leadership skill to cajole and support and motivate and engage educators to become connected. He impresses on educators the many benefits for themselves and ultimately for their students. I reflected that he sounded just like me 10 years ago when, as an e-learning leader at International School Dhaka (ISD), my role was similarly frustrating—with almost the same daily conversations. In those days my colleagues were only just starting to learn how to manage our 1:1, wireless, and ubiquitous learning environment (laptops in Grades 9–12 and Palms in Grades 6–8). ISD at the time was leading the way with mobile learning with more of a top-down approach, realizing the inevitability that it just had to happen. Leading this type of change involves close communication between users of technology and those who can fix the technology (perhaps more so in those days, given certain hardware and software vulnerabilities) and many conversations with teachers who found themselves out of their comfort level with devices in the classroom. Sharing simple management skills—such as it being OK to ask students to put their devices away sometimes, and it being necessary to get up from behind the desk in the front of the room to walk around the learning (rather than complain that students were "time-wasting" on their devices)—became important conversations among teachers at the time…and those conversations are still important today!

Leadership for New Global Learning Paradigms

Leading global connection and collaboration is a much more diverse skill now—device management, online learning platforms, Web 2.0 facility, collaborative pedagogy, and more. The global education leaders featured in this chapter are teacherpreneurs and outliers in a variety of ways. They lead new initiatives tirelessly and with the conviction that making authentic global connections for an educator is the bridge to collaborative teaching and learning in both real and virtual learning environments.

Evolution of Leadership Style: an Australian Perspective

Anne Mirtschin, an award-winning Australian teacher who has led the way in global learning for many years, contributes the following excerpt. Read more about Anne in Case Study 1.1 in the ebook. Anne contributes the following for the purposes of this book in order to share global leadership goals and actions.

Evolution of Leadership Style

Leadership involves sharing—sharing experiences, challenges, reflections, learning and more in open, online spaces such as blogs, discussion groups on Nings, Google+, Skype, and Edmodo groups. It entails taking risks, willingness to experiment, determination to succeed with projects, ability to pave the way when challenges would prevent others from venturing. It may mean taking little steps when barriers come in the way.

"The role of leadership in education … is not and should not be command and control. The real role of leadership is climate control, creating a climate of possibility. And if you do that, people will rise to it and achieve things that you completely did not anticipate and couldn't have expected."

Ken Robinson (2013)

Leadership for Global Collaboration

For many, it means jumping in where few others have dared venture and exploring uncharted territory. The curriculum may have to fit the projects or collaboration rather than refusing to take part because it does not match the curriculum. It involves taking on responsibilities in organized projects, mentoring those who need help, being involved in or leading the way with Twitter chats, using hashtags that alert others to the opportunities for global connection and collaboration. It means making opportunities for sharing, such as presenting at online webinars, the annual Global Education Conference (GEC), or other online conferences. Where possible, face-to-face conferences provide wonderful opportunities for presenting. Special global days will be promoted, and leaders will get involved in Connected Educator Month in October each year.

It means busy days, actively seeking out tools that will ensure success, a willingness to take on leading roles within global projects or starting global projects of your own. Strong communication skills are essential, and broad shoulders to ignore the many "blockers" who may be out there. Global collaboration means just that in leadership as well.

In the early days, I saw my personal leadership style as being "servant leadership," as I tended to lead simply by meeting the needs of the team such as sharing experiences, participating when required, being a judge where needed, providing advice to others, recording global competencies required, and so on. I would do whatever I could to enable dynamic interactive and transformative educational experiences across borders. However, in recent years, I would like to think that I am taking on a "transformational leadership" style, trying to motivate others locally and globally through a range of options including moderating weekly online webinars, being a leader for the GEC, leading global discussions at the ISTE conference, taking on moderator of Twitter chats for "Skype in the Classroom" and the "Global Classroom," sharing experiences, projects, and contacts over Twitter, writing guest blog posts, sitting on global panels, and presenting wherever possible in both face-to-face and virtual situations.

> "Collaborative leadership is key to success. Being a leader, means that we are teaching and learning in spaces that may have never been ventured into before, leading the way to completely change the pedagogy of teaching and learning, bringing excitement into the classroom and beyond on a global scale." Anne Mirtschin

Leading for Collaborative Learning

Katie Grubb, Australia, is a Mandarin language educator and recipient of the NSW Premier's Kingold Chinese Teacher Award in 2015, as well as co-founder of "Connect with China Collaborative" that brings students, teachers, and extended community members together with the purpose of connecting with China.

"Collaborative learning can be difficult sometimes when you can't see everyone face to face and ask how their learning and contributing is going. Leadership skills in collaborative learning is definitely something I am constantly developing and became aware of when I started a Chinese teacher collaborative group using WeChat—at first everyone contributed—but then the conversation died down after the initial buzz, so I had to learn some strategies" (Katie Grubb, Australia, @katiegrubby).

Strategies for Collaborative Learning

Katie's simple checklist to support leaders:

- Does everyone in the group understand what they have to do? How do you know this? Sometimes when people aren't contributing it's because they don't understand the process. It can be worthwhile to write out what the process and steps are and to check to see if everyone understands what is going to happen.

- Can everyone access the digital tools and do they know for which part of the learning process they are to be used? It is good to double check and ask if anyone is having trouble.

- As leaders, are we commenting and giving feedback and encouragement to *every* post in our group? Being "seen" is a great motivator for students.

- What guiding questions and smaller tasks can group members do that will contribute to the bigger project?

- Checklists are good for students too. For example, "Week 1: did I share a photo of my rural area/city (on Edmodo or Padlet) and comment on another student's post? Week 2: Did I answer the guiding question? How did I research it?"

- If the usual channels of communication in the collaborative groups areas aren't working then try a personal email (to the person you would like to contribute more, or a group email to the class). If you get no response, you can email their teachers and see if they can provide extra support. You can also send personal messages on Edmodo. You are more likely to get a response to a direct message than a group message.

Characteristics of a Leader: a Mexican Perspective

Pedro Aparicio (@Aparicio_Pedro) is an education leader based in Mexico City. He is a Google Certified Teacher and leads Google Hangouts and mystery Skype calls for cultural exchanges in his classroom. He is also co-founder of the Twitter hashtag #mexedchat. When asked recently about the attributes of a global education leader, he shared the following points.

A global education leader must be someone who:

1. Can be open-minded about people from different countries and cultures.
2. Can communicate and provoke learning through global collaboration.
3. Is committed to education. If you expect your team to work hard and produce quality content, you're going to need to lead by example.
4. Has a positive attitude toward solving world's issues.
5. Has the ability to inspire and empower students and other educators to make a positive change locally and globally.
6. Is creative and original in order to make a difference in the global village.
7. Is a risk taker with a passion for using innovative technologies and approaches to improve teaching and learning.
8. Can have the desire to participate in real-time online Professional Development.
9. Is an ambassador for change and models high expectations, leadership, lifelong learning, collaboration and innovation.
10. Grows his/her PLN.
11. Can often attend and/or be a presenter at different conferences about education and technology throughout the year.

Some Global Conferences to attend:

Global Education Conference: **http://globaleducationconference.com**

Learning2: **http://learning2.org**

K12 Online Conference: **http://k12onlineconference.org/**

Grassroots Leadership in New Zealand

Award-winning New Zealand educator Sonya Van Schaijik (@vanschaijik) tells us, "My own name is associated with being a global education leader. The work I do with teachers allows me the autonomy to trial learning and gives me the confidence to develop that same confidence with the children that I teach."

I first met Sonya when she was on an award-funded education world tour. She came to Honolulu in 2013 to join the Flat Classroom Live! 2-day event where educators and high school students came together to work collaboratively on solving global issues. Sonya has a true passion for leading educational change and learns quickly from and with others across the world.

"Advice for global educators: If they want to "become" a global education leader/educator—they should be there now. [That's the] difference between thinking about the task and just doing it." Sonya Van Schaijik

Be Disruptive!

Reflective professional learning, including disruptive practices that focus on process more so than product, was a focus of the #EdBookNZ project Sonya launched in 2014. "Connected educator" is a term being used a lot now, of course, but when talking to Sonya, the realization is that it should be just what we naturally do as educators: connected learning that really has to be about collaboration and co-creation. Sonya tells us, "Through the work I do with Pam Hook and SOLO Taxonomy, I have identified this as thinking relationally because teachers working collaboratively together strengthens their understanding about making links with each other and with a topic. If an artefact is co-created then abstract thinking is extended. This was highlighted in the EdBookNZ project that happened during Connected Educators month 2014. Based on the work I did as part of the Flat

Connections Global Educator certified course I pulled together 10 educators from around New Zealand to write a digital book. The feedback after the sessions was the writers had more fun and learning with the process of having a disruptive friend."

Educators were invited to contribute to the book and to have a "disruptive friend (DF)." This challenged their thinking and also had them reflect on how their thinking had changed. Although the book was finished and went live, the real learning took place in the process, and Sonya sees this as something we can emulate as educators in our classrooms. Sonya explains the role of the DF in a bread-making analogy. The DF is like the yeast: it makes something happen, and you get a much better product through deeper thinking. The DF is not meant to be negative but fearlessly asks the questions that should be asked. They also push for the work to be finished and at the highest standard possible. I think we all need a DF or two!

EdBookNZ 2014 outcome: **http://tinyurl.com/zwpb62f**

EdBookNZ 2015 wiki: **http://edbooknz.wikispaces.com**

SOLO Taxonomy (Pam Hook): **http://pamhook.com/solo-taxonomy/**

Being a Global Education Leader Means . . .

"That I must take responsibility for creating the conditions where students can make connections personally and conceptually in a global learning community. It is about ensuring that our students have an orientation where they are learning about "what is" and "what could be" so that they feel empowered to make an impact on their world." (Wayne Denmar, International Head of School, Australia)

"To teach learners concepts and skills necessary to function in a world that is increasingly interconnected and multicultural. It also means being able to help learners to examine issues from the vantage point of the individual, the local community, the nation, and the world community. It means teaching learners about problems and issues that cut across national boundaries. Furthermore, being global education leader to me means being able to see things through the eyes and minds others—and realizing that while individuals and groups may view life differently, they also have common needs and wants. Being a global

(continued on next page)

educator at my school has a positive impact on the school as well as my learners because everyone is working hard to make sure that we keep up the standard of the school. Many teachers have used the opportunity to learn from me and to improve their teaching and learning." (Moliehi Sekese, Teacher, Curriculum and Assessment Developer, Lesotho)

"Being a global educator and leader means to be a part of building a future where diversity thrives and leads to increased mutual understanding of not only who we are, but our part in this global mosaic. Global education leaders are knowledgeable instructional leaders who are experts not only in content, pedagogy, instruction, and assessment, but also educational technology leaders who are able to integrate technology in meaningful and appropriate ways. In spite of the tremendous pressure and challenges that we all face on a local level, global educators make it their priority to advocate for global educative opportunities.

"I try to bring in a global perspective to the curriculum I cover on a daily basis. In addition, I seek out opportunities for my students to communicate and collaborate with students in different parts of the world on both small and large-scale projects. I also have mentored a fellow teacher in the district through her first experience in global collaborative inquiry by finding a partner in China for her and her students. Through these experiences, I try to lead others to developing a different mindset or way of viewing the world. Most students and teachers that I work with have never had any sort of global collaborative experience and feedback I have received is that these are "mind-altering" and transformative experiences that literally lead to walls being torn down in their mental understandings and perceptions of a different culture. Powerful stuff…" (Janice Mak, Teacher and Instructional Coach, USA, @jmakaz)

Whole-School Approach to Global Leadership

At Wilderness School in Adelaide, Australia global learning and online collaboration is taken very seriously by leaders. Recently Ann Rooney was appointed as Global Project Coordinator and has the responsibility of tracking global projects in the school, assisting teachers to connect with schools and join projects (such as Flat Connections), to build relationships with schools and to be active in global teacher organisations. She will also create an online site that teachers can access for collaborative tools and list global projects. In addition, she will teach an elective short course of one semester to senior secondary students that provides three lessons a week to participate in an online global project. This visionary approach is commendable and hopefully leads the way for other schools looking to take positive action in this area.

Online Global Communities
of Practice

Communities of practice are continuing to develop due to increased access to the internet. These communities extend beyond the immediate school. They are largely online and virtual and provide professional learning for teacherpreneurs as well as a venue for them to lead as "cosmogogical entrepreneurs." Teacherpreneurs have the opportunity to share and promote connected and collaborative excellence, and to package themselves as leaders in the educational global trade.

The examples shared here give the reader an insight into what it takes today to start, manage, and proliferate a community in order to reach the point where authentic sharing and extended learning takes place. We must remember, of course, that global education leaders are implementing these types of community-building initiatives across the world—and on top of what they do already as active educators. Enhanced skills in communication across cultures, event organization, marketing, and promotion, as well as online publishing and archival curation, are a few of the skills needed to support active online and face-to-face communities.

A further challenge for global leaders is the fluidity of community gatherings. It is hard to determine who will actually show up or contribute before, during, or after an event. A recent ISTE Learning Series webinar I co-ran for the ISTE Global Collaboration PLN was what I would call successful. Although more than 80 educators registered to attend, just over 30 came into the virtual room on the day, with everyone who registered receiving materials via email afterward. In the past I have run webinars with no one attending and tweetchats with three active at the time. It does not bother me so much, as the accessible recording and the archived material is often just as important as the presentation and interaction. It is imperative that social media be used to share before, during, and after to maximize participation and use of the learning legacy.

The following examples share the diversity of global education leadership and community development.

Tweetchats

Like it, love it, or just not your style? The tweetchat culture is in full swing right now. There are hundreds of education hashtags being used every day, and many of these have regular 1-hour synchronous chats each week, or each month. Education leaders are designing tweetchat methodology as I write. The approach and look and feel of a tweetchat session continues to evolve—some like to have seven to nine questions delivered by the moderator(s); some like to have one main theme and let questions evolve over the hour. Many tweetchats are *very* busy and the tweets go whizzing by. They are an excellent way to share ideas and resources and to collect new members for your PLN. The following shares some examples of active leadership in this area.

#AussieEd

Founded by Brett Salakas (@MRSalakas), an enthusiastic team of Australian educators now lead what is likely the largest Australian "ed chat" on Twitter. The #aussieED Twitter chat runs on a Sunday night at 8:30 p.m. AEST. Teachers run it for teachers, leaders, and administrators to share and discuss real issues. There is a blog, an interview program, and resources based on an attractive and vibrant website.

#AussieEd, co-founded by Brett Salakas, Australia, **@MRSalakas**

Find updates, archives and more on **http://aussieed.com**

#Whatisschool

Craig Kemp (@mrkempnz) is a Singapore-based New Zealand educator and Head of ICT and Learning Innovation at Avondale Grammar School, and making waves in connected learning globally (Kemp, 2014). As the 2014 Edublog award winner for the best individual tweeter and best Twitter hashtag or chat, he is influencing both the US and Australasian sides of the world.

When Craig co-founded the tweetchat in 2014 with Laura Hill (@candylandcaper), he wanted to create a space online where anyone from anywhere can say anything about the related topic via a tweetchat. The #whatisschool hashtag and regular tweetchat includes topics that cover all levels and engage educators globally to make a difference through connections. The first tweetchat surprised the founders with about 60 people turning up online. Craig relates this was "most overwhelming but also most rewarding." The record since then has been more than 9,000 tweets from 200+ educators within an hour, with averages each week being between 4,000 to 9,000 educators coming from all over the world, almost every continent! "The tweets just fly by at a fast speed!" exclaims Craig. In terms of technology, they use Tweet-Deck to manage and moderate the chat, and Twitter and Google+ as well as their blogs to get information out. They also use an app called Remind with 250 on the list each week who receive a direct email or SMS as a reminder to join in. They are currently working with Remind developers to improve the app. Storify is used to archive the chats. Read tips for managing a fast-paced Twitter chat on Craig's blog (Kemp, 2015).

#Whatisschool, co-founded by Craig Kemp (**@mrkempnz**)

Find archives for **#whatisschool** here on Craig's website: **http://mrkempnz.com/category/whatisschool**

#EdChat

One of the oldest chats for education, #EdChat, was started by Shelly Terrell (@ShellTerrell), Steve Anderson (@web20classroom), and Tom Whitby (@tomwhitby) in 2009 to focus on topics for educators (Whitby, 2012). Tom tells us, "We used the hashtag #Edchat to aggregate all of the tweets in one place so people could follow #Edchat-specific tweets and focus on the chat in real time. By isolating all #Edchat tweets in a separate column on TweetDeck, we were also able to follow and archive the entire discussion. #Edchat certainly was not the first "chat," but its quick acceptance and growth among thousands of educators within weeks ensured its place in Twitter history. We held the original #Edchat at 7 p.m. Eastern on Tuesdays. Tuesdays became known as "Teacher Tuesday," a day on which teachers recommended other teachers to follow on Twitter. Participants used the hashtag #TeacherTuesday or #TT. We quickly learned Twitter's global reach as European educators requested an earlier #Edchat to accommodate their time zones. We added a noon Eastern #Edchat in response" (Whitby, 2012).

"The use of Twitter as the platform for education chats enables not only anyone interested in the topic, but also people whose area of expertise might be that specific topic. Keep in mind that Twitter has a global reach, so the only possible barriers to anyone's participation might just be time zones. Many authors, speakers, bloggers, and thought leaders will often participate in chats." (Whitby, 2015).

#EdChat, Co-founded by Shelly Terrell (**@ShellTerrell**), Steve Anderson (@ **web20classroom**) and Tom Whitby (**@tomwhitby**)

Find more educational hashtags from Cybraryman: **http://cybraryman.com/ edhashtags.html**

Tweetchat calendar:

https://sites.google.com/site/twittereducationchats/education-chat-calendar

Read more in Tom and Steven's book *The Relevant Educator*: **www.corwin.com/ connectededucators/whitby-book.htm**

#satchatOZ

Andrea Stringer (@stringer_andrea), Sydney-based innovative education leader and #satchatOZ co-leader, shared this insight.

"After participating on #satchat, Brad Currie (@bradmcurrie), connected and asked me to co-moderate #satchatOZ. "OZ" stands for Oceania, which is an extension of #satchat. All satchat teams use Google Docs to share the topics and questions. Topics are based on our interest and the interests of our #PLN. We have struggled with time zones and daylight savings time and as circumstances have changed, so have our moderators. Currently, our hour-long chat starts at 8:30 a.m. AEST on Saturdays and our hashtag has changed to reflect the moderators location - #satchatOZ."

Moderating this weekly global Twitter chat, presents opportunities to connect with and learn from highly influential and innovative educators. These experiences allow me to share research, publish work and collaborate with some of the world's best thinkers, practitioners and decision-makers. Being a connected educator sharpens my thinking and opens my eyes to possibilities to further enhance our practice."

#satchatME

Holly Fairbrother (@MrsHollyEnglish), an expat educator based in Qatar, co-leads this new chat in the Middle East. #satchatME is an offshoot of the US-based #satchat. Holly noticed a gap in the market in terms of time zones as well as a lack of ed-tech-based initiatives hailing from the Middle East. Moving to Qatar proved a valuable opportunity to plug this gap and get educators from this part of the world sharing and learning together. #satchatME meets from 7 to 8 p.m. KSA time every Saturday—the nature of the name requires the chat to be on a "Sat," and Holly worked around existing #satchats to ensure there is a chat for every time zone. Topics are decided on among moderators, arise from chats, are voted on by chatting contributors, or are hosted by special guests. Each week, six questions based around the topic are released over the hour. Chats are archived and shared each week via Storify. Holly says, "Following the success of my experience with #satchatOZ, I wanted to be able to share this experience as well as establish and create a PLN in a new part of the world that is emerging educationally. We would like to establish a network of connected educators in the Middle East and blaze the trail when it comes to using technology in a positive and effective way to enhance the teaching and learning experience for everyone in this region."

#satchatOZ, Co-lead Andrea Stringer, Australia, **@stringer_andrea**

#satchatME, Co-lead Holly Fairbrother, Qatar, **@MrsHollyEnglish**

The #satchat tweetchat has a family across the world. See all global leaders via this Smore poster: **www.smore.com/ujyeh-the-satchat-family.**

#ISTEglobalPLN

The ISTE Global Collaboration PLN organizes regular Twitter chats using the hashtag #ISTEglobalPLN. Participants set aside an hour to network on Twitter. Participants answer preset questions and share resources, experiences, and knowledge. This practice builds global awareness and explores competencies for collaborating with others to solve problems. The energy in these chats is fantastic. Participants can learn in synchronous time or asynchronous time (through the archives and ongoing conversations) and form a like-minded community of educators who wish to pursue global learning beyond the textbook. It provides a great opportunity to develop a global professional learning network—a space to innovate, form partnerships, try collaborative technologies, learn of other cultures, spaces, and places, and find inspiration and innovation by being globally connected.

#ISTEglobalPLN

See all ISTE Professional Learning Networks at **http://connect.iste.org/connect/ learningnetworks**

#MexEdChat

The tweetchat #MexEdChat started in August 2013. For more than a year this bilingual chat was held weekly via Twitter, but recently discussions have been every two weeks. Participants come from Canada to Argentina and average 20–30 educators during the chat, with around 1,000 tweets exchanged.

#MexEdChat, Pedro Aparicio, Mexico-City, **@Aparicio_Pedro**

An archive of a joint #MexEdChat and #GEGchat March 2015

http://tinyurl.com/gp25mx7

"The global impact," according to co-founder Pedro Aparicio, "is that we have connected many teachers via Skype and hangouts. We have empowered many students to communicate their ideas and traditions, and more importantly, to break down classroom walls and make learning fun. Latino students practice their English, and US and Canadian students practice their Spanish. Engaging in multifaceted lessons, collaborating with different disciplines, students get a much deeper learning experience to understand the importance of learning other cultures. More importantly, we all have the wonderful opportunity to learn about and reflect on how we are all similar and uniquely different as people."

Founders Dominique Dynes and Pedro Aparicio have plans to have a #MexEdChat website and share resources with more teachers, as well as to add another hashtag, #GEGchat, to invite Google educators to inspire more teachers around the world to make learning an exciting journey.

TeachMeets

While researching for this book I was pleasantly surprised to find how the "Teach-Meet" community has developed globally. There are TeachMeets almost everywhere now (so it seems) with the main idea that teachers learn from each other and that there is a technology focus. At the five-year TeachMeet "birthday," the originator of TeachMeet, Scottish educator Ewan McIntosh (@ewanmcintosh), shares his dislike of traditional conferences where participants lack a synchronous voice and encourages teachers everywhere to be part of this personalized and vital gathering in their own communities (vitalsteve, 2011).

A TeachMeet is an organized but informal meeting (in the style of an unconference) for teachers to share good practice, practical innovations and personal insights in teaching with technology.

http://en.wikipedia.org/wiki/TeachMeet

Read more on Ewan McIntosh's blog **http://edu.blogs.com/edublogs/teachmeet07/**

Find a TeachMeet—Create a TeachMeet! **http://teachmeetinternational.wikispaces.com**

The TeachMeet in Australia

Matt Esterman (@mesterman), Sydney, has led the way in designing TeachMeet experiences for educators in the Sydney area and beyond. Henrietta Miller also hosted the first Primary TeachMeet in Sydney.

On Matt's blog he tells us, "For professional learning, I love TeachMeets. Sure, I still go to conferences and seminars and lectures. I still listen to podcasts and do professional reading. I still sit in meetings and listen to discussion panels. But where I really get the chance to test ideas, to converse and confer, is at a TeachMeet," and

"The beauty of TeachMeets is their focus on ideas, not on egos or brands or products. By the end of a TeachMeet, the participants will have heard several new ideas to take into their classroom, spoken to many new colleagues from all types of schools and institutions, and also—another special aspect of the TeachMeet—is that the participants ARE the presenters. At the best TeachMeets I've been to, the participants are tweeting, chatting and laughing their way through a series of excellent (but short and sharp) talks by their colleagues. On top of that, they get to speak to them in the breaks" (Esterman, 2013).

TeachMeets have been recognized by several institutions and networks as powerful ways to engage teachers in professional learning. The Australian Institute for Teaching and School Leadership (AITSL) awarded the TeachMeet Sydney network with an Innovation Grant that allowed the hosts to provide more opportunities for TeachMeets to occur and for some members to travel to other parts of Australia to assist in supporting the growth of new TeachMeet communities. TeachMeets are not only an Australian phenomenon: they run in the UK on a fairly regular basis and have also become a model adopted in the USA, such as in New Jersey. Matt has joined TeachMeetNJ to share learning across the world, and this has culminated in the organization of a series of TeachMeets on the day before ISTE 2015. The session filled up quickly soon after it was posted on the ISTE website.

TeachMeets are often accompanied by a Twitter hashtag and other forms of back-channeling. This has allowed teachers to learn with colleagues from around the world, from the Czech Republic to New Jersey to London to Melbourne, and everywhere in between.

The idea of TeachMeets is about open, free, teacher-driven professional learning, and the successes that have been found in particular places, such as Perth in Western Australia, are a testament to the fact that something truly inspiring happens when passionate teachers make the time to come together and share their craft. They may look different, function differently, be run by non-teachers from time to time, be sponsored to various degrees, but TeachMeets are by far some of the best professional learning experiences anyone can have.

TeachMeet via Hangout

Over the ditch from Australia (as they say in that part of the world) to New Zealand, the virtual and global power of online TeachMeets is brought to us by Sonya Van

TeachMeet Australia Resources

The TeachMeet Sydney wiki (**http://tmsydney.wikispaces.com**) and the TeachMeet Australia website (**www.teachmeet.net**) share this vibrant professional learning activity across Australia.

Schaijik, developer of the online TeachMeetNZ (based on the TeachMeet international model that is also virtual). It initially enabled her to better support her Newmarket School colleagues through the expertise and connections she made, but more importantly it provided a regular session (in the form of a hangout) for teachers anywhere in the world. The format is fast-paced, with short presentations from contributors (usually invited guests) over the hour. Sonya works hard to not only provide the full one-hour recording of the entire TeachMeet via YouTube, but also to segment each contribution into a bite-size video available for global consumption afterwards. In October 2014 I was a guest for TeachMeetNZ as part of Connected Educator month and presented on "Beyond global connectedness, What's next?" (Van Schaijik, 2014b).

The New Zealand Ministry of Education (2014) recognizes Sonya's work as futuristic. A more recent gathering, TeachMeetNZ Science in March 2014, was again a truly global event. In a recent conversation, Sonya told me, "The TeachMeetNZ meets Science session was a collaborative process between myself and Catherine Battersby from the Science Learning Hub. However, what began as a duo chatting face to face soon became a full group of science educators making connections on Twitter and Google+, creating a presentation to share in a Google Hangout, learning and supporting each other with the tools, celebrating during and after the event and then sharing via a reflective blog post for the education community."

Sonya also shares that, "My goal for TeachMeetNZ is for the process to continue to evolve. I have identified that my work with teachers and the site is moving into relation thinking using SOLO taxonomy because each year I have had a teacher take on the task of hosting an event. Therefore other educators are making the link of the importance of teachers sharing their practice." More importantly, Sonya says, "TeachMeetNZ is about teachers leaving a legacy for the education community. This can be in the way of Twitter microblogging and being curated using Storify, it is in the YouTube clips, the slides that are made available to the community via the wiki, it is in the reflective blog posts that eventuate about the sessions and the process. It is

Resources

TeachMeetNZ, Sonya Van Schaijik, New Zealand, **@vanschaijik**

TeachMeetNZ website: **http://teachmeetnz.wikispaces.com**

TeachMeetNZ meets Science—**https://youtu.be/A4wimf6NXtw**

important for teachers to run their own sessions and have ownership of the Teach-Meet and more importantly to understand how they can "lift their game" by seeing globally what others are doing."

Webinars

A webinar is an excellent opportunity to bring learners together across time zones for sharing, discussion and taking action. A variety of tools can be used; see Chapter 2 for further details.

Webinar: a seminar that is conducted over the internet

Classroom 2.0

Classroom 2.0 co-founder Peggy George, PhD, USA (@pgeorge), shares her reflection and excitement about this ongoing webinar and associated global community. As a retired elementary principal and university pre-service teacher educator, Peggy wanted to continue to mentor and support teachers and to remain connected with other educators and current technology best practices in schools, and she decided this was a perfect way to do that from her own home. She is actively involved in many online global communities and webinars, which allows her to find and recruit outstanding presenters for the show.

Classroom 2.0 LIVE, now in its seventh year of production, originated in 2009 as a way to extend the learning, connections, and conversations begun in the already-thriving Classroom 2.0 Ning community created and maintained by Steve Hargadon (@stevehargadon). It is a community of educators from around the world who welcome the opportunity to gather with other educators in virtual real-time events hosted in Blackboard Collaborate, complete with audio, chat, desktop sharing, and video. The weekly Saturday webinars are freely open to all, last for an hour, and have participants from across the USA and Canada and frequently from other countries including Italy, Thailand, Serbia, Brazil, the UK, and more. They are always recorded and archived for later viewing and/or sharing. In addition to posting the video recordings in a blog post, the video and audio files are also posted on iTunes U and YouTube.

The purpose of these webinars is to help educators learn about new technology tools and teaching strategies important to 21st-century teaching, and to learn to use technology effectively both as professionals and with students, parents, colleagues, and administrators. Professional development certificates are offered to all participants, whether they participate in the live sessions or view the recorded sessions.

Learn more about Classroom 2.0 and Peggy George

http://live.classroom20.com, **www.classroom20.com**

https://about.me/peggy_george

Tech Talk Tuesdays

Tech Talk Tuesdays is a weekly webinar series that runs for one hour every Tuesday during Australian school terms from 4–5 p.m. AEST. Its focus is on the use of technology in teaching and learning. It varies in format from featuring guest presenters through to "unwebinar" style sessions where participants interact, determine the direction of content, and share their questions and experiences. Presenters have come from Australia, the USA, Asia, and England. Most are practicing teachers; others may be pre-service teachers, casual replacement teachers, retired educators, or community members who are interested in teaching and learning. All educational levels have been represented, ranging from preschool through to university and on to the senior members of our community. Webinars are held in Blackboard Collaborate. Most sessions feature application sharing so that tools or websites being discussed can be walked through so participants can see what it looks like. Sessions are recorded and links shared for those in different time zones or for those who cannot attend. Everyone is encouraged to have a voice, get connected, and empower learning with technology.

Tech Talk Tuesdays is hosted by Anne Mirtschin. Details can be found at **http://techtalktuesdays.global2.vic.edu.au** Twitter: **@techtalktue**

Hangouts

Since the rise of Google Hangout as a tool, it has become another popular way to gather locally and globally. It is similar to a webinar, but characteristically different in that it takes more of a talk rather than show approach.

Google Hangout: a communication platform developed by Google that includes instant messaging, video chat, SMS, and VOIP features. The service is accessed online through Gmail or Google+ websites or through mobile apps. Read more: **https://en.wikipedia.org/wiki/Google_Hangouts**

Google Lunch Hangout

Google Lunch (www.gglelunch.com) is an open discussion about technology in education and how these tools that can help the learner, teacher, and administrator in the school environment. Founder Chuck Pawlik (@deanpawlik) says, "We tried to address all international educators who wanted to improve their school and classroom with new tools for teaching. The goal of Google Lunch is to be informational, educational, technological, and entertaining. We like to smile!"

"The global educational leader reveals their classrooms, their schools, and themselves to the many influences from around the world allowing all involved to grow from a wider perspective and worldview. The global educational leader shares their knowledge worldwide through "flat" channels, enabling them to reach more people than ever before in educational history" (Chuck Pawlick, @deanpawlick).

ACCE Learning Network "Hangouts"

The Australian Council for Computers in Education Learning Network (ACCELN) is a regular series of live education webcasts from Australia hosted by thought gurus Amanda Rablin and Roland Gesthuizen. Or as they describe themselves, "lost souls drifting across the education landscape as they tinker with the learning gears, united by a sense of wonder and geeky backgrounds."

These shows or hangouts are recorded live on a Monday evening or Saturday morning and feature an international panel of guests and regular viewers. The hangouts have been broadcasting for around five years, with an archive of more than 100 shows and more than 3,000 followers.

Connect with AACELN Hangout hosts Roland Gesthuizen (**@rgesthuizen**) and Amanda Rablin (**@ackygirl**): **http://about.me/rgesthuizen** and **http://about.me/arablin**

ACCE Hangout Archive: **http://acceln.wikispaces.com**

YouTube Channel: **www.youtube.com/channel/UC4HVi4RbwJBMZArECmx-WPg**

As Roland shares, "We started with a Google Hangout when it was first released and we had never really explored it before. It seemed to meet our needs so we jumped in and learnt along the way. At first, we were really informal with our approach but once we decided to record the conversations we had to step up our organization."

Australian Council for Computers in Education (ACCE): **http://acce.edu.au**

Twitter: **@ACCE_AU**

According to Roland, "It took us a while to get a handle on how to best do this, and we now have an officially branded ACCELN YouTube. We have also have a wiki at acceln.wikispaces.com and a Google+ community that we post to. We share a common vision about education and passion for learning. With over 100 shows under our belt, we have learned a lot about running these webcasts and have built up a huge respect for some of the wonderful things that are happening around the

ACCELN website: **http://acceln.wikispaces.com**

Twitter: **#ACCELN**

globe. It has been a humbling experience to be part of this dialogue between a global community of educators with visiting guests and fans spanning Australia, New Zealand, Europe, the US and Asia."

Podcasts

Although not a new technology, the educators mentioned here share solid work and goals to connect ideas and learning through this largely audio-based product.

Podcast: a digital audio file made available on the internet for downloading to a computer or portable media player, typically available as a series, new installments of which can be received by subscribers automatically.

Teachers' Education Review Podcast (TERpodcast)

The TERpodcast was started in 2013 by Australian educators Corinne Campbell, @corisel, and Cameron Malcher, @Capitan_Typo.

Listen to TERpodcasts: **http://terpodcast.com**

Follow on Twitter: **@TERpodcast**

Campbell and Malcher wanted to bridge the perceived gap between developments in educational research and classroom practice. They shared, "Often research seems to stay within institutions, or be presented at academic conferences that most teachers can't access. Over time, it is filtered down to a classroom level, but this happens slowly and selectively, often controlled by gatekeepers." They wanted to create an opportunity for teachers to hear directly from the academics researching education and, as classroom teachers themselves, to ask the kinds of questions that classroom teachers would want answers to.

In terms of global outreach, the TERpodcast listeners tune in from countries all around the world. Most are from Australia, including a number from rural and remote schools who comment that the podcast exposes them to information and ideas they would otherwise not be able to access. Some of the most popular episodes have featured international guests such as Sugata Mitra, Pasi Sahlberg, and Richard Gerver, but many episodes featuring local guests, such as Simon Breakspear and Jenny Luca, are also popular.

Education, Productivity, Technology (EPT) Podcast

The Education, Productivity, Technology Podcast was created by Adnan Iftekhar, @adnanedtech.

Listen to episodes from the Education, Productivity, Technology (EPT) Podcast:
http://ai2020.com/category/podcast/

Learn more on the AI2020 website: **http://ai2020.com/**

Based on the US west coast, Adnan is a technology and innovation specialist and host of the regular EPT Podcast. He shares, "Connection is the first thing I think of when I hear the word podcast. Not just connection in terms of connecting with the people I interview but connection with the people listening in. The beauty of podcasting versus other media is that in some ways it's more intimate yet it is also very unobtrusive. Video, as well as text, requires all of your attention and focus, whereas with a podcast, you can be listening while washing the dishes, out for a run or walk, driving or even grocery shopping. It's a lot less demanding on your attention than pretty much any other medium. One of my goals is to have interviewed 300 people by the end of the year and at least half of them from countries outside the USA."

Absolutely Intercultural Podcast

Produced by Anne Fox, Denmark, and Laurent Borgemann, Germany, Absolutely Intercultural started in 2006 when podcasts had just started to break though as a popular online medium. The producers decided to try it out, lured by the idea that it was not so complicated from a technical point of view. The key ingredients are good-quality audio and the courage to approach people to speak to us. Free tools such as Audacity and WordPress helped to make this a low-cost, low-risk experiment. Notable shows included the ones featuring people from Lebanon and Israel during the conflict in 2006 and inspiring stories such as our continuing coverage of Shai Reshef and his University of the People that aims to bring a university education free of charge to anyone in the world.

Connect with Absolutely Intercultural

Website: **www.absolutely-intercultural.com**

On iTunes: **http://tinyurl.com/gn65z27**

On Facebook: **www.facebook.com/AbsolutelyIntercultural**

Being a Global Education Leader Means . . .

"Being a global educator and leader means that you set an example of passion, excellence and integrity for others to follow. A leader and an educator holds themselves to the highest standards, does not follow the herd of the nomenclature or the flavor of the month educational pedagogy, but rather views teaching and learning as two sides of an ever-evolving dynamic that is influenced by the changing nature of our societies, our culture and the technology that enables us to share our perspectives, insights and best practices with "edulearners" on every side of this world. We share what we know, who we are and how we see the opportunities to connect with our fellow inquisitors and we listen to those in other lands with differing worldviews, experience and insights and we bring them to whatever place we go. A global educator is a leader who insists on connecting everyone they meet to the vision that he/she has conjured from demonstrated practices in and out of the classroom. The global educator does more than bring about visions of the future of how we could engage in an improved paradigm of learning. He or she models those visions, shares the tools with which to bring a special kind of learning about and then listens to the insights of the person with whom they are connecting and adds that to the reservoir of insight from which the leader draws.

"The challenge of the global education leader is to set the example and persuade all teachers and learners that seeking out dynamic change and embracing it is not the act of someone who is reckless and dangerous, but is the very instinct we need to foster so that our youth can continue to embrace and shape a world that is changing at a faster rate than at any point in our earth's history. A global education leader must confront those who are stuck in the past and afraid to step outside of themselves and bring forth examples of those who have risked and have been rewarded with deeper learning, empathetic understanding and the opportunity for a more just and certainly a more interesting world where each and every one of us has the ability to create their own future. The challenge for the global education leader is creating a structure that will afford every individual the opportunity to control that narrative themselves."

Brian Mannix, Teacher and Game Designer, USA, @mannixlab

Global Education Leader Case Studies

As a culmination to Part Two, Leadership for Global Collaboration, we explore the activities of nine global education leaders. These educators are diverse in location and include a mixture of government and private institutions and also leaders of non-profit groups. They share stories of cultural and global significance and help us to understand the challenges faced by leaders whose goal is to broaden and deepen the learning for those around them. I am reminded of a presentation by Canadian colleague, Dean Shareski, from a few years ago when he talked about "rigor" and "relevance" in learning. Much had been written about rigor in the first decade of the 21st century and Dean's advice was it is time to carefully consider the meaning of rigor and the relevance of what we do as education leaders and how learning without relevance is not acceptable now (Shareski, 2011). The global leaders represented here have worked hard and show true global leadership qualities through their ability to embrace different contexts and make global learning relevant—it is possibly our responsibility to take these ideas and build in the rigor for learning. The expanded version of the case studies can be found in the ebook.

Case Study 2.1 Yvonne Marie Andres: GlobalSchoolNet

Yvonne Marie Andres, Phd, is President/Co-founder of GlobalSchoolNet.org and founder of iPoPP (International Projects or Partners Place). Andres serves as the US co-chair for the US-Russia Social Expertise Exchange's Education and Youth working group. She is the creator of International CyberFair and the US State Department's Doors to Diplomacy programs, has met with President Bush to launch the Friendship Through Education Initiative, and speaks at conferences worldwide. Andres was named one of 25 most influential people worldwide in education technology for her innovative e-learning projects, involving 5 million students from 194 countries. Andres was awarded the Soroptimist International Making-a-Difference-Award for advancing the status of women and children. In 2012, Andres was one of San Diego Magazine's

Women-Who-Move-the-City, which recognizes dynamic women who create positive change and contribute to the community.

My global link with Yvonne, and my first real online global collaborative experience, goes back twenty years to 1996 when the International Schools Cyberfair project ran for the first time. I entered my school at the time, Eltham College in Melbourne, into this international online competition and worked with willing students after school to complete it. My students and I chose environmental awareness as a theme for the Cyberfair entry and were charged with connecting to different parts of the community and developing an informative website. A website? How could we do that? I madly rushed out and bought an off the shelf website creation tool becoming popular at the time, only to find the students were very happy to use HTML and build it themselves from the ground up. This global project was a whirlwind of activities beyond the essential website creation; it linked us with local communities and teachers who shared what they were doing at the time to implement and teach environmental awareness. It was hard work and we received an honorable mention. Wow! Was I hooked on global connections after that experience!

I remember meeting Yvonne each year at the NECC/ISTE conference where she tirelessly shared global collaborative projects and best-practice approaches and learning designs—as she continues to do today. There are many more educators now moving into global connected and collaborative learning with Web 2.0 being a major catalyst, however my message to all is to look at and learn from the work Yvonne and others in the Global SchoolNet (GSN) developed—this is one place where quality telecommunication-based education started, and there is a lot to learn from the project designs, how they have been sustained and how the community around GSN has supported each other.

Yvonne is a global collaboration expert, and I am honored to be able to share some of her story. In the ebook case study she shares an historical perspective alongside current ideas to do with global education, global leadership, emerging technologies and their impact on global collaboration, challenges and benefits to students and teachers.

Connect with Yvonne Marie Andres

Twitter: **@YvonneMarieA**

Website: **www.yvonneandres.com**

Case Study 2.2 Mahmud Shihab: Leadership to Connect

Mahmud Shihab is currently Director of the Educational Resources Center (ERC) and Head of Educational Technology at International College (IC) in Beirut, Lebanon. He started working at IC in 1996 as an IT teacher where he taught applications in the secondary school and trained all teachers every Wednesday afternoon. He still trains the teachers but now as part of a coaching program where his role is to train the trainers. He now has a team of over 20 IC faculty serving as educational technology facilitators to support technology integration college wide. When IC started the IB Diploma Programme in 2001 Mahmud started teaching Information Technology in a Global Society (ITGS), and over the years he has contributed to ITGSopedia, an online resource for all ITGS teachers in the world. In 2001 he also became Head of IT to oversee IT integration across K–12. He was also twice winner of IC's distinguished teacher award.

I first met Mahmud Shihab at the ISTE conference in the USA when we were both appointed to the International Committee of ISTE. Having worked in the Gulf region for five years in Arabic schools I was familiar with some of the challenges peculiar to that area of the world. Mahmud was always willing to share his particular initiatives, his needs and solutions to improving teaching and promoting a more global perspective within the ISTE ranks. In 2014 I was delighted to be invited to Mahmud's school to run both student and educator workshops to introduce and share pathways for action to do with social entrepreneurship. This gave me an excellent insight into the college and into the education system as a whole in Lebanon. It can not be stressed enough in this book how important it is for all educators to take advantage of other global educators when they can—either in their home country or through travel—to learn more about learning environments and how vital connections can be made to improve understanding of the world. I am very pleased to be able to feature Mahmud as a case study. Read more about Mahmud, IC and the ERC in Case Study 2.2 of the ebook.

Connect with Mahmud Shihab

Twitter: **@mahmudshihab**

Case Study 2.3 Ed Gragert: Global Connections

Ed Gragert has four decades of experience in global education. He is Interim Director of iEARN-USA. From 2012 to 2015 he served as the Director of the Global Campaign for Education-US, an advocacy coalition in Washington, DC of 80 organizations committed to securing a quality education for all young people worldwide. Earlier, for 23 years he served as the Executive Director of iEARN-USA, pioneering and expanding online collaborative learning among schools worldwide. He also served as Executive Director of ICYE-US, an international youth exchange program, and worked for the International Relations Committee of the US House of Representatives. Ed received a BA in Japanese political science from the University of Washington, and an MA in Korean History and a PhD in Japanese History from Columbia University. He has authored numerous articles and book chapters on educational technology and teacher professional development and has a column on Huffington Post.

It was 11 p.m. on a Friday evening on east coast Australia at the end of another long and busy week, but that did not deter me from connecting with Ed Gragert to talk about his life as a global educator and leader. When I left Australia at the end of 1997 to become a computer teacher at Simba School, Ndola, Zambia I was able to implement iEARN Learning Circles as an after school activity. In my non-networked, non-internet computer laboratory I had a room full of students from Grades 8–11 excited about sharing what they knew and about connecting with others beyond. Each week I took small groups from the activity room to walk across to the other side of the school where our one internet-ready computer was locked up. Once there we logged into the iEARN website and checked messages and communicated with the world. I connected with Ed at that time, and then when I moved to my next international position in Kuwait, Ed reached out again and said "Are you the same Julie Lindsay who was in Zambia last year?" When I started attending NECC/ISTE conferences from 2003 I found Ed was always there at the iEARN stand, at the international reception - talking, encouraging, and sharing his passion for taking learning global.

Like me, I think Ed always took it for granted and thought it was very obvious global education and collaboration are imperative—however although we are a long way from the "tipping point" we did agree during conversations for this book that things have come a long way in 30 years. I am proud and pleased to be able to share the following insights into the work Ed has done across the world to bring global learning and understanding to many teachers, students and education leaders. He is certainly one of my top global collaboration gurus.

Learn more about Ed and the history and development of iEARN, as well as thoughts about global collaboration, new technologies, goals for educators and leaders, and advice for the future!

Connect with Ed Gragert

Twitter: **@egragert**

iEARN website: **http://us.iearn.org**

LinkedIn Profile: **www.linkedin.com/in/ed-gragert-668b54**

Case Study 2.4 Cameron Paterson: Leading a School to Be Global

Cameron Paterson is a history teacher and the Mentor of Learning & Teaching, responsible for the strategic leadership of learning and teaching, and promoting excellence in teaching practice, at Shore School in Sydney. He has worked at Harvard Graduate School of Education as a Teacher Education Program Advisor (2010–2011), and as a Fellow at the Project Zero Classroom and the Future of Learning Institute (2013). He holds four postgraduate degrees and he has received several awards for teaching and leadership. Last year, his lesson on the Ho Chi Minh Trail was animated and published online by TED-Education.

I came to know Cameron online when he signed up to bring students to the Flat Classroom Conference in Beijing in 2011. Circumstances prevented him from coming at that time, but further online discussion resulted in Shore School hosting a new iteration of that event, the Flat Connections Conference in 2014. When I met Cameron for the first time at ISTE 2013 his enthusiasm for improving learning opportunities through global connections was very evident.

Cameron shares developments across the school as a case study of developing a global connected learning environment. Cameron states up front that although Shore does not yet consider itself a globally connected school they are focusing on steps that are leading in that direction, including technology and curriculum objectives. Cameron also shares activities with his students that reveal the essence and power of global connections. Through despair at the bias of Australian history textbooks

Connect with Cameron Paterson

Twitter - **@cpaterso**

Blog - **http://learningshore.edublogs.org/**

Cameron connected his classes to other students across the world and together they have shared stories including about World War One (with Turkey) and World War Two (USA) showing clearly how students become the textbook for each other!

Read more in the ebook case study about Cameron and how he is leading learning with technology. This includes the adoption of Project Based Learning and Visible Thinking; leadership for integrating mobile and ubiquitous technologies for learning; and global collaborations implemented to support his students perspectives and engagement with the world. He also shares reflections about hosting the Flat Connections Conference at Shore in 2014, an event based on the theme "What's the other story?" from Chimamanda Adichie's (2009) extraordinary TED talk, The Danger of a Single Story, where Adichie relates how impressionable and vulnerable we are in the face of a story.

Case Study 2.5 Ann S. Michaelsen: Teacher, Global Collaborator

Ann is a teacher and administrator at Sandvika High School in Oslo Norway. She has promoted the use of computers in school since 2002, working at the county level to implement the Skillsoft LMS in 34 schools. Sandvika high school was Norway's 2009 Pathfinder school in the global Microsoft Partners in Learning Innovative Education Forums, and Ann presented at the same event in South Africa 2010. She has been recognized by Microsoft Partners in Learning as a "Global Hero in Education" in August 2012 and June 2013. She is an active writer of the blog Teaching Using Web Tools, where she offers advice to fellow educators. She was on the 2013 Horizon Norway Advisory Board and the 2014 Horizon Report Europe Advisory Board, and the Scandinavian Horizon board. In 2013 she wrote the book *Connected Learners: A Step-by-Step Guide to Creating a Global Classroom* with 27 high school students. She was featured on the BBC News Technology page after speaking at BETT (a large edtech conference in the United Kingdom) in 2013.

Ann understands the need for students to share their learning and to interact globally. Her student's blogged, co-wrote a book with her, and collectively have been

Connect with Ann Michaelsen

Twitter: **@annmic**

Blog: **http://annmichaelsen.com/**

acclaimed across the world for how they learn in a connected way using technology. Ann has pushed boundaries in a country that supports a conservative curriculum, amongst a student body that usually learn in a competitive, exam-based environment. A recent student-initiated project with a school in Lesotho has produced students with social entrepreneur skills and a new school for local students. There is much scope to Ann's global outlook and ability to forge new learning modes. I first met Ann in Qatar at the iEARN Conference and then in 2014 I invited her to Australia to help facilitate the Flat Connections Conference.

In the ebook case study Ann shares her experiences of teaching and leading in Norway, how she is connecting teachers and students to the world, technologies for collaborations, new pedagogies, a vision for the future and how she led the rebuilding of a school in Lesotho.

Case Study 2.6 Eva Brown: Teacher Education Goes Global

Eva Brown is a teacher educator at Red River College (RRC) in Winnipeg, Manitoba, Canada. She is a Flat Connections Global Educator and a Microsoft Innovative Teacher. Eva is continually seeking opportunities for her pre-service teachers to acquire skills to infuse technology and global education into the curriculum to prepare their students to be competitive in the global economy. Her pre-service teachers have participated in the Flat Connections Project as lead teachers, expert advisors and judges as well as other global projects such as The Global Education Conference. Eva demonstrates her passion as a lifelong learner and believes modeling is key to teaching. She is in her doctoral studies in education in a blended learning program at The University of Calgary, with a specialization in Learning Sciences.

Connect with Eva Brown (@ebrownorama)

Blog: **https://sites.google.com/site/ebrownorama/**

Eva is a strong advocate for global education being infused into the curriculum so that it no longer becomes a choice for educators but a requirement. Teacher education across the world is challenged by the impact of emerging technologies and the diversity of situations across schools. A typical pre-service teacher has a unique experience depending what schools are available for workplace experiences with often less than satisfying outcomes when using digital technologies. As a teacher educator Eva and her students are forging new modes of sharing understanding including "flipping PD" and community outreach. The enthusiasm coming from Eva is totally matched by her students as she places them in one professional learning opportunity after another.

Read more in the ebook case study about how Eva is taking learning global, the role of technology in embedding global learning into teacher education, and how she is changing the learning ecology at RRC.

Case Study 2.7 Michael Furdyk: Social Entrepreneur, Global Educator, Technology Guru

Michael Furdyk, Canada, is the co-founder of TakingITGlobal, which provides innovative global education programs that empower youth to understand and act on the world's greatest challenges. In the past, he turned his interest in technology into several successful online companies, including MyDesktop.com, which sold to Internet.com in 1999. In 2008, he was named by Contribute Magazine as one of 10 Tech Revolutionaries Redefining the Power and Face of Philanthropy.

Michael has led the way in connecting educators and all learners across the world using digital technologies for many years. TakingITGlobal (TIG) was formed out of the growing disconnect between the way young people are living and the way they are learning, a successful attempt to close the gap and create a learning community. Through the tagline "Inspire, Inform and Involve" the organization strives to engage students through resources and tools that form a pathway to action.

Michael was inspired through his own experience teaching an evening high-school program for at-risk students, gaining a better understanding of how they use technology to engage students develop programs to support education. Through a Microsoft Partners in Learning Grant, which included mentorship from Chris Dede, in 2006 TIG launched TakingITGlobal for Educators (TIGed), a dedicated program for educators.

"Openness to change and innovation will be key to future success, no matter how established a school might be in a city or country - their students will be competing in a diverse global market where the brand of most schools won't matter as much as they once did" (Michael Furdyk, Canada, @mfurdyk).

What is immediately evident when you meet Michael is his boundless energy and enthusiasm for cross-cultural and global learning. In recent years he has worked tirelessly for the non-profit organisation, TakingITGlobal he co-founded in 2006. Educational change and how to foster this amongst teachers is uppermost in the work Michael does around the world. Michael shares his vision for informal and formal changes that need to take place with a focus on implementing and measuring global digital citizenship in a process that embeds ongoing reflection, learning and action.

In the ebook case study Michael shares his views on the current state of global connectedness across the world, the state of education leadership, education in Canada and his vision for the future. More formally, the vision for Future Friendly Schools is a framework for a whole school approach to improvement and change. A school leader could assess themselves and work towards improvement through committing to values for change on a daily basis.

Connect with Michael Furdyk (@mfurdyk)

TakingITGlobal: **www.tigweb.org**

Future Friendly Schools: **www.futurefriendlyschools.org**

Case Study 2.8 Alan Preis: National, International, Global Educator

Alan Preis is currently the Director of Technology at Shanghai American School. He has had extensive experience in technology planning and the integration of technology to support and transform student learning. Alan has been involved in a number of collaborations with other schools and organizations around connected learning, design thinking, and instructional innovation. He has made numerous presentations on the effective use of technology in schools at IT and educational conferences, both throughout the United States and abroad.

Alan makes it quite clear he is an national / international / global educator. His previous position was at an international school in the USA. How does that work? Well, in fact it works very well, and Alan shares this experience as well as his thoughts about the move to China. Alan has forged connections beyond his school and country and is passionate about making connections that benefit all learners. His story shares another side to what it means to be a global education leader.

Connect with Alan Preis (@apreis)

Case Study 2.9 Matt Harris: A Cosmopolitan Life

This section on global education leaders concludes with Matt Harris, EdD, a US educator with deep passion and vast experience around educational technology currently working and leading in international schools in Asia. In his career, Matt has worked as an educational leader, teacher, instructional technologist, author, presenter and researcher. He has taught at all grade levels from preschool to university graduate school as an ICT and mathematics teacher. He has worked as a senior administrator at independent schools and universities in North America and Asia. Additionally, Matt works as an educational consultant for schools and Ministries of Education in the Middle East, Africa, North America, Australia, and Asia. He has also been an active member of the ISTE Board. In 2015 he moved from Singapore to Indonesia to take up the position of Deputy Head for Learning Technologies at the British School of Jakarta.

Matt shares a very important perspective on the myriad of challenges associated with "expat" living and teaching with special insight into cultural complexities. As an astute leader he also shares his views on "cosmopolitanism" and how educators can become citizens of the world and develop a global vision regardless of whether they leave their home country or not. He also discusses organizations that move from the "local to global." Read more about Matt's goals as an international global leader, Third Culture Kids and global connections in the ebook case study.

Connect with Matt (@MattHarrisEdD)

Blog: **http://mattharrisedd.com**

EdTech Vlog: **http://bit.ly/MattHarrisEdDVlog**

Part Three

Online Global Collaboration

"We are witnessing the birth of the world's first truly global civilization. Rather than being places where students learn about the world, schools are now places where students truly can learn *with* the world."

AL GORE (2013, P. 92), USA, @ALGORE

As my colleagues, friends and family will attest, this section of the book is the closest to my heart. Online global collaboration is an area I have been working with for 20+ years in different learning environments, as a global education leader, and as a consultant, speaker and author. My Doctorate research is about online global collaborative educators, how and what they are doing that may in fact be influencing pedagogical change. The next four chapters will share ideas and practices to do with online global collaboration and include many current examples of global educators and leaders who are connecting and collaborating for a multitude of reasons using a diverse basket of tools and strategies. This is where you as a global educator should become more inspired and determined to forge these vital relationships across the world and embed rich collaborative learning into the curriculum.

What Is Online Global Collaboration?

I t is one thing to connect with the world and appreciate the diversity and significance of "them" and "us" learning opportunities, however it is a whole other challenge to be able to collaborate globally with different learning partners. The latter is what all educators and learners should be aspiring to but the reality is you cannot run before you can walk. Unless educators understand and experience digital and online collaboration in a local context first it is likely jumping into global contexts will not be successful.

What Is Collaboration in a Digital World?

As I start to write this chapter my thoughts go back to my school years in the 1970s and how as an "A student" I never really liked collaborating with others. Why should I do the work and they benefit from the result? (An assessment challenge for teachers at that time that continues today.) As I moved into education and designing learning activities the music teacher in me immediately knew the value of collaboration within a group and how each member contributed something unique and valuable, however the educator in me struggled with providing adequate tasks to meet all learning needs, and to assess groups and individuals fairly. Today digital technology has completely changed how I work with students and educators and in fact has changed my whole perspective on the value of collaboration for learning. Digital technology provides for differentiation, accountability and visibility in the learning process. Emerging approaches to digital scholarship question what knowledge is, how it is gained and how it is shared, amongst other things. Veletsianos and Kimmons (2012) share a new form of scholarship called "Networked Participatory

Pay it Forward

Emerging approaches to digital scholarship question what knowledge is, how it is gained and how it is shared, while digital technology provides for differentiation, accountability and visibility in the learning process.

Scholarship" that reflects scholarly practice and participatory technologies. For collaborative learning online technologies provide a platform for engaged learning, deeper understanding and exciting outcomes.

Collaboration is not a new pedagogy for learning. Much has been researched and written about collaborative learning including the work of Dillenbourg (1999) who drills down into different collaborative situations for learning. Authors Fullan, Langworthy and Barber (2014) share collaboration as a "deep learning task" and skill for the future and state, "Collaboration in learning is easy to consider on the surface, but tough to do well in practice. One of the most complex transitions for students and teachers to make is the move from a pedagogy that centres on *individuals* demonstrating their learning to a pedagogy that embraces *groups* demonstrating their learning" (p. 26).

"Educators do not understand how to collaborate in a meaningful way. Some have gone through Google training for example and are beginning to understand the tools and techniques and methodology. It's a very small percentage of teachers doing this" (Yvonne Marie Andres, USA, @YvonneMarieA).

In the collaborative learning process learners share and discuss and build on the outputs of their peers. The building of something through participation and negotiation with peers or others requires coordination, regular contribution, shared conception, and agreement on what drives the iteration and construction of new shared ideas or artifacts (Laurillard, 2012). In a collaborative environment there is usually no personal ownership; there is shared ownership and contribution that leads to co-created artifacts such as a text-based wiki or a piece of multimedia.

The development of digital and online learning modes and access to new tools and online networks means the practice of collaboration can take on a whole new

"In the broadest sense 'collaborative learning' is a situation in which two or more people learn or attempt to learn something together. As distinct from cooperative learning where the required tasks are distributed amongst the learners" (Laurillard, 2009).

persona. Collaboration as an inquiry-based, higher order thinking and problem solving skill is now just as possible virtually as it is face-to-face. Online collaboration by its very nature implies synchronous as well as asynchronous working modes. As educators we need to know how to bring digital collaboration into the learning environment. The paradigm shift to include digital collaboration as a norm is shared by Lee and Ward (2013), "While insular, "stand alone" teaching has characterized the teaching of a paper-based world, collaborative teaching could well characterize that of an increasingly digital and networked world; a world where collaboration and integration are the norm."

Moving into the age of online collaboration means understanding the importance of contribution and shared practice, including shared research and co-creation. It also means "learning about" can become "learning with" and this is enhanced by contact either virtually or in person (or virtually in person). The video "Collaboration: On the Edge of a New Paradigm" (Collaborative Society, 2013) discusses a shift from a world about "content" to a world about "context". It shares with us the imperative of collaboration to solve global issues in health, society, science and economics.

'Collaboration: On the Edge of a New Paradigm'

https://vimeo.com/77240879

http://wecollaborate.org/

Learning does not happen in isolation, learning is social and individual creation can, or more pointedly should, become collaborative creation in many instances. Students develop understanding about the world through working together with others, by sharing ideas, sharing outcomes and sharing benefits in both synchronous and asynchronous modes. Videoconference interactions and asynchronous online discussion forums or blogging, as examples, provide a full agenda of globally connected activities. As global educators we therefore need to consider how to bring online collaboration into our learning environment. We also need to understand how to go beyond synchronous to also support asynchronous online collaborations. This involves embracing new pedagogies and new pedagogical capacity, namely a teacher's repertoire of teaching strategies and partnerships for learning. We can always learn "about" something however, the goal for online (leading to global) collaboration is to learn "with" others and build understanding together.

> ### Pay it Forward
>
> We can always learn 'about' something however, the goal for online (leading to global) collaboration is to learn 'with' others and build understanding together.

Pedagogies for Online Global Collaboration

It is possible that online global collaboration affords new pedagogical approaches. If we understand pedagogy to mean the method and practice of teaching, especially as an academic subject or theoretical concept, then perhaps it is time to consider a new approach that informs the art and science of teaching and learning across the world while using online technologies. A global collaborative pedagogy, which I introduced in Chapter 6 as "Cosmogogy" is based on constructivist learning theory and connectivism as a learning approach and uses online digital technologies as an essential scaffold for learning objectives.

A flat and connected learning environment where participants collaborate globally requires educators take a different and "cosmogogical" approach. An online global collaborative project requires consideration and curriculum redesign to embed into everyday learning. In fact, conversely a cosmogogical approach can be embedded across the entire curriculum regardless of whether a "global project" is taking place.

In the past 20 years online global collaboration using technology has evolved from the 1.0 version of information exchange, to the 2.0 version where artifact exchange as well as information exchange takes place. With the development of faster internet and better technology tools, online global collaboration 3.0 allows us to network, collaborate, co-create information and artifacts, and build knowledge together online to share with the world. Shown in Fig. 9.1, all three versions are currently practiced and valid in today's education scenarios and each can be transformational for learning in their own way.

Online Global Collaboration 1.0	Online Global Collaboration 2.0	Online Global Collaboration 3.0
Information exchange	Information exchange and artifact exchange	Information and artifact co-creation, building knowledge together and sharing with the world

Fig. 9.1: Evolution of Online Global Collaboration

"While good pedagogy should be the driver, pedagogy can be amplified and accelerated with technology. However, the real revolution is not technology, it is global collaboration" (Cameron Paterson, Australia, @cpaterso).

Attributes of Online Global Collaboration 3.0

Let's explore the 3.0 version of this evolution: information and artifact co-creation, building knowledge together and sharing with the world.

You know you are implementing Online Global Collaboration 3.0 when you have:

- Engaged, connected and digitally fluent educators who know how to communicate using Web 2.0 and other online tools
- Carefully planned and designed global collaborations that are implemented and managed with a view to effectively join classrooms together to enhance learning and support co-created outcomes
- Common assessment objectives between global partners
- High expectations and requirements for connectivity, contribution and collaboration on educators and students
- Community partners who provide new knowledge, skills and resources for the online learning community
- Use of multimedia to pitch ideas to solve real-world problems
- Educator or student initiated themes, student-managed learning
- Student autonomy in learning and an ability to initiate online collaborations

- Peer-to-peer learning that transcends cooperation and supports new collaborative digital modes
- Online publishing and sharing modes that make use of Web 2.0 platforms and social media

Many educators are not embedding online global collaboration into their curriculum and lack of technology access, as already mentioned, is usually not the reason. There must be realistic expectations of what online global collaboration is—and in fact it is hard work. It is relatively easy to have the occasional Skype call and bring the "wow" factor into the classroom. Going "beyond the wow" requires planning and curriculum redesign. Both learners and leaders need to be engaged with authentic topics and uncomplicated accessible technology tools. Yes, it does take a shift in traditional pedagogies to integrate technology into learning so that it is transformative and so that it expands the learning environment walls to include and embrace the world.

Pay it Forward

There must be realistic expectations of what online global collaboration is—and in fact it is hard work.

Putting the "Global" into Online Collaboration

At this point in the chapter we need to have a serious discussion and reflection about terminology. Educators have used the term "global collaboration" even before telecommunications and the internet allowed digital connections teacher-to-teacher and class-to-class. Many have used and continue to use other non-digital means to connect and collaborate such as mailing/posting furry animals and sharing hand-written travel journals across the world to be manually completed and sent on. These practices are also considered as "global collaboration" and provide rich, engaged learning without the hassle of using technology! However, in today's digital learning landscape we need to redefine global collaboration.

The dictionary and accepted definition of "global" is "all embracing, relating to or covering the whole world." In some respects "global collaboration" is a misnomer. Many educational collaborations take place that are not "global" in practice but do join learners for connected and collaborative learning. Two classrooms in the same school, for example, can use digital technologies to collaborate online. In this instance students are not in an environment where they work immediately face-to-face, and at the same time are not "global" either, but do work virtually online to collaborate on outcomes (such as a shared Google Doc or wiki). The same skills with the technology and with the learning process are required, whether the collaborators are in the next room or on the other side of the world. Perhaps the key word here is "online" rather than "global"? Maybe we should be talking about "online collaboration" and leave the global out?

My dilemma is that "global" is a word I use often, in fact my professional branding and my work for the past 20 years is based around global experiences and understandings of what it means to travel, learn and teach globally and in a global context. It is through the use of emerging technologies, especially Web 2.0 tools, that learning has become more globally accessible. The word "online" is used to indicate attachment to digital technologies and implies the connection and collaboration could be either local or global. Online learning in the context of a K–12 school is a developing concept and a general definition could include a school-based blended and/or flipped approach. Therefore, when referring to "online global collaboration" the question is what does the word "global" add to the concept of "online collaboration"? Is it in fact redundant?

Do all educators use the word "global" when embarking on classroom collaborations? From the tertiary perspective it is not a word used readily. Online or distance education courses and degrees today include students from anywhere, and no distinction is made because the delivery and learning is largely or totally online. My recent work as an Adjunct Lecturer and as a Quality Learning and Teaching Leader (online) with Charles Sturt University (CSU), Australia, has supported the objective to create all distance and internal subjects with an adequate online interface and navigation and system that fosters student-teacher and peer-peer online learning in a variety of modes. CSU has students from around the world – but at the same time they are not practicing online global collaboration, as there is little or no connection with other institutions and no embedded learning that joins students from these institutions for enhanced collaborative learning. This is not a criticism as such; it is a statement of fact and an observation that the logistics for such an endeavor are huge—although this book does feature some leaders in this area.

The K–12 perspective is different however. There has been a tendency to use the word "global" to indicate connections with others beyond the immediate school or situation. It does not always mean these connections are geographically distant; it could mean learners are in fact in the same town or state or country. What educators are inferring is a desire to have a cultural ("global") and learning exchange with others who are not in their immediate presence and who are therefore "different".

"Often we think we have to go around the world to make it valuable—but it does not have to be around the world. If we go to another local community, like my Microsoft Innovative Teacher project where I went 200 miles away in the same province, the learning becomes totally different because connections are made between urban and rural students. Global connected learning helps students become acquainted, helps them to learn about other cultures and helps them to learn to not only accept but appreciate other people. Staying in the same Province such as Northern Manitoba with Red River College students is still globally connected learning" (Eva Brown, Canada, @ebrownorama).

At this point I will let the reader decide if the word "global" is redundant, however for this book, with a focus on global education infused with digital technologies, I have used the full term "online global collaboration". I believe there is no redundancy of words here, "online global collaboration" broadly refers to geographically dispersed educators, classrooms and schools that use online learning environments and digital technologies to learn with others beyond their immediate environment in order to support curricular objectives, intercultural understandings, critical thinking, personal and social capabilities, and ICT capabilities. This applies to K–12 educators who are striving to connect the learning in their classrooms and by their students to others beyond their school, at a distance, embracing the world, "globally". A school integrating new tools and practices entirely for the purposes of supporting learners within, namely online "local" collaboration is relevant to the term "online collaboration". The same or similar online collaborative practices, possibly using many of the same digital tools, evident in K–12 schools today takes learning into a global realm with learning partners beyond local and this practice is correctly labelled "online global collaboration".

Online global collaboration broadly refers to geographically dispersed educators, classrooms and schools that use online learning environments and digital technologies to learn with others beyond their immediate environment in order to support curricular objectives, intercultural understandings, critical thinking, personal and social capabilities and ICT capabilities.

Pay it Forward

True online global collaboration in the classroom requires a shift in teaching that allows teachers and students to 'flatten' the learning experience in order to bring the outside world in and put themselves out there—to build bridges for global empathy and create workable structures where all participants can learn with and not just from each other.

Online global collaboration can take many forms. The effective application of online global collaboration is not easy and not always achieved, nor is it generally supported by standard curriculum and assessment, both of which are traditionally focused on individual response. True online global collaboration in the classroom requires a shift in teaching that allows teachers and students to "flatten" the learning experience in order to bring the outside world in and put themselves out there—to build bridges for global empathy and create workable structures where all participants can learn with and not just from each other.

Pay it Forward

We have the tools; we have the pedagogies, let's connect the world!

Why Online Global Collaboration?

Global competition for jobs means that today's students must not only be well-educated, creative problem solvers but they must also be equipped to collaborate globally and be culturally aware to the point that they communicate effectively in person and digitally. This is not just about economics however; it is about knowing how to connect and learn with others anywhere in the world and ultimately to solve global problems through collaborative practices.

It is vital that schools develop integrated curriculum and new assessment models while pursuing opportunities for learners to adopt techno-personal skills allowing them to engage in both synchronous and asynchronous collaborative work that is local and global.

"Global collaboration encourages teachers to engage on an equal basis internationally in a model in which 'everyone recognizes that no-one knows so much that they can not learn from the other and no-one knows so little that they cannot teach the other' (quoted this from a teacher in Argentina). This give and take is the heart of global education, it's not giving up but learning from, it's educating for and with each other. Students come out of the experience knowing there is real value and wisdom everywhere in the world and they can benefit from it and contribute to it" (Ed Gragert ,USA, @egragert).

Concept 1	Concept 2
Online Global Collaboration Is Imperative for All Learners to be Globally Competent	Online Global Collaboration Provides a Focus for Digital and Online Technologies

Concept 3	Concept 4
Online Global Collaboration Is a New Paradigm for Modern Learning	Online Global Collaboration Supports Glocalization

Fig. 10.1: Four Concepts of Global Collaboration

Online Global Collaboration: The Four Concepts

The essence of this chapter (and book) is encapsulated in these four concepts to do with global collaborative practice, flat connected learning, and the use of online technologies. These concepts (shown in Figure 10.1) collectively form what could be termed as an "elevator pitch" that should help readers put forward the case for global education and online global collaboration in their own learning environments.

Online Global Collaboration Is Imperative for All Learners to Be Globally Competent

Online global collaboration is imperative for modern teaching and learning. It supports global competence, defined here as the cross-cultural skills and understanding needed to communicate outside one's environment and to act on issues of local and global significance. Global competence allows students to frame an understanding of the world through connected experiences that go beyond the textbook, beyond the limitations of face-to-face or local interactions. It improves global awareness and fosters intercultural understanding and the realisation that although everyone is not like me, everyone is like me in some way. Intercultural differences can become intercultural understandings and break down stereotypes, cultural superiority and socio-economic dominance.

"Focusing on the 'global' is the moral and ethical and logical approach to education. It's almost unimaginable that we are not preparing young people to live in a world where they can collaborate with and learn from one another" (Yvonne Marie Andres, USA, @YvonneMarieA).

Global competence is the cross-cultural skills and understanding needed to communicate outside one's environment and to act on issues of local and global significance.

Online Global Gollaboration Provides a Focus for Digital and Online Technologies

Online global collaboration is one of the major reasons for using mobile and ubiquitous digital and online technologies for learning. This practice goes beyond merely integrating technology. It is a disruptive innovation and includes a new category of tools and learning habits that support modern learning skills and global collaborative objectives. Working with others in the world virtually provides new understandings about the power of technology for humanity. A balanced curriculum not only encourages computing and the discovery of programming and coding skills but also embeds flat and connected learning approaches with the view to collaborating online. This practice is immersive and ongoing. A lack of digital access and fluency through internet blocking and filtering will hinder a globally collaborative learning environment.

"It is clear there are more people doing things with technology—Skype allows you to have a conversation anywhere in the world. In terms of pedagogy it has not changed that much because teachers still are learning how to use the technology to enhance teaching and learning" (Ed Gragert, USA, @egragert).

Online Global Collaboration Is a New Paradigm for Modern Learning

Online global collaborative practices can change the way we teach and learn—it already has for the many teachers and students who have taken the opportunity to connect and collaborate. An "unflat," non-collaborative classroom is disconnected and isolated. Learners must be able to go beyond the "textbook" in order to connect, not just with current content, but also with people who are the voice—peers, experts and more. A modern learning environment provides opportunities for all learners to connect and collaborate without barriers for deeper understanding about the world.

Online Global Collaboration Supports Glocalization

Online global collaboration across disciplines and learning modes supports true glocalization and a "think global and act local" mantra. Glocalization is about accepting differences and applying to the local context without homogenization. The goal is not for one culture to emerge but to find differences as well as commonalities. A glocalized curriculum supports global collaborative practices and goes beyond the usual institution handbook statement of having a global approach to community learning.

Glocalization is a combination of the words "globalization" and "localization'" and is used to describe products and services that are both developed and sold to global customers but designed so that they suit the needs of local markets.

Norms of Online Global Collaboration

Educators who participate in online global collaboration need support understanding how to build engaging and successful relationships with others at a distance so that deeper global learning is realized. The Norms of Online Global Collaboration are typical or usual behaviors and actions to be practiced in synchronous and asynchronous modes when collaborating globally. As a global educator and education leader, following these eight norms will likely ensure successful collaborations. Figure 10.2 shows the eight norms and is followed by a deeper look at each of them in turn.

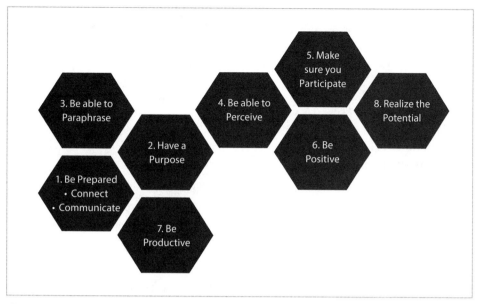

Fig. 10.2: The Norms of Online Global Collaboration

Norm 1: Be Prepared

So many potentially excellent global collaborations fail because educators are not prepared, largely because they do not know what to prepare for.

Objectives	Actions	Guiding Questions
Have a plan for connecting	Use your PLN and PLCs to find like-minded partners for global collaboration. Determine what common tools you will use to connect and collaborate. Test all tools beforehand to make sure you have access at school (and at home as needed). This may be the first time you use online collaborative tools to connect your students beyond the classroom therefore choosing and testing is most important. Work out time zone differences and what is possible.	Is it clear who this global project is for? Is it clear how participants will join? Is it clear how participants will connect? What common tools will be used? What time zones will participants be working in?

Objectives	Actions	Guiding Questions
Determine how you will communicate	Work out how teachers will communicate during the collaboration and test this well before students come together.	Is it clear how teachers will communicate during the project (with project organizers and with each other, and with students)?
	Decide what communication activities will take place between teachers and then between students (e.g., synchronous meetups, asynchronous sharing).	Are there any synchronous communication activities pre-planned (e.g., Skype calls, online teacher meetings, other)
	Work out student communication protocols and make sure all participants agree on these.	Are there any asynchronous communication activities pre-planned (online introductions or *handshakes*, topic brainstorming, other)?
	Determine the expectations for communication during the collaboration (every day? every week? students? teachers?).	What are the communication protocols during the project?
	Agree on the READ, RECEIVE and RESPOND systems and protocols for all participants.	What are the communication expectations during the project?
	Collect holiday and out of school information from each participating school so everyone knows when there may be no responses.	Are school holidays and hemisphere differences between schools being accounted for?

For online collaboration to take place it is first essential that global partners be connected through tools that everyone can easily access and use. The differences between synchronous and asynchronous tools and objectives should be discussed and decisions made as to use. Next, communication conduits must be established with all partners understanding how to contribute to planning, discussions and collaborative work. The reality of online communication is that once sent, it usually takes time to be received and read and then responded to. Some communication may be synchronous in nature, such as an online chat, however for global collaborative partnerships, most will not be. Therefore communicating asynchronously from different parts of the world means at least a 24-hour buffer needs to be allowed for partners to respond. Do not become frustrated if in fact it takes longer than this, but you are obliged to nudge for a response beyond 48 hours. This is where collaborative tools such as Google Docs or wikis have set the standard for what can be called "effective" communication between distant partners. New text, images, links, and comments can be left asynchronously for global partners to respond to on the document or page.

Pay it Forward

For online collaboration to take place it is first essential that global partners be connected through tools that everyone can easily access and use.

Norm 2: Have a Purpose

Every connection, communication and eventual collaboration must have a purpose. Planning is the key to success!

Typical Purposes	Guiding Questions
Cultural exchange	Is the purpose of the project clear?
Inquiry and exploration into a topic or topics	Is the length of the collaboration clear? Is it a set length or flexible?
Global project, short or long, curriculum-based	What are the shared inputs from participants?
Shared outcomes, student summit	What are the shared outcomes?
Artifact exchange and/or co-creation	Will there be artifact exchange? Will there be co-creation of outcomes?

Think carefully what it is you are trying to achieve, what learning experiences you are fostering and also align your needs with those of your global partners. Once a purpose is established then the collaboration should unfold. Collaborating without a common purpose causes confusion and eventual abandonment and frustration.

The purpose of the collaboration will determine the amount of planning and curriculum design that needs to take place by the individual teacher and the global teachers as a group. It will also determine whether activities are largely synchronous or asynchronous—an important part of the collaboration design. If a simple cultural exchange is the goal and synchronous connection is possible then the global collaborative design may be to do a series of Skype calls, with each subsequent call providing deeper learning experiences for the students beyond the initial handshake.

Pay it Forward

Collaborating without a common purpose causes confusion and eventual abandonment and frustration.

Norm 3: Be Able to Paraphrase

The norm "paraphrasing" is about fostering clear communication skills for intercultural understanding.

Paraphrasing Considerations	Guiding Questions
Use clear, global language at all times	Does project material use global language? Is it biased toward one culture?
Use alternative language for better understanding	Are all aspects of the project clear to you and culturally neutral? If not, is there a reason why?
Do not expect colloquial sayings and local phrases to be understood without explanation	
Question actively for intercultural understanding	

In a global context it is important that online communication is understood and to support that clear, global language is expected at all times. Remember there is often more than one way to spell a word or to describe a thing or situation. Therefore global partners are not "wrong" when they spell differently to you or use different words for common situations. Initial clarity and understanding is achieved by using common language. Some typical examples include referring to months rather than seasons ("Fall" and "Autumn" both refer to the same season, and remember each hemisphere has seasons at different times!); providing time zone conversion charts (e.g. http://timeanddate.com) for meetings; and being able to convert temperatures and measurements as needed.

Misunderstandings between global partnerships can be avoided with more careful questioning in either synchronous or asynchronous modes. Nations have unique cultural sayings that, although sometimes very funny to global partners, do not support understanding unless questioned and explained. For example, a typical Australian statement might be "I will put my case in the boot before we go". How

Pay it Forward

Encourage an atmosphere of inquiry-based collaboration at all times for intercultural understanding.

odd this must sound when in North America the case is usually called a bag and the boot is called the trunk of the car! Encourage an atmosphere of inquiry-based collaboration at all times for intercultural understanding.

Norm 4: Be Able to Perceive

True perception or understanding takes astute communication. Make sure you…	Guiding Questions
understand the parameters of the global collaboration.	Do you understand all parameters of the project enough to join?
are comfortable asking for help to keep on track.	Is it clear what teachers have to prepare and share before and during the project?
share knowledge and understanding in order to propel the learning.	Are you willing to share lesson resources and advice with others to support collaboration?

It is imperative that all members of the collaboration understand or perceive what they need to do, where the meeting places are (synchronously and asynchronously) and what the timeline is for the collaboration. All participants must feel comfortable asking questions at any time to support further understanding. Imperceptions lead to classes and teachers dropping out of the collaboration because they feel overwhelmed or lack confidence in continuing. A successful global collaboration is where all members work hard to share knowledge and understanding in order to propel the learning. This is a lot easier of course with another teacher in the same school. With a teacher(s) in another country it is harder work, but not impossible.

Pay it Forward

A successful global collaboration is where all members work hard to share knowledge and understanding in order to propel the learning.

Norm 5: Participate

Make sure all members of the collaboration understand how and where to contribute and what the expectation is for doing this reliably.

Participation Includes:	Guiding Questions
Being visible online during the collaboration	How will learning be visible online during the project?
Being a reliable and regular contributor	What will teachers and students need to contribute and when?
Responding to others in a timely and constructive manner	Are the timeline and main contribution times clear and detailed?

When collaborating around a table face-to-face it is almost impossible to not contribute as the norm is to request, encourage and allow time for opinions from all. However in an online scenario it is VERY easy to be "invisible" by not responding or contributing to emails, online discussions and collaborative spaces. Determine shared communication protocols so that all learners understand how to connect and communicate with partners. Make sure students have access to spaces and know what is expected of them.

Online global collaboration is successful when partners contribute and respond often. To avoid the breakdown of collaborative relationships contribution expectations and regularity of interaction and responses should be agreed upon. An overall timeframe for responses including expectations for frequency of responses can be established at the start of collaboration. Productive collaboration relies on these being adhered to. Adding ideas and material to an online space and then becoming invisible is also not acceptable in a collaborative environment. Responses to individual contributions fosters problem solving and co-creation of outcomes through ongoing discussion and knowledge building.

Pay it Forward

Online global collaboration is successful when partners contribute and respond often and are not 'invisible.'

Norm 6: Be Positive

Positive intentions are assumed at all times. The goal is for the collaboration to be constructive in an educational context.

Stay positive by...	Guiding Questions
encouraging a positive and constructive approach at all times.	Are there guidelines for encouraging positive and constructive approach at all times?
sharing global citizenship best practices	How will global citizenship objectives be shared and understood?
building empathy among learners	How will participants in the project be monitored for best practices?
celebrating achievements along the way	How will empathy be built among learners?
	How will achievements throughout the project be celebrated?

Global citizenship skills come into this norm as well. A constructive learning environment assumes a positive working environment free from criticism, misunderstanding, and "localized" colloquialisms that block global partners. Positive empathy between collaborators can be built through sharing local images, occurrences, statistics and other data. Sharing things that are familiar in daily life, although seemingly too "normal" to the owner are a good way to start the "handshake" process of getting to know a working partner. Share questions about global topics—do not be afraid to say you do not understand or do not know—this is where global partners, in true collaboration, will support new understandings via their frequent responses to questions and comments. Celebrations and reflections are an important part of the process of global collaboration and help construct better understandings between partners and enhanced outcomes.

Pay it Forward

A constructive learning environment assumes a positive working environment free from criticism, misunderstanding, and 'localized' colloquialisms that block global partners.

Norm 7: Be Productive

A well-designed online global collaboration is about flattened learning and creating something to share or co-creating artifacts between students and classrooms.

Productivity means you...	Guiding Questions
collaborate and share information and ideas	How will participants collaborate and share information?
create outcomes to share and encourage responses	What artifacts will be created?
make outcomes visible to the outside world	Will artifacts be co-created? How?
encourage students to compare, contrast, reflect	How will feedback and responses be gathered based on the student work?
aim to build knowledge together and co-create artifacts	Are outcomes going to be visible to the outside world? How?
	How will students interact in order to compare, contrast and reflect?

Productivity is an important norm. What did you actually produce during this collaboration? Where is the evidence? Consider as part of the global collaboration design what the outcomes will be and work towards this. Consider also making these outcomes visible to others, and if possible making the process visible as well.

As part of the productivity, develop an understanding of what co-creations are possible between students and how this could be implemented and encourage collaborators to work towards this. It may be a co-created statement or document that all have contributed to, or a co-created multimedia artifact, or a co-hosted online summit, or something quite new!

Pay it Forward

As part of the productivity, develop an understanding of what co-creations are possible between learners, how this could be implemented and then encourage collaborators to work towards this.

Norm 8: Realize the Potential

Serendipitous learning happens when you least expect it. This final norm is about being aware of and fostering these unintended learning opportunities whenever and wherever they happen during the global collaboration. It may be that some plans are altered on the run, it may be that outcomes are tweaked or it may be that connections and working time is extended in order to fully maximize the learning.

Make sure you are...	Guiding questions:
prepared for new experiences and unintended learning outcomes	How can the potential of individual learners be realized while completing this project?
flexible and are able to deviate from the plan to support enhanced learning opportunities	How flexible are the parameters of the project to allow this potential to be reached?
able to realize the potential of individual learners as they connect globally	

The message here is for all learners to be aware that learning is not always "planned" and connecting learners globally leads to many exciting outcomes, many of which are unexpected. Be wary of overplanning global collaborations to the point where there is no flexibility for the transient learning community at that time to make decisions and alter the pathway. By allowing that extra weekend, maybe two more classes could finish their videos to submit. By allowing students to gather in a virtual classroom and give them leadership opportunities they can assume a globally competent approach— even if the conversation wanders from the project work to fruit (as happened to me when students from the Middle East and USA came together in a synchronous summit and talked for five minutes about fruit, the catalyst being when one of my students in Qatar mentioned a mango and the US students did not know what that was!).

Pay it Forward

Online global collaboration provides personalized learning opportunities and supports students to excel in different ways. Global educators know how important this is for individual learning and design flexible outcomes to support this potential.

Barriers and Enablers to Global Collaboration

et's now explore some practicalities to do with embracing global collaborative learning. In an online world, the global collaborative classroom is defined by the following characteristics.

- connected learning
- engagement with multiple audiences
- engagement with diverse resources and tools
- authentic, collaborative learning outcomes

There are TWO main types of communication in an online global collaborative classroom—synchronous and asynchronous. Collaborators must be able to sustain connections beyond the face-to-face experience and beyond the virtual, synchronous experience and be able to build networks and online communities to support collaboration.

Schools across the world vary in a multitude of ways including approaches to curriculum, access to digital technologies, teacher expectations and much more. Beyond the typical school concept and practice, learners at all levels and all ages are impacted by different factors as to how they connect and collaborate globally. Gaining a deeper understanding of these factors can implicitly start to shift learning environments to be more conducive to online global collaboration.

There are two basic challenges to global collaboration: language and time zones.

Language: "Not having a common language, limits the level and depth of communication you can have with the partner school. Collaboration is still possible but takes a bit more creativity where the written or spoken word is not part of the collaboration."

Time zones: "Educators are just now beginning to understand the concept of blended learning. This means where you do certain activities online, some offline, and when you add the dimension of global to it you have to add synchronous and asynchronous. The very sexy, jazzy and provocative thing is to do synchronous stuff, it's really cool and in the moment… but the reality is you are not really solving a lot of problems or accomplishing a lot synchronously."

(Yvonne Marie Andres, USA, @YvonneMarieA)

Barriers to Effective Online Global Collaboration

What are the typical deterrents to online global collaboration? How should educators overcome these?

Technology Infrastructure

Technology infrastructure refers to the hardware, software and networking setup and capability within a digital learning environment (DLE). The question is, "Does your DLE allow you to collaborate globally?" Maybe you need to start with the question, "Does your DLE allow you to collaborate locally?" and see what the pressure points are? Effective online global collaboration requires access to the internet and access to a range of tools that are usually not part of a typical learning management system (LMS). As technologies emerge it is not useful to generalize across schools and countries however it is usually Web 2.0 tools that provide the bridge to global partnerships and collaboration. These include collaborative writing spaces like wikis, blogs, social bookmarking and artifact creation tools. In addition the technology infrastructure must allow learners to connect, communicate and create multimedia artifacts and share them online. Older digital equipment may not have the facility required. On the other hand it is NOT necessary to have the latest device or laptop at all! The goal is to examine the technology infrastructure available at the school with a view to making modifications if needed. Wireless networking is a major consideration if the learning environment is going mobile. It always helps to find a friendly IT support person and discuss this challenge, remembering that educational objectives must trump what IT support personnel may prefer!

Technology Access

Implementing online global collaboration does not mean you need to be a 1:1 or BYOD or BYOT (or other acronym) digital learning environment. Many of us have implemented global collaboration in the classroom with one computer, 30 students and a weak internet connection. More importantly you do need regular internet access and an understanding of new responsibilities when connecting with external partners. Online collaboration only works if all partners contribute and respond and share often across the project or collaboration timeframe. Once reliable technology access is established then the essential toolkit for connections and collaborations can be determined. Questions to consider include, "Does access include the same tools that others are using?"; "Can you negotiate with the collaboration partners to use different tools if needed?"; "Can you open your own access (blocked websites) in order to collaborate globally?" Typical technology access challenges across the world include sites being blocked beyond the control of the classroom teacher or even the school leader. Both schools and/or governments block certain tools often because of the social media aspects of usage and the fear they might be either misused or unwanted outsiders may infiltrate the collaboration. It may also be purely to preserve bandwidth in a situation where it is in short supply. In many examples these tools can be unblocked if teachers know how to state their case for online collaboration and understand how to design, implement and monitor collaboration beyond their classroom walls. In my experience teaching across six countries, including the Middle East and especially China where blocked tools are a way of life, there is always a way to connect and collaborate without breaking the law of the country or the requirements of the school and without resorting to other offline modes.

Technology Fluency

Once infrastructure and access barriers are solved, the next barrier may be a learner's ability to work with the technology. To make online global collaboration a success certain digital fluency is required by the teacher and the students. This can be gained through initial practice and carefully planned usage of online collaboration tools. Skills such as being able to join or initiate and host a Skype call, or initiate a Google Hangout or edit a wiki or join students to Edmodo can cause some stress at first. Regular usage promotes fluency. Regular experimentation with new or different digital tools also promotes fluency. Educators are encouraged to become learners and move out of their comfort zone in this respect and reach out to their PLN (and the students!) for help and support as they explore new tools. Learning new tools opens more doors for global collaborative experiences!

Global Digital Citizenship Skills

Often there is focus on digital citizenship skills through commonly accepted topics of safety and privacy, netiquette, copyright and legality. The next step for global collaborative learners is to understand more fully what it means to be a global digital citizen and learn skills that will support this. This is a barrier to online global collaboration when learners do not know how to interact and learn online with others at a distance; when they do not know how to be reliable and responsible users of shared online spaces; and when cultural and global areas of awareness are not discussed before and during the collaboration. What is known as the "fear factor" can be evident here. A typical scenario is where a teacher assumes students are not going to be reliable online learners and therefore thinks online global collaboration will not work. This is a false assumption and a major barrier. All learners, at all ages, need to learn how to learn online in collaborative situations, and yes they will make some mistakes. Most mistakes made by learners (of all ages) are not a reason to suspend or shutdown the work. Most are easily fixed through discussion between teachers, maybe taking something offline if needed, and continuing to share best practice. Teachers must also model good global digital citizenship skills at all times through their connected learning habits.

For schools it is good practice to have global digital citizenship guidelines in place that support online learning with distant partners (and do not inhibit by being too draconian). It is also good practice to meet with parents and students together to review and discuss the objectives for global outreach and global collaborations that are part of the curriculum, including expectations for online learning approaches and learning beyond the school day.

Curriculum Conformity

Are you a "teacherpreneur" or an "outlier"? In any education setting these global educators who are willing to take risks and bring new learning opportunities to their students often hit major barriers with what we call "curriculum conformity". This means, for example, if one Grade 3 teacher wanted to do an online global collaborative project, the school position may be that unless ALL Grade 3 teachers can do it, then it is not possible within the curriculum confines. A typical scenario often follows where the other teachers are NOT interested so therefore the inspiration for collaboration by the first teacher is dropped. Once again, to overcome this barrier much discussion and forward planning of curriculum design and global connections to support collaborative objectives needs to be in place. With careful planning it is valid for pilot classrooms or students to lead the way one year in a new global collaboration and then bring the others along with them the following year.

The "we are already collaborating and don't need anything more" Approach

A deeper barrier to why more classrooms and schools are not collaborating globally is the lack of a shared understanding of what embedded, curriculum-based online global collaboration is. The typical scenario is a classroom or school who may have a focus on a particular country or project that becomes all consuming for a few, but in reality results in non-involvement for most. The established global connection may already involve rich learning activities and country-to-country exchanges for teachers and students, but may not provide a structure for all students to learn with others at a distance collaboratively within the curriculum.

Another scenario is where a particular activity, for example video conferencing (rich learning experiences that may include additional hardware or software such as Polycom or Skype), is being implemented across grades and subjects but learners are not encouraged to move to essential asynchronous collaborations. The "online global collaboration" box has been ticked through this one activity and everyone is happy, especially if a lot of money has been spent on video conferencing hardware and software. However, one approach using one type of technology does not afford embedded global collaborative curriculum objectives. More must be done at an individual classroom level to support diverse collaborative learning objectives.

Attitudes Toward Using Digital Technology

Research is showing us the educator is a major barrier to adopting new modes of learning with digital technologies. Laurillard (2009, 2012) shares research that shows "first order" challenges such as infrastructure, access to technology, policies, curriculum development and so on, are more easily fixed than "second-order" challenges, namely teacher attitudes and beliefs about technology integration. This includes beliefs about the role of digital technologies and beliefs about the adoption of more innovative pedagogies for online learning locally and globally.

This attitude barrier can translate partly to the "no idea where to start" problem which may be solved through exposure to other global educators, learning from them and following their lead. The deeper problems of a non-constructivist approach and lack of understanding about transformative use of digital technologies by the educator adversely impacts learners and is a major barrier to the adoption of online global collaborative practices.

Enablers to Effective Online Global Collaboration

Typical enablers for online global collaboration are described in this next section.

Building an Effective PLN and PLCs

A connected educator is, by the very nature of those connections, global. Educators who build a strong personal learning network (PLN) will find other educators ready and willing to support their entry into global collaborative learning. This is such an important enabling step. Professional learning communities (PLCs) (such as the ISTE PLNs) bring like-minded educators together to share, discuss, and build collaborations for future learning. A popular and effective tool to build a PLN now is Twitter. Much has been written about its efficacy, and a global educator knows how to use hashtags to connect with diverse global communities, and how to join or review tweetchats to share and learn with others. Examples of other global communities are found on Facebook, Google+ and Ning networks. Being a reliable contributor to some of these networks is advized, however it is physically impossible to be active in all places all the time. The advantage of continuing to join communities is that they will always be there when you are ready to contribute and collaborate and learn from and with them.

Finding a Reliable Partner(s)

It is an inspiring and exciting time when you start to reach out globally to find partners and other global educators who also want to join their classroom to the world. For a start it may be the first time you as an educator have worked and collaborated on something with someone in another place. Secondly, all sorts of new collaboration skills will be employed such as how to communicate effectively and where to share meeting notes and action points. Sometimes, despite good intentions on all sides, the intended collaboration fails. It can be a confusing time—the failure can be due to extraneous pressures within or beyond the school, or it can simply be the teacher did not follow through. The message here is DO NOT give up! Learn, reflect, and work out what to do better next time, find a more reliable partner(s) and try again! Make sure you enable the partnership through careful pre-planning of the online collaboration first, including a timeline, tools to be used and learner expectations!

Learning Standards and Frameworks

Have you looked at accepted standards and learning frameworks recently? Have you really looked? Don't they say things like "intercultural understanding" or "collaboration with others at a distance"? What are you doing about this? The ISTE Standards for Students state: "Students use digital media and environments to communicate and work collaboratively, including at a distance". The ISTE Standards for Teachers state teachers will, "Collaborate with students, peers, parents, and community members using digital tools and resources to support student success and innovation."

Learn more about the ISTE standards for students and how they relate to global collaboration at **iste.org/standards**

There are a number of frameworks available to support global competency and intercultural understanding. The Asia Society provide a free downloadable resource, Educating for Global Competence, that shares pillars for global competence and states globally competent students must have the knowledge and skills to investigate the world; weigh perspectives; communicate ideas; take action; and apply disciplinary and interdisciplinary expertise. The Partnership for 21st Century Learning provides a Framework for State Action on Global Education (US-based, but a great resource for all). The framework along with a Teacher Guide to K–12 Global Education Grade Level Indicators are also available for free download. The Australian National Curriculum document has "Intercultural understanding" as a general capability and shares online a learning continuum that includes recognising culture

Asia Society: Educating for Global Competence: **http://asiasociety.org/global competence**

Partnership for 21st Century Learning: Global Education: **http://www.p21.org/ our-work/global-education**

Australian National Curriculum: **http://www.australiancurriculum.edu.au/**

and developing respect; interacting and empathising with others; and reflecting on intercultural experiences and taking responsibility.

In reality the occasional Skype call is NOT enough to fully cover these 21st century or modern learning standards and expectations for learning. Teachers are encouraged to meet with curriculum or learning and teaching coordinators within their subject and grade level groups to discuss the possibilities. Discussion and combined problem solving within a school is a BIG enabler to moving forward with global learning and collaboration.

Curriculum Design

Embedding meaningful global learning experiences into the curriculum takes some redesign and pre-planning. Online global collaboration, as a modern learning objective, requires careful design and preparation. Often teachers start planning a global collaborative experience for their students 12 months beforehand! This includes connecting and communicating virtually with partner teachers and determining the structure and timeline of the collaboration, the outcomes, the shared knowledge and the co-created products. Curriculum redesign is a wonderful challenge for teachers at all levels but should not be viewed as a barrier to global collaboration. Global collaboration fits into any and all curriculums—it is a matter of refocusing and realigning approaches to learning and adopting more innovative pedagogy. See the following chapter for more details about learning design for global collaboration.

Web 2.0 Tools

Access to Web 2.0 tools is the bridge to collaborative learning, both locally and globally. When you want to "go global" all participants need the same online places and spaces to connect, communicate, collaborate and share creations and co-creations. It is very rare that a school LMS will allow "outsiders" to join therefore independent platforms must be set up such as Edmodo, Wikispaces, Google sites, and so on. The beauty of Web 2.0 tools is they are mostly free or inexpensive and they are web-based therefore potentially accessible by learners everywhere. Some tools may be pass-worded by design (Edmodo requires a join code); or choice (Wikispaces or Padlet can be public or private with password access). Individual schools can create accounts and pay for Web 2.0 services and then invite outside collaborators quite easily.

Learning Is 24/7 for Everyone

When collaborating globally learning does not stop when the class or the school day is over. Often that is when your partners are starting their day. Many places in the world now have internet access in the home as well as at school. Or they may access online spaces via a community portal such as a library or internet cafè. One major enabler for global learning that leads to online collaboration is expecting students (and teachers) to blend learning modes and hours. This concept and practice has deliberately been added to the "positive" enablers list, rather than the more "nega-tive" barriers list. It is a reasonable expectation that "homework" include connecting with others beyond the immediate learning environment for the purpose of seeking information, sharing ideas and artifacts and collaborating on new concepts and prototypes. It is also reasonable that teachers attend online planning meetings and communicate virtually with global partners outside of the usual school day—how else will global collaboration ever take place if they do not? Those schools or teachers with draconian regulations and attitudes about working hours must become the minority in a global learning environment otherwise the positive change we want to see will not happen.

Online Global Collaboration: Design for Action

S uccessful online global collaborations require some structure and planning. Elongated projects that continue for 3–6 months or even up to a year take considerable thought as to how to engage the participants and what the outcomes will be. This chapter examines a range of online global projects and provides strategies and formulas for design of learning that includes global objectives. This is a vital chapter for global educators and global education leaders to review and understand.

Design for Action!

The protocols for successful online globally collaborative learning can be summarized simply as:

- **Find** like-minded educators
- **Design** curriculum and outcomes
- **Select** tools that all participants can access
- **Manage** the collaboration for success

It takes careful design, implementation and management to embed online global collaboration across the curriculum. I call this "design for action!" If you are new to online global collaboration it may be easier and more worthwhile to join an established project with experienced educators who are leading the collaboration so you can learn from them. If you are already experienced and/or ready to jump in and design your own collaboration then you are ready for action! Remember, this is not always easy work, but has profitable outcomes for better understanding of the needs of online global collaboration.

This chapter shares many ideas to do with online global collaborative design for learning. Some global projects shared have taken years to develop, with many iterations and evolutions. Some have remained pretty well intact with the same design that they started with. Others are fairly new and continue to evolve.

Online Global Collaboration Taxonomy

As a way to classify types and levels of online global collaboration the Online Global Collaboration Taxonomy (Table 12.1) has been created. It covers types of interactions, purpose, communication mode, and local-to-global learning modes. Let's explore what each facet of this taxonomy means and then examine useful examples. First, a word about communication modes.

Synchronous Communication

Synchronous means in real time. It applies to learners interacting and communicating at the same time. Learners are always highly engaged and motivated when interacting with new friends or experts synchronously. This can be, for example, a Skype call that brings different cultures and experiences directly into the learning environment and allows students to share ideas and inquire on the spot. Synchronous connections such as Skype or other forms of interactive video conferencing are excellent for kicking off a more extended interaction and collaboration. They provide a way for participants on both sides to "handshake" virtually and learn about each other through visual and audio communication. Simulated synchronous communication is possible through the use of tools like online chats or Google Docs when participants are online contributing at the same time.

Asynchronous Communication

Asynchronous means not in real time. It applies to learners interacting and communicating at different times. Asynchronous communication is vital for sustaining connections beyond the face-to-face experience and beyond the virtual, synchronous experience. Online global collaboration by its very nature implies asynchronous collaboration. Successful online global collaboration hinges on asynchronous communication strategies that support ongoing interactions across time zones. Effective asynchronous communication provides a scaffold for learners and fosters deeper understanding and community building. Through this mode trust can be built that leads to viable working opportunities where learners collaborate at a distance and co-create products together.

Asynchronous communication is where text and other multimedia can be posted online at any time and then added to or responded to at any time by global partners. It is not reliant on all collaborators being online at the same time. This includes discussions such as with the tool Edmodo; artifact development using a tool such as VoiceThread; and online sharing tools such as Padlet. The line is a little blurred sometimes as these tools also work quite well in a synchronous mode with almost fluent responses being given to simulate being in the same space at the same time.

Local-to-Global Learning Modes

Before we classify the levels of online global collaboration here is an explanation of local-to-global learning modes.

A) **Intraconnection:** This is when connection, communication and collaboration occur within a confined learning environment such as a classroom (real or virtual). Collaborative tools, often Web 2.0, are used to connect learners who are brought together as a community for learning (an inner circle) within the same school or institution.

B) **Interconnection:** This mode is when a learning environment is connected with another one (or more than one) anywhere in the world. Typically students interact asynchronously although connections in the same town, state, country or between countries that are within similar time zones afford real time synchronous meeting opportunities (in person or virtual).

C) **Teacher global connections:** This is where educators join their students to existing (or possibly self-created) projects and complete certain agreed-upon requirements. Typically students are not joined to one another for direct discussion and group co-creation; however there may be opportunities for real time meetings such as a Skype interaction. In this example educators manage the collaboration and the "product", such as a website, ebook, or video, may become a focus. Uploading and sharing the finished artifacts becomes a responsibility of the educators involved.

D) **Managed student connections:** In this mode students make direct connections with each other on an individual basis, often in groups of two or more. Some form of online community may be built that allows individual students to introduce themselves and respond personally to others not in their immediate vicinity. Each student may have a unique learning goal through cross-classroom team formation that aligns with the overall project and global collaborative goals. Powerful peer-to-peer learning experiences may be designed and implemented.

E) **Student collaboration:** A powerful learning mode is student-to-student where the learning is "flattened" such that students take on leadership roles and manage interactions and collaborations across learning environments. Educators are present as facilitators (or Learning Concierges) and monitor any cultural disconnections or non-participation and intervene as needed. Student autonomous learning is ideally practiced to enrich the online global collaborative experience.

Table 12.1: Online Global Collaboration Taxonomy

Level and Activity	Purpose	Communication Mode	Local-to-Global Learning Modes	Examples
Level 1: Online interactions	To share online learning environment activities and expand communication from local to global through online digital platforms	Asynchronous	Mode A, B	Blog posts and comments (class and individual) Posting digital artifacts for others to view and comment on

Level and Activity	Purpose	Communication Mode	Local-to-Global Learning Modes	Examples
Level 2: Real Encounters	To connect in real time to external learners and experts	Synchronous	Modes B, C, D, E	Skype interactions Google Hangouts Video conferencing Online chats
Level 3: Online Learning	To encourage learning through digital interaction and sharing of artifacts	Asynchronous, could also be synchronous depending on the tool used	Modes A, B C, D, E	Online communities to support curriculum objectives May be localized or more global May be teacher led or student led MOOCs, discussions, sharing multimedia
Level 4: Communities of Practice	Designed for specific learning objectives where students initiate or join deeper global collaboratives Foster online global collaborative practices	Synchronous and Asynchronous	Modes A, B, C, D, E	Global collaborative projects
Level 5: Learning Collaboratives	Fosters learner autonomy for online global collaboration	Synchronous and Asynchronous	Modes A, B, C, D, E	Extended collaborative communities

Examples to Support the Online Global Collaboration Taxonomy

Level 1 - Online Interactions

This "getting started" level applies to asynchronous communication and "Intraconnection" as well as "Interconnection" modes. A simple explanation is that of a class or group of learners who design learning activities to share in a local mode with a view to expand communication to global through online digital platforms. As an example, a class blog might be used for students and the teacher(s) to share ideas and connect. It might even be shared with the wider school community, including parents and other classes, and it might even be shared online with other interested teachers and students across the world. Whoever this is shared with may have the option to not only read but to make comments thereby creating that interactive, almost collaborative relationship. This applies also to digital artifacts posted online, such as a video, that others can view, share and comment on.

Quadblogging

The original quadblogging idea came from David Mitchell in the UK. Typically four classrooms are grouped for the purposes of sharing their blogs for student comments on a rotation basis. It has been an extremely popular global project since 2011. Watch the video that shows David speaking about the success of blogging in his elementary school and how this practice raised achievement.

Quadblogging website: **www.quadblogging.com/**

Quadblogging, linking learning to global audience: **http://youtu.be/w8J8Jrr_eq4**

100 Word Challenge

This is a weekly creative writing challenge for children under 16 years of age. Writing is posted to a blog and linked to the 100-word challenge blog. Students are encouraged to visit other blogs and leave comments. There is also a showcase feature where individual students are recognized each week.

100 Word Challenge website: **http://100wc.net/**

The Not Perfect Hat Club - Global Blogging Challenge

Based on a series of books that feature life struggles through dog personas, students (ages 6–13) are encouraged to craft and share stories of their own that share they are not perfect.

The Not Perfect Hat Club website **http://nphcblogit.com/**

Twitter Hashtag: **#NPHCBlogIt**

Founders: Jena Ball **@JenaiaMorane** and Beverly Ladd **@BevLadd**

Travelling Teddy Bears

These cute bears are sent out to classrooms around the world for students and teachers to blog and share images and videos of their adventures together. This project encourages very young students to participate in digital media, including blogging and promotes intercultural understanding through the inanimate object of a cuddly teddy bear.

The Traveling Teddy Bears website: **http://travelingteddybear.com/**

The Traveling Teddy Bears blog: **http://travelingteddybear.com/?page_id=19**

Kindergarten Around the World

A Twitter-based virtual exchange project that encourages classes to build relationships to share daily life, develop an awareness of other cultures, and use technology to communicate, amongst other objectives.

Kindergarten Around the World website: **http://kindergartenaroundtheworld .blogspot.com.au/**

Twitter hashtag: **#kinderchat**

Coordinator: Amy Murray **@happycampergirl**

Projects by Jen

Jen Wagner has been organising online projects for elementary school levels since 1999. Interesting creative ideas and fun simple products make these popular amongst North American classrooms. This is ostensibly a Level 1 collaboration, although synchronous meetups are encouraged.

Projects by Jen website: **http://projectsbyjen.com/**

Jen Wagner: **@jenwagner**

Global Math Task Twitter Challenge

This challenge is for students of any age, anywhere in the world. Twitter is the tool used to share math tasks. Organizers have set up an excellent slideshow to share how to get more out of your tweets by using images.

Global Math Task Twitter Challenge website: **http://gmttc.blogspot.com**

Twitter hashtag: **#GMTTC**

Organizers: Beverly Ladd **@BevLadd** and Heidi Samuelson **@swampfrogfirst**

Level 2 - Real Encounters

To connect in real time to external learners and experts is the parameter of this "Real encounters" level. It employs digital tools that provide those essential connections such as Skype, Google Hangout and other video- and chat-based apps. It is applicable to all local to global modes, except of course for Mode A (Intraconnection) although for practice purposes "intraclass" real encounters online are a viable activity.

Skype in the Classroom

The Skype in the classroom website has excellent ideas and links to resources. It encourages three ways to use Skype in the classroom: collaborate with other classes, find guest speakers and take a virtual field trip anywhere in the world!

If you have not explored this possibility this is one to take on—every teacher should be able to embed some form of Skype interaction into the curriculum. Skype

Skype in the Classroom website: **https://education.microsoft.com/ skypeintheclassroom**

Twitter: **@skypeclassroom**

first came to the classroom in about 2006, maybe a little earlier. I was teaching in Bangladesh at that time and my high school students discovered the power of synchronous connections before I did (of course!). It opened a new window to the world and complemented the online global collaborative work we were doing with Flat Classroom.

The "Taxonomy of a Skype Conversation" (Tolisano, 2014) focuses on the pedagogy and shows how to develop communication skills during a Skype call from ping-pong to free-flowing conversation.

It's Exciting Face-to-Face!

These global educators are piloting and refining synchronous connections.

Edna Pythian, USA, tells us, "My favorite easy way to get connected is the mystery Skype process. You can use Skype or Google Hangouts as a platform as it is so easy. It is non-intrusive, takes little preparation, and the kids love the game. The other thing is it can be placed regarding location, number, animal, or anything."

Toni Olivieri-Barton, USA, shares her practice when she says, "My school and students enjoy the interaction with others. There are some students who excel at the video or audio aspect of our project. There are others who learn to excel at the typing portion of our projects. In a large global project there are so many ways students can show their strengths. The students and teachers understand how simple it can be to connect with others to discuss a topic. One great example of this is we have Skyped with a classroom in California after we have studied the Colorado Gold Rush and they have studied the California Gold Rush. The students compared and contrasted the facts that we both learned about in their own classrooms. We did the same thing with a school from Chile when we were both studying rights and responsibilities of citizens."

School in the Cloud

We can learn a lot from Sugata Mitra and the School in the Cloud initiative. Originator of the infamous "Hole in the Wall" implementation in rural India, Sugata Mitra (academic and researcher) won the 1 million dollar TED prize to develop the School in the Cloud.

The School in the Cloud initiative includes:

- SOLE: Self Organized Learning Environments. From the website, "A Self-Organized Learning Environment, or SOLE, can exist anywhere there is a computer, internet connection, and children who are ready to learn. In a SOLE, educators pose Big Questions to students. Anyone can create a SOLE."

- Granny Cloud: From the website, "A global community of mediators who use Skype to work with children in SOLEs across the globe. Granny Cloud members, or Grannies, are both young and old, male and female. The goal of the Granny Cloud is to stimulate children's curiosity, develop their confidence, and generally to have fun."

School in the Cloud website: **www.theschoolinthecloud.org**

Twitter: **@schoolincloud**

Video conferencing

There are many examples of video conferencing for learning, also called interactive video conferencing. In Australia, all state schools in New South Wales have H.323 video conferencing equipment, usually Polycom or Tandberg units. Victorian schools are also rolling out H.323 platform equipment. The advantage of this equipment is the ability to send multiple content streams—main camera, second camera or document cameras, Powerpoint presentations, and content from a DVD. Sue Beveridge from Electroboard tells us, "Whilst it wasn't global our experience with a collaborative project run nationally demonstrated the power of creating new knowledge. Students across eight Australian schools shared their first contact stories as part of a project based on the novel *Nanberry* written by Jackie French, the Australian Children's laureate. Jackie spoke to the children about the perspectives of the characters in the text and then students were to research first contact in their local areas. They developed a digital product to communicate their research with the other schools. These shared learnings were powerful as students learned that for some areas of Australia, first contact had been with whalers and gold miners, whilst students from NSW Gymea Bay explained that it was Captain Cook. Last year we supported a panel of experts speak to a live audience at Gunghalin College about issues of migration and refugees. We connected other Australian schools and American schools to engage with the panel via video conference which enabled students to understand the global nature of this issue."

Sue also adds that, "There are important learning outcomes from this kind of global connected learning. Seeing and hearing student peers from other countries engaging in similar topics and sharing their views broadens our students perspectives and their capacities in terms of oral language having to communicate to an audience of this complexity and size."

See material from Sue Beveridge **https://interactivewhiteboardnetau.wordpress.com/** and **www.virtualexcursionsaustralia.com.au/**

Another exciting opportunity for video conferencing comes from Ben Newsome at Fizzics Education. Ben, a science teacher, received a Churchill Fellowship to develop a viable video conferencing format that would bring science to students and teachers in support of the curriculum. Ben and his team provide a pedagogically improved video conferencing experience that has hands-on student involvement in science experiments and inquiry learning.

Connect with Ben Newsome

Fizzics website: **http://fizzics.com.au/**

Twitter: **@BenNewsome_** and **@FizzicsEd**

Fizzics Education: **www.fizzicseducation.com.au/Schools/video%20confer-encing.html**

Level 3 - Online Learning

The aim of this level is to encourage learning through digital interaction and sharing of artifacts. It applies to the development of online communities to support curriculum objectives and may be localized (between classes or schools in the same geographic region) or more global. The learning focus is asynchronous, although some unintentional (serendipitous) synchronous communication may take place, especially if a chat facility is provided for participants. Design at this level includes tools for sharing all forms of multimedia, encouragement of student and teacher engagement and online contributions that lead to collaborations. A MOOC, a project wiki, or a Ning community may align with this level.

Global SchoolNet - Cyberfair

The Cyberfair project, under the umbrella of Global SchoolNet, is a community engagement project where students in a school create a website to share their community service and learning based on a choice of set topics. Peer review of other students work is a key feature. Read more about Yvonne Marie Andres, founder of Global SchoolNet, in Case Study 2.1.

Cyberfair website: **www.globalschoolnet.org/gsncf/**

PenPal Schools

PenPal Schools provides curriculum-guided online exchanges and has connected 70,000+ students across 70 countries. It is now a free service. They pair up classes and match each student with a PenPal for a 6-week exchange. Multi-lingual objectives, world news and US-based discussions are the main curriculum focus for students of age nine and up.

PenPal Schools website: **https://penpalschools.com/**

Twitter: **@PenpalSchools**

eTwinning

eTwinning is the community for schools in Europe where teachers can freely and safely connect, develop collaborative projects and share ideas. Many global projects are available for review on the website (great for getting new ideas) however only schools within Europe can join—it is very much a closed shop to others in the world. eTwinning applies to the Member States of the European Union: Austria, Belgium, Bulgaria, Croatia, Cyprus, the Czech Republic, Denmark, Estonia, Finland, France, Germany, Greece, Hungary, Ireland, Italy, Latvia, Lithuania, Luxembourg, Malta, Poland, Portugal, Romania, Slovakia, Slovenia, Spain, Sweden, the Netherlands, and the United Kingdom. Overseas territories and countries are also eligible. In addition, Albania, Bosnia and Herzegovina, the Former Yugoslav Republic Of Macedonia, Iceland, Liechtenstein, Norway, Serbia, and Turkey can also take part.

eTwinning offers an online platform called the Twinspace that schools can use to work together on their project. This platform offers a chat facility as well as spaces to share and showcase work. The annual eTwinning conference has over 500 teachers attend. Other professional learning sessions are held throughout the year.

Connect with eTwinning

Website: **www.etwinning.net/en/pub/index.htm**

Twitter: **@eTwinningEurope**

eTwinning in the UK website: **www.britishcouncil.org/etwinning**

Twitter: **@eTwinningUK**

There are many projects showcased on the general and UK sites

www.britishcouncil.org/etwinning/what/case-study

www.etwinning.net/en/pub/collaborate/project_gallery.cfm

Level 4 - Communities of Practice

As distinct from Level 3, this level, called "communities of practice", is designed for the purpose of specific learning objectives as a global community of learners. All local to global learning modes may be employed and both synchronous and asynchronous communication modes are expected. The community of practice would normally have a shared objective such as a global collaborative project, and probably a set timeline that dictates workflow and communication patterns. The goal of this level is to foster diverse online global collaborative practices that may be teacher and/or student led.

Global Read Aloud

The Global Read Aloud (GRA) is an award-winning project that runs for six weeks starting in early October. It helps classrooms find partners for the purposes of reading a book over that time and interacting and sharing in different ways. Founder Pernille Ripp shares that, "Online collaboration takes many forms, such as commenting on blog posts, video blogs, Twitter feeds; shared writing experiences; and the use of Google Docs for collaboration. Skype calls are also good, but time zone challenged. The strength of the GRA is that once the project is over that's when all of the other stuff begins. Teachers now have confidence with tools and collaboration experience and have a huge community they can tap into for continued collaborations. Another strength of GRA is global collaboration is now not scary." Read more in Case Study 3.7.

Global Read Aloud website: **http://theglobalreadaloud.com/**

Founder, Pernille Ripp: **@pernilleripp**

Out of Eden Walk

A unique learning community has been built around the journey of Pulitzer Prize-winning journalist Paul Salopek as he retraces on foot the global migration of our ancestors in a 21,000-mile, seven-year odyssey that begins in Ethiopia and ends in Tierra del Fuego. It is an initiative of Project Zero at the Harvard Graduate School of Education. The global community interact with Paul in different ways and respond

Connect with Out of Eden Walk

Website: **www.outofedenwalk.com/**

Twitter: **@outofedenlearn**

Registration information: **http://learn.outofedenwalk.com/**

Watch video: Out of Eden Learn: Portrait of Practice, Natalie Belli: **https://youtu.be/ IlZmd1DhyuY** with multimedia reflections and other artifacts. Tweetchats, live Skype calls, blogging, and local activities such as neighborhood walks and mapping are features of things this community participates in. The website is alive with opportunities.

Rock Our World

Since 2004 Rock Our World led by Carol Anne McGuire has worked with students around the world to collaborate in original music composition and movie making. Students also meet each other via video chats and discuss various curriculum topics. Apple's GarageBand is used to co-create music and important partnerships have been made with supporting companies including Fablevision, Discovery, Smart Technologies, and NASA. They even have an app!

Rock Our World Website: **www.rockourworld.org**

Facebook: **www.facebook.com/rockourworld1**

Twitter: **@rockourworld**

Flat Connections: "A Week in the Life…" Project

This project is for upper elementary students, ages 8–11. It is an exciting, challenging and unique experience that allows young people (and their teachers) to connect, communicate, explore global topics and issues, and create digital artifacts together that share solutions. A learning community of educators is developed to support project objectives. Students are grouped in cross-class teams and use Edmodo for initial communication, Google Docs for collaboration, and VoiceThread for final co-created products.

A Week in the Life website: **www.flatconnections.com**

Twitter: **@flatconnections #flatconnections**

Level 5 - Learning Collaboratives

This final level is a little harder to explain and for many it may be difficult to visualize based on lack of experience to date. The purpose is to foster learner autonomy for online global collaboration. All communication and local to global modes may be used in order to cement relationships and trust for learning so that each member has the confidence to initiate, respond and co-create within the collaborative. Learning collaboratives redesign the learning paradigm to encourage students to take the lead in connecting and collaborating and in doing so co-create solutions to global problems and challenges.

Flat Connections Global Project

The Flat Connections Global Project is the "ultimate" collaboration for high school students aged 14–18. It involves mixed-classroom teams of students co-creating understanding of topics based on the Horizon Report and emerging technologies for the next five years. An extended community supports student activity with expert advisors, a keynote to interact with, and external judges who review the final multimedia communication piece created by each student (which includes an outsourced clip from another student across the world). What puts this project into Level 5 is the community that is built around this project and the student leadership piece where students are encouraged to be autonomous learners and step up to manage and propel the project themselves. Read more about the Flat Connections Global Project in Case Study 3.2.

The Flat Connections Global Project Community: **http://flatconnectionsglobal project.net/**

Twitter: **@flatconnections #flatconnections**

Flat Connections: Connect with China

Connect with China Collaborative is a learning environment where ways to connect between China and other places are explored to increase global collaborative opportunities for learning. This collaborative approach aims to bridge the global gap and engage with the world in authentic ways to support effective 21st century learning that includes educational institutions and independent learners.

Connect with China website: **www.connectchinacollaborative.com/**

Design for Global Collaboration – Design into Action

Designing a global collaborative experience involves transcending the obvious real time linkup, fostering higher order thinking and providing opportunities for cultural understanding while usually making a product that impacts others in a positive way. Educators are encouraged to continue searching for better ways to join multicultural classrooms for authentic learning through effective collaborative design. One of the first challenges of this design process is finding an effective topic that can support a global collaboration, however with creativity and application just about any topic is suitable!

Pay it Forward

Designing a global collaborative experience involves transcending the obvious real time linkup, fostering higher order thinking and providing opportunities for cultural understanding while usually making a product that impacts others in a positive way.

Pre-planning Global Collaborations

Figure 12.1 shares one way to approach design for online global collaborative learning. We need to design in order to connect; construct collaborative possibilities and leave a legacy of learning; and amplify this legacy in order to impact others... even the world.

Pre-planning global learning experiences to support intercultural understanding in a global collaborative context involves being able to **Connect**, leave a **Legacy**, and **Impact** the world.

- As global educators we need to **connect** ourselves, our schools and our students with the world
- Once connected the outcomes and products of the collaborations will leave a **legacy** for ourselves and others
- This legacy can **impact** the world in positive ways and in fact make a difference

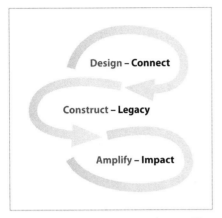

Fig. 12.1: Design into Action – Planning Flow

This also means it is necessary to **Design** experiences to **Construct** outcomes and **Amplify** these.

- Global educators need to **design** fruitful connections. Just as we design curriculum and other activities for learning, connected learning also requires careful design and planning
- Global educators must plan to **construct** or create the legacy not just hope it will happen
- They then design to **amplify** the impact of these connections and legacies. Tell the world! Involve the world! Spread the word! Plan for more and better experiences

Questions to consider:

- Who can you collaborate with? (Connection, Collaboration)
- What can you create together and where will this creative legacy be shared? (Legacy)
- What are the actionable outcomes to change the world? (Impact)

Designing Global Communities

Designing a global community for learning is part of the design process for online global collaborative learning. It may be a community of educators who gather to determine what the collaboration will look like and then go about implementing it. It may be a community of educators and learners who collaborate across a number of objectives during the global project.

Figure 12.2 shows how a simple global community starts with a network of learners brought together for a purpose, often transient in nature (e.g., a short online global project). Around this is built collaborative learning opportunities and around this is a design for how learners will interact with and share with the world.

When wanting to "cultivate a community of practice" Wenger, McDermott and Snyder (2002) provide a useful set of seven principles. These are shared here with some additional observations as to relevance and alignment with online community development for global objectives.

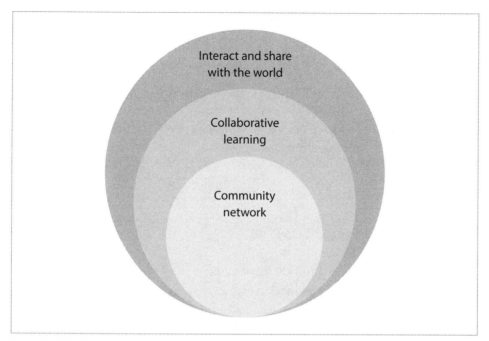

Fig. 12.2: Global Community Structure and Purpose

1. **Design for evolution.** Communities are dynamic and as new members join different interests and community focus may occur and structures may evolve to accommodate emerging needs. Design elements must be able to catalyze community development.

2. **Open a dialogue between inside and outside perspectives.** -An insider's perspective helps lead the community however the possibilities for achievement by the community are best realized through bringing in outside dialog and experience and capitalize on new ideas—and in a global community ideas are often divergent given the multitude of backgrounds and experiences.

3. **Invite different levels of participation.** Consider the reasons people join communities and what they can contribute. It is unrealistic to expect all community members to contribute equally. A well-designed community has a coordinator who organizes and connects members, however leadership comes from others as a core group. Other levels include the "active group" and the "peripheral group" as well as various onlookers who may

join in when the topic becomes relevant. Design of community activities is important to give all members an opportunity to contribute and move across levels.

4. **Develop both public and private community spaces.** Both formal and informal "gatherings" can be designed that are either public or private. It is important to have a public persona, while at the same time creating a private place for community interaction.

5. **Focus on value.** Communities thrive when they give value to the members. Activities within the community may be small daily exchanges or larger events, and each of these has some value that members can use to feel included and worthwhile.

6. **Combine familiarity and excitement.** Encourage regular interactions where members share and seek advice as well as promote alternative activities that may stretch understanding of a topic or ask for different collaborative practice. Each of these helps community members develop relationships for learning.

7. **Create a rhythm for the community.** Regular happenings and activities provide a sense of movement and liveliness. Too slow and the community stagnates, too fast and it feels overwhelmed.

Design Thinking for Online Global Collaboration

The Design Thinking Cycle (shown in Fig. 12.3) is useful for online global collaboration design as it is an iterative process that builds in consideration for stakeholders, curriculum objectives, and outcomes as well as feedback loops to ensure reflection and improvement. The steps of the cycle are outlined below.

Step 1: Empathy

Build **EMPATHY** for the global collaboration design vision.

- Discuss and take notes about what the vision is for this global collaboration
- Talk to stakeholders and potential and/or real global partners

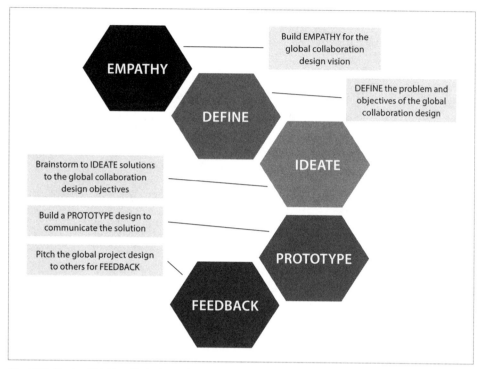

Fig. 12.3: Design Thinking Cycle for Online Global Collaborative Projects

Step 2: Define

DEFINE the problem and objectives of the global collaboration design.

- What are you trying to achieve by joining classrooms and students?
- Discuss and be clear on the purpose and problem to be solved

Step 3: Ideate

Brainstorm to **IDEATE** solutions to the problem/task.

- Choose the best solution and pitch to others for feedback
- Discuss the essential parameters; these must include:
  ‣ Topic and subject area(s)
  ‣ Timeline
  ‣ Expectations of participants
  ‣ Shared outcomes

Step 4: Prototype

Build a **PROTOTYPE** design to communicate the solution

- Use the "norms of online global collaboration" from Chapter 10.
- Focus on 1) Project goals, 2) Process, 3) Timeline, and 4) Global online interaction and collaboration

Step 5: Feedback

Pitch the global project design to others to gather **FEEDBACK**

- A true test of a good global collaboration design is in the successful implementation, however being able to pitch and explain to others will provide valuable feedback beforehand

Collaboration to Action–Online Global Project Design Examples

The following examples share diverse online global project collaborative design ideas and hopefully will inspire readers to a deeper understanding of curriculum-based global learning and design approaches.

Level 1: Online Interaction

Project	Goals	Process	Timeline	Global Online Interaction
The Monster Project Designed by Dr Terry Smith the Monster Project has been running for many years.	Describe parts of a "monster" so other classes anywhere in the world can "create" their own monster	Students choose a monster part and write a description that is added to a shared chart. Each class then builds its own monster based on chosen descriptions. Students learn how to work together and make group decisions.	Sign-up in September and create monster part descriptions. Build monsters in October and send pictures no later than October 31, in time for Halloween.	Coming up with monster descriptions and other interactions with global classrooms through sharing videos and blog posts and the final monsters!

Connect with the Monster Project

Website: **www.smithclass.org/proj/Monsters/index.htm**

Level 2: Real Encounters

Mystery Skype

Mystery Skype is a global game that gets kids learning about the world via Skype. The Mystery Skype website helps link classrooms and provides ideas for curriculum use.

Activity	Goals	Process	Timeline	Global Online Interaction
Mystery Skype	Connect two classrooms from different schools (usually different geographic areas) in order to "inquire" and "guess" where the other class is located.	Find another classroom, organize a time to Skype, prepare objectives and activities for the live session.	Skype can be up to one hour. Preparation may be a week or more, less for teachers experienced with Mystery Skype.	The Mystery Skype website provides ideas including '20 Questions" and "Mystery Skype Jobs".

Mystery Skype website: **https://education.skype.com/mysteryskype**

Twitter: **#MysterySkype**

Virtual Field Trip

An excellent example of what a virtual field trip provides for global learning is the Polar Bears International (PBI) organisation. Julene Reed, global education leader, directs the PBI Tundra Connections program, which connects scientists and educators in the field with students in remote classrooms. Tundra Connections, as well

Connect with Polar Bears International

Twitter: **@polarbears**

Website: **www.polarbearsinternational.org/**

as connecting students to experts, provides live footage of polar bears on the tundra during the migration season. It is easy for schools to sign up and many educational resources are provided on the website. The website also invites input from members via comments, shared images, a commit list and more.

Level 3: Online Learning

Activity	Goals	Process	Timeline	Global Online Interaction
Global Youth Debates (GYD) Formal debating online in an asynchronous format using a tool called VoiceThread. This exciting format has transformed debating and encouraged research and sharing of global perspectives around pertinent issues.	Provide a facility for students to connect globally in order to explore, share and debate pertinent issues. Use Web 2.0 technologies	Schools sign up one or more teams and each is paired to another. Teams research topic and prepare material for debate. Brackets for each round change (based on who wins the previous round). Teachers of the two debating partners must agree upon a schedule for recording and sharing responses. International judges review each round and nominate winners.	At least three debate rounds per semester, three weeks to complete each round. In semester two there is set of semi-finals and then finals so that one debate team emerges as the overall winners for that year. The final debates are often held synchronously in a virtual classroom with a live judge.	In addition to the actual debating, students are encouraged to share ideas and questions and get to know each other in a GYD Edmodo group.

Global Youth Debates website: **www.globalyouthdebates.com/**

Twitter: **@debateglobal**

Level 4: Communities of Practice

Activity	Goals	Process	Timeline	Global Online Interaction
iEARN Learning Circles Learning Circles have been around since 1994 and are highly interactive, project-based partnerships among a small number of schools located throughout the world.	Join classrooms together for intercultural understanding and interaction that leads to collaboration.	Learning Circles groups/classrooms come together to interact around a topic or theme. iEARN organizers group classrooms depending on geographic diversity and topic interest. Participants determine communication method and how they will share and produce evidence of research and learning.	There is a set timeline and expected output of some sort of publication. Currently Learning Circles run twice a year (September and January).	Authentic student work and true international collaboration through creation and co-creation of artifacts such as ebooks, books, websites, and more.

iEARN Learning Circles website: **www.iearn.org/circles/**

Twitter: **@iEARNglobalLC**

"As an instructor, the challenges in participating in a global project are not very different from the challenges of day to day school: getting students to buy in or see the value in what you are asking them to do. I typically have 36-40 year 9 students per semester in my course; I would estimate that 60-70% of them give the global project their best effort and do really well working within the structure of the project. Of the others, probably another 10-15% come around to a better understanding and a more complete learning experience as the project develops. The remainder only respond when missing grades show up in the grading portal" (Brian McLaughlin, USA, @brian326).

Level 5: Learning Collaboratives

Activity	Goals	Process	Timeline	Global Online Interaction
Flat Connections Global Project Designed for high school students featuring an extended community of learners including expert advisors and judges, Flat Connections Global Project frames the sociability of online learning into a context that can be embedded across the curriculum.	Flatten classroom walls so that instead of each class working in isolation, two or more classes are joined virtually as one large classroom. Develop cultural understanding, Web 2.0 skills, experience in global collaboration and online learning, online community interaction and co-creation. Educators interact with students not in their immediate class to support their learning.	Students are placed into mixed classroom teams. Each team explores one of the current Horizon Report K–12 topics for emerging technologies. Introductions and open discussion via online community. Co-research and co-authoring of material based on the topic leads to a team ebook or infographic. Individual students create a personal communication piece (usually video) to share their learning. Part of this piece is outsourced to another student in the project from a different part of the world.	Three months *Month 1:* Orientation, 'handshakes', team allocation and theme/topic explanation. Keynote speaker leads interactive webinar. *Month 2:* Collaboration, shared research, multimedia design and request for out-sourced artifacts. *Month 3:* Digital artifacts are uploaded, shared, judged and an Awards Ceremony announces the best projects for the semester. Classes connect and run live online summits showcasing their learning through short presentations supported by creative slides.	Encourages a deeper level of collaboration from all participants. Educators invited to weekly synchronous meetings (held at differing times to reflect time zone needs). Each project must develop a learning community around the collaboration to support the process. Student leadership group meets regularly, online in real time, to support teams and encourage students.

The Flat Connections Global Project website: **www.flatconnections.com/**

New Media Consortium Horizon Report website: **www.nmc.org/nmc-horizon/**

Global Educators Share Their Global Collaboration Experiences

Other global educators have differing approaches to global project design and participation that is useful for us to learn about here.

Building Communities for Global Learning

Theresa Allen (USA) is a Flat Connections Educator and for many years has been a global collaboration Project Manager. She is now the Director of Instructional Technology at the Archdiocese of Chicago. At her previous school, Cathedral of St. Raymond School in Joliet, Illinois she worked as the Technology Teacher and Coordinator. She shares with us her experiences building capacity for connected and collaborative global learning in her school. I also recommend you watch the Brainwaves video where Theresa shares further thoughts about flattening the classroom walls.

Theresa Allen's Website: **https://about.me/theresa.allen**

Twitter: **@tdallen5**

Brainwaves video 'The Flat Classroom': **https://youtu.be/xW7Khu0KzTE**

Recently I asked Theresa to share her experiences integrating global collaboration at her school. She contributed the following.

Connecting with the World and School Learning Ecology

"Having the students from early childhood to eigth grade connecting with students and educators around the world allows students the opportunity to share and find commonality with each other as well as learn about new cultures and lands. It is almost natural to Skype another classroom, and students inquire when the next session will be. They also like to learn from each other using Edmodo as a tool to connect. They not only share subject matter but their favorites. Other teachers have mainly used Skype to communicate with other classrooms and people who share information about a topic, book or theme. They have used Google Apps to share documents and presentations with schools (poem critique in 5th and Animal study in 2nd)."

Integrating Global Collaboration

"Other teachers have mainly used Google Apps and Edmodo to collaborate with others around the world. Second grade use Edmodo in the Global Pen Pal Project. K, 3, and 7th use Google Apps, Edmodo and Skype for Flat Connections Projects. 4th uses Skype to connect with classrooms from the Global Monster Project. 5th and sixth-graders use Skype, Google Apps, and Kidlink to connect poems and their face descriptions for a partner to draw and share. First grade used Twitter to connect with classrooms in Taiwan and Massachusetts for a coding project without using the computer. That was fun! (Teachers do these projects with me.)"

Building an Online Community for Global Collaborations

Theresa is also an Edmodo certified educator and expertly uses and trains others to use this useful online community building platform. Edmodo connects students asynchronously to communicate via discussion forums and foster sharing and collaboration. She talks often about developing online communities for global collaborations and uses the metaphor of building a house to help explain the stages of community development.

Construction to Community

- **Excavation:** This is what happens in the background before a collaboration. Teachers connect; Edmodo provides for a "teachers only group"; common meeting times and tools for meetings are explored.
- **Foundation:** Introductions, replies (getting to know each other), students connecting. Edmodo can attach a link and a video, handshake. Skype cements the foundation via a synchronous gathering. Focus on digital citizenship skills.
- **Framing:** Gather information (photos, media) and use different platforms to share. Edmodo has a folder option to store collections.
- **Mechanics:** Fostering discussions, modeling skills, further digital citizenship skills for communication.

- **Drywall:** Research, move into smaller groups as needed. Edmodo supports groups and containing conversations within them. Further sharing, research, commenting.
- **Finish:** Building the final action projects and co-created artifacts.
- **Final Product:** Presenting, celebrating and showcasing products from the entire project.

International Dot Day

Kate O'Connell is a passionate educator and learner with 19 years of classroom experience, teaching a variety of age levels including: 4 year olds, 5 year olds, Grade 1, Grade 2, Grade 3 and 7 grade Science. Kate is originally from the United States and has taught both at home and abroad in China, Tanzania and now Thailand. This is in her words.

One of my favorite Global Adventures in Education was celebrating International Dot Day. It was one of the first Global Projects that I participated in and therefore maybe it has the advantage of being a first! For this project, we read the book: *The Dot* by Peter H. Reynolds. I love the book's message of creativity and individuality and the power of a teacher. You can find out more about this project on the website (www.thedotclub.org/dotday/). Essentially, we read the book by watching a video of the book on Youtube. Then the students created Dot Day Posters. They had the ability to interpret the assignment, "How do you want to make your mark?" by either creating a piece of artwork or expressing what their passion was through artwork. On the back of the poster, the students wrote out what they would tell other students around the world about their Dot Day poster. Finally, we Skyped with various classrooms around the world including Greece and Australia. The students communicated their passions and listened to others in authentic contexts. I loved how each teacher interpreted the project differently. The International Dot Day project connected us individually and globally.

The benefits? On a student level, I loved that this book and this project inspired kids to think creatively, build their self-esteem, find their passions and then communicate with others around the world. On an educator level, it was a very easy project to tailor to the curriculum, jump in as much or as little as you would like, and it was very easy to connect with different parts of our curriculum, for me it connected to my unit of inquiry on Who We Are. Fabulously, this book was available on Youtube, read by the author, which is great for international educa-

(continued on next page)

tors who may or may not have access to this book in their library. I felt that this project was truly transdisciplinary in that it "transcended" traditional curriculum subjects, yet used many.

This project was significant to my development as a global educator as I met other like minded teachers that have been my partners and friends in exploring the new digital learning landscape. The proof that this project was significant to my students came through their end-of-year reflections which said that doing International Dot Day was one of their favorite things that they did in second grade.

Connect with Kate O'Connell

Twitter: **@innovatecreater**

Blog: **http://innovatecreateandrelatewithkate.blogspot.com/**

Connecting Students to the World

The following contribution is from Jacqueline Liesch, USA.

"I have worked as a library media specialist with students from nursery through high school. I have been connecting students with their global peers since 2007, fostering global understanding. Working in schools in Wisconsin and Ecuador and studying, volunteering and traveling the world has given me a truly global perspective of education. I have become a more patient and understanding person as a result of these experiences. Showing students that the world is bigger than their immediate community is so rewarding. Modeling empathy and understanding is immensely gratifying. I love seeing students so engaged and excited to learn about other cultures and countries. Connecting students globally made me more adventurous. I started volunteering more with WEMTA (Wisconsin Educational Media and Technology Association) and ISTE."

"My most memorable connections were the ones that I facilitated from South Africa. I was part of a group studying the impact of information poverty on the HIV/AIDS pandemic as part of my Master's program and was ecstatic to share this experience with students. Prior to my departure, I worked with elementary teachers at my school while two district middle and high school library media teachers collaborated with classroom teachers at their schools to prepare students for our connections. First graders learned about the physical geography of the country while fourth graders compared the United States government to that of South Africa. Middle school students learned about the history and tenth grade sociology students researched the HIV/AIDS pandemic. A challenge for these connections was technology. After learning I was selected to participate in the study abroad, I immediately contacted my professor to ask if these connections would be possible with our intense schedule. Given a week where we would have reliable internet access, I proceeded to plan as many connections as possible, with the eight hour time difference. Since the Kenosha schools were connecting with me, we were able to connect later at night, South Africa time. I was sure to pack an ethernet cable in my luggage to facilitate the connections. Thankfully, everything went smoothly. Students were thankful to hear about South Africa. Students at the elementary school where I taught were especially excited to see me and hear more stories upon my return."

More Inspiring Examples from Global Educators

Aaron Maurer (USA, @coffeechugbooks) shares, "We just worked with a class from Spain with our Spanish classes and teacher. At the end of the day we learned two very important things that happen time and time again.

1. We really don't know enough about ourselves, and working with others reminds us that we assume too much about what we think we know about our area and where we live.
2. No matter where you live, conditions of school, school operations, cultural differences, and so on, kids are kids. We laugh the same; we find the same things funny, interesting, and peculiar.

Every time I work with a new school this is the case. Kids are kids and we are doing our best to make sense of who we are in this world."

Becky Morales (USA, @kidworldcitizen) says, "I have always been trying to open my students' eyes to the world outside their community, even before all of the amazing global education tools were available. Maybe 10–12 years ago I had students in my Spanish class writing to a Peace Corps volunteer in Bolivia, watching videos sent (on a CD!) from a class in Mexico, and interviewing a visiting student from Mexico, plus numerous other projects we invented. I remember one student whose parents were from Mexico told me that for the first time in her life, a teacher highlighted her culture and made her feel proud. She told me she only ever heard negative things in the media about immigrants being lazy, and she had been rebelling against speaking Spanish. She was a shy student who had never spoken up in class, but that day after class she told me "Ms. Morales, you have to keep teaching kids about other cultures because it changes your whole perspective. I want kids to learn that Mexican kids are just the same as kids in the US- they like the same things, they have boy problems and girl problems, and they're just trying to figure things out just like us." I will never forget that student... Even though I don't have students like this every day, I do believe that our lessons change the way kids view the world." See more of Becky's work at http://kidworldcitizen.org/

Michael Roemer, Director of Global Initiatives at Trinity Valley School (TVS), USA, coordinates virtual (online) and in-person exchanges between TVS students and students and adults around the world, K–12. "In addition to increased knowledge about various parts of the world, I think that the most important impacts our Global Initiatives Program has made are lifelong friendships with our international guests, a deeper understanding of human dignity, and a desire to learn more from, and an increased comfort level for working with, people from diverse backgrounds and perspectives."

Connect with Michael Roemer

Global Initiatives Program Website: **http://trinityvalleyschool.org/gip**

Danielle Hartman (USA), is Supervisor of Instruction, Burlington County Institute of Technology. This is her story.

I have been using global collaboration as a part of my curriculum for years now. As I've improved my pedagogy, my collaborations have become more sophisticated as well. When I began, my collaborations mostly revolved around culture. My students would work with another country (or several) and at unit's end create a project of some sort that related to the collaboration. Once the students completed a digital storytelling project, several times an iMovie, and another time they participated in the International Mock Trials.

My project varied in rigor, but they always kept the students engaged. Invariably, when I distributed my end-of-semester questionnaires, global collaboration was the favored activity of the students. At times, I wondered how I could address both student interest and meet our standards. I searched for classes who had similar semester goals with little luck.

I find that as an American teacher, I have to work much harder than my international colleagues to find a partner. Whenever I would post a project or classroom profile on ePals (my platform of choice), I would not receive any solicitations from potential partners. Instead, I would have to create a form letter that I sent out to any classes or teachers I thought would work well with my students. From fifteen or so emails, I would receive possibly five replies. I would then email back and forth a few times before committing. You can usually tell if a teacher will follow through with a project depending on how quickly they respond to your queries.

When we rewrote our English Language Arts curriculum to conform to the Common Core State Standards (CCSS), we decided to make sophomore English an authentic world literature course. The unit asks classes to choose a geographical area, read contemporary literature from the area, complete research, and participate in a collaboration with a class from that country. Obviously, we can't mandate the collaboration, but we do strongly suggest it. The CCSS are utilized by states across the country, and at one point, they were used by almost everyone. As usual, though, the US can't stick to anything for long, so many states have dropped out. It's unfortunate. The standards are quite good and urge 21st century skills and globalization.

Last year, to my surprise, my sophomores decided that Italy was the country they were interested in. I really thought they would want South America or Africa. Luckily I was able to find an awesome teacher to work with! Miriam is an ELL teacher from Italy. So though her goals weren't the same as mine, she was flexible in her curriculum. Her goal was to encourage her students to speak and write in English.

(continued on next page)

Our students worked together all semester. They read common literature, viewed a movie about the difficulties that arise when cultures collide, participated in chat room discussions and even live video chats (not easy to orchestrate with the time difference). They also researched each other's countries and created flyers based on something they found. It was interesting to find out that what we find on the internet is not always an accurate portrayal of your country!

At year's end, we decided that we wanted to participate in a student exchange. Miriam's students would visit the US and stay with my students, and then we would visit Italy. Though we were fully committed to this project, problems on my end are making that seem less probable. My students are poor (we are a Title I district) and my administration is concerned with Miriam's student's housing. Additionally, they are concerned with our students staying there. However this goal turns out, I know that my students increased skills across all of our standard strands, and they had fun doing it. Beyond the standards, they gained in life experience.

Connect with Danielle Hartman

Sophomore curriculum: World literature website: **http://bcitla.com/E2U2Cultural Awareness.html**

Twitter: **@danielle6849**

Donna Adams Román (USA) shares a poignant and inspiring story:

I was contacted by a colleague requesting we partner with a classroom she knew of in Jericho, West Bank in Palestine. I had never met the teacher or worked anywhere near this area before, but I agreed to meet the teacher online. We set up weekly classroom Skype meetings to work on a science project together. To make the time zones work, the ten 14 year old boys in Jericho went to the local radio station after school for adequate internet connection. We came in an hour before school started. For the first two weeks, the students would not talk. They just sat in awkward silence while the teachers tried to start conversation.

My class had no idea what to make of this, but they felt very uncomfortable. By the third meeting we had each done some research on our partner schools' location, and it was a whole different feeling. The students asked all sorts of questions and it was apparent that the boys from Jericho had a lot of misconceptions about Americans, and we had a lot of misconceptions about people from the Middle East. As we all realized how silly our questions were sounding on both sides, the palpable hostility that had been there the first couple calls melted away. That was very powerful. If schools and classrooms understood that power globally, it could change the type of world we have now. I know I am idealistic, but teachers could literally change the face of the planet. By looking other kids right in the eyes and seeing how similar they are, and by teachers working directly with other teachers, we can shift the fear, misunderstanding and hostility we see all around us. I don't know how to make that happen, but I rcan eally see the power of it.

Connect with Donna Adams Román

Jericho to Geneva website: **https://sites.google.com/site/jerichobridgeand millcreek/**

Twitter: **@donnaroman**

Online Global Collaboration Case Studies

This collection of case studies features educators and online global interactions, collaborations and projects. There are many stories of struggle and resilience, joy and hope. Educators from Australia, South Africa, Denmark, USA, Canada, and more are featured as they share what they are doing to embed online global collaboration and how they are doing it. Some educators are award winners and/or may have great acknowledgement within their own country, others are classroom teachers who are pushing the boundaries of what "school" looks like and what "learning" should look like in a modern and global learning environment. You will be inspired!

Case Study 3.1 – Mali Bickley: Global Collaboration Is Good Teaching

Mali Bickley from Canada has 34 years experience as a classroom teacher. Over the past 12 years, she has used ICT and successfully integrated literacy and content area curriculum to have her students connect, communicate and collaborate with several classes from around the world. As a classroom teacher, Mali is using Global Education Projects to integrate reading and writing strategies into meaningful projects that connect students globally. Mali's students have successfully collaborated with each other and students around the world to make a difference in the lives of others. Her

> "The first time we needed to connect with a class live in Japan we bought our kids in at 8p.m. at night, the kids in Japan were 8 a.m. in the morning and we struggled with the technology at first, but we were there and made it happen and it was like the magic of the world opened up. I will never forget that first video conference" (Mali Bickley, Canada, @dreamteam51).

students won the My Hero Project's Ron Kovic Peace Award for their film "Imagine Peace": An International Art and Music Collaboration. Mali is the assistant country coordinator of iEARN Canada and designs and facilitates many international projects.

Mali has given workshops on Collaborative Global Education projects and integrating ICT into classroom practice to several schools, districts, universities and interested organizations, such as TakingITGlobal, World Vision, ECOO, NECC and ISTE both nationally and internationally. She clearly sees how students become highly engaged in global collaborative projects that use ICT. Mali feels the rewards of teaching include seeing how students become passionate about the connections they have made with others.

I first connected with Mali at an ISTE conference many years ago when, along with Jim Carleton, she keynoted and shared her global adventures. Her involvement with iEARN Canada, and now closer working mode with TakingITGlobal sees Mali spread her influence across many classrooms and countries. This is a compelling case study about transformation in the classroom.

Connect with Mali Bickley

Twitter: **@dreamteam51**

Website: **iearn-canada.org**

Case Study 3.2 – The Flat Connections Global Project

Flat Connections offers online global collaborative projects for K–12. This case study applies to the high school project called the Flat Connections Global Project (FCGP). Individual educators as well as the Berea school district in the USA share their global collaborative journey through this project.

The FCGP is a merge, redesign and rebrand of what was originally the Flat Classroom Project that started in 2006 and the NetGenEd Project that started in 2009. The project is for high school students and each year uses the most recent K–12 Horizon Report on emerging technology trends as a catalyst for collaboration. It challenges all learners to connect and communicate beyond their immediate classroom and school. It also encourages collaboration and co-creation of final artifacts as well as student leadership, while exploring emerging technologies and envisioning the future of learning.

Global educators have embedded this project into their curriculum in various ways, and have learned how to manage this type of project through immersion while being supported by a community of educators that is built around each semester-length iteration of the project. Here are some stories that share their goals and successes.

The ebook case study for this project shares the real stories of Ann Rooney, Australia, Cindy Nickodam, USA, and Perla Zamora, Mexico as they joined the FCGP as new global collaborators. It also shares the journey of Roger Crider, USA, Brian McLaughlin, USA, and Andrew Churches, New Zealand, and how they have embedded the global project across the curriculum year after year. The story of Berea District schools in Ohio, USA is retold by Flat Connections Educators Amy Jambor and Sheri Williams as they share their district and personal journey into new learning modes that shifted classrooms into interdisciplinary, collaborative and eventually global paradigms. They account for the many challenges and joys of embedding global collaboration into the curriculum and how they integrated the FCGP with Computer Science, Social Studies and English standards.

Connect with Flat Connections

Twitter: **@flatconnections**

Website: **http://flatconnections.com**

Case Study 3.3 – Leah Obach and Devon Caldwell: Early Years Collaboration

Leah (an early years teacher in rural Manitoba, Canada, currently teaching at Hamiota Elementary School) and Devon (a junior and senior kindergarten teacher at Oak Lake Community School) are global educators based in Manitoba, Canada. In this case study they tell a vital story about how their students connect across a whole year for collaborative learning and share many online global collaborative projects, tools and resources. A "must read" for all early years educators!

Connect with Leah Obach

Twitter: **@LeahO77** and **@mrsobachsclass**

Connect with Devon Caldwell

Twitter: **@india0309** and **@olcskinders**

Joint Blog: **http://kinectingclassrooms.wordpress.com**

Case Study 3.4 – Toni Olivieri-Barton: Leadership for Successful Online Global Collaboration

Toni Olivieri-Barton has been teaching 21st Century Skills to adults and children for over 20 years and is currently a Library Technology Educator at Fountain Valley School. In her previous job as a librarian/media specialist and IB Coordinator at Woodmen-Roberts Elementary School in Colorado Springs she facilitated all 2nd through fifth-graders to have an opportunity to flatten their learning by connecting with students from around the world. Previously, she worked at Shanghai Community International School, China, as technology coordinator. In 2011 she won an ISTE Award in Online Learning for creating opportunities for Online Independent Studies at the middle school and high school level.

As a Flat Connections educator Toni has taken on the role of Project Manager and supports other educators through regular global collaborative projects. The following case study is Toni's own account of leadership for online global collaboration within and beyond her school and shares how planned connections supports serendipitous collaborations.

Read in the ebook case study how Toni has participated in and led many online global projects across K–12 levels. She is truly a master global teacher!

Connect with Toni Olivieri-Barton

Twitter: **@toniobarton**

Blog: **https://toniobarton.wordpress.com/**

Website: **http://toniobarton.wikispaces.com/**

Case Study 3.5 – Tracey Winey: One Million Lights

Tracey Winey is the Media Specialist and STEM Integration Specialist at Preston Middle School in Colorado. Tracey has been named the Fort Collins Teacher of the month, a SMART Certified Instructor, a SMART Exemplary Educator, a SMART Concept Design Trainer, a Google Certified Teacher, and a Flat Connections Global Educator. She has presented at the local, state, national and international level at conferences for the National Science Teachers Association, Technology in Education, ISTE, International Technology and Education Development, and the National Network for Educational Renewal.

As part of the Flat Connections Global Educator course Tracey Winey redeveloped an existing project in her school to align it more strongly with online global collaborative and co-creational needs. The concept and practice of 3D printing was used to create this authentic, multi-age global entrepreneurship project. To do so she forged connections with other K–12 and tertiary level educators. The essential question is, "How can students use technology to impact the world and themselves?" In conjunction with an engineering focus and a problem kids can solve "One Million Lights" has been designed as an amazing and unique global opportunity. Basically students will design 3D lights that can be used in other parts of the world. The goal is to share these with less-advantaged communities so they have light to read and study at night.

One Million Lights (OML) has three primary leaders, Tracey, Ian Fogarty (high school Chemistry, Physics and Science 12 in New Brunswick, Canada) and John Howe (Assistant Principal at Preston Middle School, USA) who tend to be early implementers or even better, pioneers.

"Having a 14-year-old in the US and a 2-year-old in Uganda look at the camera, smile, and giggle. It was such a emotional moment that guided Preston's work" (Tracey Winey, USA, @premediawine).

Read their story as they connected USA and Canadian students with students in Uganda with the purpose of working together to provide lights for reading at night. It is a powerful and cutting edge story of how to use emerging technology and online global collaboration to change the world.

Connect with Tracey Winey

Twitter: **@premediawine**

Hashtag: **#OMLights**

Blog: **http://mediawine.edublogs.org/**

Case Study 3.6 – Janice Mak: Global STEM Learners

Janice Mak is a global educator and STEM teacher from Arizona, USA. In addition to living and teaching abroad for 11 years, Janice has been working intensively in the area of global collaboration since 2013.

The experience shared in this case study involves mentoring two educators (American and Chinese) through science/STEM-based collaboration on Genetically Modified Organisms (GMOs). It provides a window into the frustration and joys of global collaborative learning and how, in addition to the hard work, all participants learn many lessons and ultimately students are the overall beneficiaries.

Connect with Janice Mak

Twitter: **@jmakaz**

Blog: **http://supercodingpower.blogspot.com**

Case Study 3.7 – Pernille Ripp: Global Read Aloud

Pernille Ripp is the creator of the Global Read Aloud (GRA) and winner of the inaugural ISTE Global Collaboration PLN Award for Innovation in Online Global Collaboration (2015).

GRA is a global reading project that has connected more than 500,000 students on six continents since its inception in September 2010.

I met the dedicated and delightful Pernille at ISTE 2015 in Philadelphia. During the time we had to talk she shared with me her background, motivation for new global learning modes and success with the GRA project.

This case study shares how Pernille came to develop the Global Read Aloud, the impact of global collaboration on students, and thoughts for future development.

Connect with Pernille Ripp

Twitter: **@pernilleripp**

Blogging through the Fourth Dimension: **http://pernillesripp.com/**

Global Read Aloud: **http://theglobalreadaloud.com**

Case Study 3.8 – Karen Stadler: The Travelling Rhinos Project

Karen Stadler is the Head of Digital Learning at Elkanah House, Cape Town, South Africa and the founder of The Travelling Rhinos Project.

Karen was the ISTE Online Learning Network Award Winner in 2014 for the Travelling Rhinos Project, a global project to raise awareness of the dire poaching situation in South Africa. Karen tells her story in this case study of global collaboration and of raising awareness globally for possible Rhino extinction.

Connect with Karen and The Travelling Rhinos Project

Twitter: **@ICT_Integrator** and **@travellingrhino**

Website: **http://saveourrhinos.wikispaces.com**

Facebook: **www.facebook.com/TheTravellingRhinosProject**

Host: **http://theglobalclassroomproject.org/**

Case Study 3.9 – Craig Chidgey and Krista Brakhage: The Working World

Craig Chidgey, Australia, and Krista Brakhage, USA are classroom teachers and Flat Connections Global Educators. Together they joined from opposite sides of the world to create the global project "The Working World".

Like many global educators, Craig and Krista have never met in person, only online. This case study shares how "The Working World" connected students and teachers from Australia and the US. It also shares how the online global project was designed, implemented, and managed, and what the outcomes were.

Connect with Craig Chidgey

Twitter: **@cchidgey1**

Connect with Krista Brakhage

Twitter: **@kmbrak**

Case Study 3.10 – Flat Connections Global Educator Cohort 15–1

In February 2015 a group of globally minded educators came together virtually to become the 15–1 cohort of the Flat Connections Global Educator online course. This accredited course is one that I have designed and teach online. Each cohort runs for about ten weeks and requires weekly synchronous meetups, readings and tasks to do with connected and collaborative learning (such as blogging, participating in discussion forums, and exploring global project design), and takes learners deeper into online global collaboration and curriculum design such that they not only discuss and observe but "get their hands dirty" practicing it. I always tell each cohort that I want them to "feel the pain" of what it is really like to connect with others in different world locations, of working through best approaches to communication, of collaborating to solve issues and co-create products—all in preparation for when they will do this with students or lead other teachers through it. As an outcome for the 15–1 cohort the group co-wrote this case study to share what they are doing, thinking and where they are going with global learning. This particular cohort became a true online learning community as this piece was put together—each participant developing confidence and momentum as the stories unfolded. I thank them for their resilience and dedication to online global collaboration! Throughout this case study contributors share their favourite adventures in global education, and a range of global collaborations across the curriculum and across the world. Kate O'Connell, @innovatecreater, is a passionate educator and learner with 19 years of classroom experience, teaching a variety of age levels including: 4-year-olds, 5-year-olds, Grade 1, Grade 2, Grade 3 and seventh grade Science. Kate is originally from the United States and has taught both at home and abroad in China, Tanzania, and now Thailand.

Katrina Harriman Conde, @KHC222, is a fifth grade language arts and human-ities teacher at Rippowam Cisqua School in Bedford, NY. During her 19 years as an educator she has taught a range of students from preschool to high school.

Louisa Polos, @MsPolos, teaches middle school English and history in Bedford, NY. In addition to her teaching responsibilities she coaches field hockey, basketball, and lacrosse.

Dianne Shapp, @dshapp, is Tech Integration Specialist and Design/Maker Educator at SDJA in San Diego and over 13 years has worked with a variety of grades spanning PK–fifth grade.

Katie Grubb, @katiegrubby, is a Chinese language educator, working at Southern Cross School of Distance Education, NSW Australia and manages a community-based business, Mandarin Pathways. Her passion for the environment and interconnection has enabled her to build authentic learning experiences between business, community and education for global learning.

Bonnie Hermawan, @BonnieHermawan, works with the Asia Education Foundation (AEF) in Melbourne, Australia on various projects promoting global skills such as intercultural understanding and proficiency in multiple languages.

The Flat Connections Global Educator online accredited course is found on the Flat Connections website **http://flatconnections.com**

Part Four

Take Learning Global

It is ironic that after four years of online study I graduated in 2005 with a Masters degree in Educational Technology Leadership from George Washington University and that during this time I did not blog, use a wiki, or a Google Doc because they just did not exist in a form that was usable or known by me then. I did use the university Blackboard portal as a collaborative online tool that in those days did help students to connect in meaningful ways through sharing files and discussion. But the birth and heyday of Web 2.0 in 2006 leading into 2007 changed the learning paradigm completely, for me and many other educators.

The final two chapters focus on pathways to become a global educator and even more ways to take learning global. Chapter 13 demonstrates through compelling examples how collaboration yields rich results. Chapter 14 features specific activities and organizations and gives the reader the opportunity to connect with individuals and communities. The book concludes with a call to action, brings together essential concepts and ideas throughout the book, reviews again what some of the obstacles are, and makes a firm case for why (and how) educators need to consider a global approach and connect themselves and their students with the world.

I remember the flurry of excitement sweeping the world (well my connected world at least!) as Web 2.0 tools provided educators the ability to connect easily and the opportunity to collaborate in new ways. The sharing that started to emerge was like a mini-revolution in learning for some, not all, educators. Conversations and experimentations using new tools pushed the limits of the classroom as innovative educators glimpsed, trialed and then implemented new ways of working that did in fact join themselves and their students with the world. The Flat Classroom Project, launched in November 2006, was just one example of how new tools for synchronous and asynchronous learning without borders and boundaries could support global collaboration and intercultural understanding. The world was our oyster, new tools for connection and collaboration were emerging everyday and there were no real limits—as long as you had connection to the internet many things were possible!

Global Educator, Global Community

By now you should have a much better idea of what a global educator and global education leader is and does. You should also be much more aware of the different levels and requirements of global collaboration and reflecting on how you as a global educator and global education leader can design and embed global learning across the curriculum—or at the very least make a start by joining others who are leading the way. This chapter shares ideas for where to get started as a global educator and how to extend your global activities if you have already started. We come back here to the notion of a learning ecology, introduced in the first half of the book, in terms of the fluidity and agility of technology-supported learning as individuals connect and learn across different settings, interests and times. You are encouraged to build personalized and learner-centered communities of practice, social networks and collegial groups (An & Reigeluth, 2011) in which educators can share and explore new teaching methods and tools and help each other find the pathways to becoming global.

Authentic Examples of Global Learning

Compiling information for this book, educators were asked to share a favourite global adventure in education and why this was important or significant to them. The stories, examples and glimpses into authentic global learning shared below reveal diversity and determination amongst the educators. There are many new global project and collaboration ideas here—and new colleagues to add to your PLN! Despite the rich learning experiences and variety of global connections possible, these examples only "scratch the surface" of what is and could be possible. Global educators are only limited by their imagination and determination to succeed!

Yes, Younger Students Can Collaborate Globally!

Dianne in California, shares, "I dreamed up a collaboration with a school in Illinois to partner our students and debate the hot topic of Sugar: should it be regulated? It was important because it utilized technologies that broke down the walls of our classroom PLUS the subject matter was relevant and meaningful for the students. Active learning took place" (Dianne Shapp, @dshapp).

In Beijing, China, Lara, a Grade 1 educator working in an international school loves doing Skype interviews looking at peoples' homes in other countries. The students also use Aurasma and trigger images that allow families to view their school work from anywhere in the world. This fosters a truly global audience.

Maggie in Mumbai, India shares the following:

> I think there are two of these that stand out for me, and both involve learning with, as opposed to learning from, others around the world. I have done Quad Blogging with Grade 4s as action research to see how student blogging can be used to teach quality writing—this class connected with other students in the USA, the Czech Republic and Thailand. Our Grade 2 students also connected with other students worldwide as they investigated how the weather and climate affects us. Our students were involved in global learning that was based on the connections that myself and the homeroom teachers had built through our personal learning networks. Knowledge is distributed widely across these networks and instead of learning from others the hope was to learn with others through inquiry and the co-construction of knowledge. (Maggies Hos McGrane, @mumbaimaggie)

Global Awareness and Impact

Eric from USA talks about the inaugural 2015 Student Technology Conference! "It was quite a journey. The conference started as a small potential collaboration between six schools, but due to the determination of our students and from adults invested in global education, the willingness of other schools to jump right in, and my willingness to turn over the planning to the students, the conference grew into a global phenomenon. To see my students uncover leadership skills they never believed they had, to see the faith they had in the process, to hear them ask for help when they needed it, and to see them realize that they could trust their peers to contribute what they sought was both transformative for them and for me" (Eric Walters).

Marymount School Student Technology Conference

http://studenttechnologyconference.com

Katie, Australia, shares that her all time favorite global adventure in education has been the Australian Marine Debris Initiative that went global. "I designed a marine debris education kit for Australian students to use all around Australia that involved beach cleaning, source reduction and students putting their data into a live database. Each school or group could set up their own micro blog or news channel and share their beach cleanup initiatives with other schools and do data comparisons and analysis. The project was then picked up in the USA, which has made the marine debris database go global. Synchronous collaboration included community beach clean-ups in Sri Lanka and China with asynchronous collaboration such as groups of students from different schools featuring on Channel 10's Totally Wild program, radio shows and sustainability forums. Students created their own national marine debris awareness program using art, workshops and competitions. There is even one school that created their own cash for container program that recycles and creates a small income for the school."

Connect with Katie Grubb, a Chinese language educator at Southern Cross School of Distance Education, NSW Australia and founder of Mandarin Pathways.

Twitter: **@katiegrubby**

WeChat: **katiegrubby**

Website: **www.mandarinpathways.org**

Sophie, USA, shares the example below saying, "This type of learning is the learning that matters in my opinion. It's relevant, it has real world application, and it helped the students to grow as a citizens of our global community!"

"My favorite global project was a food, nutrition, and hunger project we did in 2013. In it the students learned all about food nutrition, food waste, GMOs, food costs, hunger/poverty rates, sustainable farming, and food industry practices. The result of this unit changed the students eating habits and reduced the food waste in the school significantly. They learned about how these topics varied country to country and even designed an aquaponic gardening system for the school based off a similar concept they'd learned about from a farm in Africa. They became well informed of the "true cost" of their food and were inspired to make lifelong changes. One boy even started his own cricket farm as a way to attain protein more cheaply and with less impact on the environment. He branched off from this unit of study and is now farming crickets and using them as ingredients in his meals. Just recently he brought in a batch of his cricket brownies to share with the class and they were delicious!" (Sophie de la Paz, @gpsteach).

Adam, a USA educator currently in Egypt, provides numerous global learning experiences for his students and this example shares how technology can be the bridge to global awareness.

"In our CONNECT class we were doing a unit on people with disabilities. We did some role-play which allowed the students to feel empathy for some of these people with these hardships. I then showed them a video of how I was able to assist a project in the slums of Calcutta that helped deaf children. They enjoyed it so much; I asked if they would like to speak to someone from the project on Skype. I then set up a call with one of the workers but didn't realize he was deaf until our chat began and he typed his answers. The students were able to type their questions and read his responses on the screen (projected on our wall). They had so much respect for him and walked away with a new appreciation for their sense of hearing and for the commitment people have made to improving the lives of people with disabilities" (Adam Carter, @SocialActionCol).

Stephanie, USA, shared that she worked with seventh grade students to fund a microfinance loan as part of a unit on hunger and malnutrition. They discussed hunger and malnutrition as global issues, and then took a look at microfinance as a way to alleviate poverty and thus, hunger. Building on a partnership the school had with the Rift Valley Children's Village, Tanzania, she reached out to Rift Valley to see if the class could finance a microloan in support of their community. A woman who needed financial assistance to support her jewelry-making business came forward, and Stephanie's students were able to work together to raise the $500 necessary to fund the loan, the profits from which the woman used to lay bricks for her family home.

Stephanie shared, "As a service-learning coordinator, this experience was so significant because it was the first time that service-learning was successfully integrated into a classroom at my school, and it provided direct, tangible support for a global community in need. The students were thrilled to be a part of it, and the loan client was able to purchase the bricks needed to lay her home. We plan to continue the project this winter, raising the funds to build a chicken coop in the same community to finance school fees" (Stephanie Wujcik, @StephWuj45).

Sonya, New Zealand, shares: "I have several, however my most significant was meeting other global educators face to face when I visited 13 countries in 11 weeks and met over 20 educators. One of them was Julie Lindsay whose work I admired greatly and had been watching from afar. This led to us meeting again at a GAFE conference and then to me training with her as part of a Flat Connections Global Educator Certificate. The learning I have had from this course has developed my personal capabilities even further. I have had an amazing learning experience learning from and with other educators like myself that has allowed me to align much of what I know instinctively about being a global educator/leader into a working and learning framework" (Sonya van Schaijik, @vanschaijik).

Matt, Australia, shares how a history learning project between students in Sydney, Australia, and in Pennsylvania, USA was significant because it showed students the possibilities and challenges (not least of which is time zones) of international communication and working together on a project. Students were put into multi-national teams and had to work together to research a historical event or issue in the 20th century that affected both Australia and the USA. Their final product was a seminar, which they delivered live on Skype as a team. Matt also had students construct wikis in lieu of a live presentation. Students have mainly been volunteers and have given positive feedback each time the project was run.

Mahmud, from Lebanon, reflected how exchanging between his school's drama team and a team from a school in Norway was a fabulous experience for students with each school now becoming friends for life. Larisa in Boston talks about her work with NASA, NASA GRACE, NASA 4D, Hubble Telescope; Projects on Arctic Research; International Ice Patrol Expedition....and much more! She shares, "We will never forget the parents of some of our students from a country in a war zone...they asked us to continue working with them despite all these real challenges...they said it's helping their children to survive" (Larisa Schelkin, @Larisa_Schelkin).

Gaming Goes Global

Brian Mannix, USA, tells us about his favorite global adventure being an Alternate Reality Game that he created where teachers, learners, businesses and local and national media around the globe are working together in the name of deep, experiential education, not just for our students, but for every member of the global community.

"The name of the game is Skabe din Fremtid (www.skabedinfremtid.com) and there are over 100 classrooms across 15 countries who are participating in a storyline that breaks down the classroom walls, invites participants to actually be involved with the creation of, archiving of, and restoring of the historical accuracy of all of human history and scientific thought. Through clues that are embedded in local businesses, local newspapers, and blogs as well as in online sites that people use every day, there is a call by "The Rez" of the resistance to rewrite human history due to the fact that our history is being corrupted by the "Raybot Spiders," an artificial intelligence agency that is systematically altering the internet's traditional version of all of recorded history to weaken the impact of humans throughout our time here on earth, and bolster the scope, impact and sensibility of machines in our lives. Participants across the globe are given "directives" or challenges to investigate "the corruption," interview historians and scientists and rewrite and re-archive on Skabe din Fremtid's website the major components of human history and the evolution of scientific thought. Skage din Fremtid means "Create Your Future" in Danish and that is what the over 100 classrooms across the globe are engaged in doing as we speak. This journey has just gotten started and I feel that this might be my greatest contribution to individuals who are dedicated to deep, experiential, and transformative learning. Either way, I'm giving it my best shot" (Brian Mannix, @mannixlab).

Marianne, USA, tells us, "My students created an original game for the Minecraft Platform. A variety of students from grades 3–6 worked on developing and refining the design for over a year. John Hunter's World Peace Game inspired the game. We asked students to develop a game where three nations had to solve an epic problem where each nation had one resource needed to solve the problem. We wanted the game to be created in the spirit of Minecraft games that are shared and modified freely. Students generated the narrative of a world about to be destroyed by a meteor shower. The one chance to survive was to build a spacecraft. Each nation had one of the components needed for the ship or the fuel. The game is called Escape To Morrow and debuted at ISTE 2013" (Marianne Malstrom, @knowclue).

Global Game: Escape to Morrow

http://morrowcraft.wikispaces.com/Escape+To+Morrow

See the example of Yvonne Harris in Perth, Australia, playing the game with her Grade 5 students

www.flickr.com/photos/98577611@N06/sets/72157650018885762/

Carly, Australia, is excited about her favourite global adventure, which is the experience of setting up a two year Senior English program using iTunes U. She says, "While it was ultimately done to accommodate a group of students in my own school, it was quite exciting to realise that the numbers were growing significantly by making the course available publicly. To this point, one of my courses has over 1000 students, several others over 100. The idea that other students and teachers can make use of my work makes me feel like I am giving as many people as possible an opportunity to learn and teach" (Carly Damen, @CarlyDamen).

Moliehi, Lesotho, shares, "To be nominated as a world most innovative teacher in the category of Educator's choice. It is important because I got an opportunity to connect with other teachers from different parts of the world. And as results of that I managed to secure funds from my international friends to build classrooms, s computer laboratory, and to pay school fees for the orphans at my school" (Moliehi Sekese,@moliehi4sekese).

A teacher from the USA, Tina shares that her first major global adventure was the Flat Connections "A Week in the Life" Project. "I was a newbie to Twitter, Google, Edmodo and global connections. This project was run by some amazing educators who were there to lend support to all of us newbies. I wasn't afraid to try new things or to ask for help when I needed it. My students and I worked together to learn how to use the technologies needed. When I saw the wonder, excitement and learning going on in our classroom from this project, I was hooked! I am now happy to call many of the teachers from that project my friends. That project gave me the foundation and support in global education that I needed and I then had the courage to go out and try other new things" (Tina Schmidt, @MrsSchmidtB4).

Judy, Australia, tells us, "Joining and becoming involved in the International Association of School Librarianship gave me the most humbling of experiences, and the biggest challenges in refocusing my connections with people and their local experiences and contextualizing my own work for a bigger purpose" (Judy O'Connell, @heyjudeonline). Read more about Judy in Case Study 4.6.

Wayne, Australia, shares, "My personal global adventure in education would have to be participation in online webinars and conferences. I love the notion of sharing professional development with an international cohort—there is nothing more stimulating than learning with a coalition of the willing. It is inspiring to share your stories with people beyond your national borders" (Wayne Demnar, @wdemnar).

Holly, Qatar, shares that "Reading is more than print, Writing is more than ink." To engage her second language learners, she developed a blended learning unit on picture books that utilised both traditional and new literacies, and both analogue and digital tools. Her Year 10 students in Singapore created the ebooks and Year 3 students in Malaysia read them and completed an online review. They then conducted a Skype interview, where the Year 3 learners asked questions to particular authors about their books they had read. They asked about where they got their inspiration from and how they went about writing and publishing. "It was really exciting to meet our reviewers and talk to them face to face. My learners are all intermediate English learners, and this unit helped address many important terms and skills required for them to pass their IGCSE Second Language exams. It also went way beyond that and gave them essential digital and media literacy skills; it engaged them through writing stories based on their own life and allowed them the chance to create through technology. The use of technology meant we also were afforded an authentic audience to easily share with and receive real feedback from" (Holly Fairbrother, @mrshollyenglish).

Read Holly's blog post for the full story: http://mrshollyexploringlearning.blogspot.com/2013/12/more-than-ink.html

Supporting Organizations and Resources

T here exist across the world organizations and associated online resources that will help global educators build a solid PLN and provide opportunities for global exchange and collaboration as well as professional learning. The associations are mentioned here as a starting point and not a definitive list. Reach out across your current networks and explore further—you'll find there is always someone and something available to help. Remember, it is not always necessary to reinvent the wheel when starting to go global.

Connecting Classrooms – Finding Global Partners

iEARN - International Education and Resource Center

iEARN is a global K–12 project-based collaboration network whose motto is "Learning with the world, not just about it." This organization has been around since the 1980s (see the interview with Ed Gragert, Case Study 2.3). There are now more than 2 million participants and collaborations take place in many languages. The main website provides access to iEARN general discussion space, global projects and learning circles. There are many iEARN organizations located in countries around the world—maybe your country has one that you can connect with?

In 2004 I completed an online course through iEARN USA and was awarded a "Certificate of Achievement as a Master Teacher". This was my first experience thinking about and designing online collaborative experiences to embed into the curriculum. Follow the Professional Development menu on the iEARN website and see a range of courses, webinars and workshops being offered to global educators anywhere.

Connect with iEARN

Website: **http://iearn.org/**

Website for collaborations: **https://collaborate.iearn.org/**

iEARN USA

Twitter: **@iEARNUSA**

Website: **http://us.iearn.org/**

Global SchoolNet (GSN)

The Global SchoolNet was founded in 1984 (see the interview with Yvonne Marie Andres in Case Study 2.1). Its mission is to support 21st century, brain-friendly learning, and improve academic performance through content-driven collaboration. It has a large online global community and a projects registry for K–12 classes. The International Cyberfair project is run through GSN.

Connect with Global SchoolNet

Twitter: **@globalschoolnet**

Website: **http://www.globalschoolnet.org/**

TakingITGlobal and Future Friendly Schools

Future Friendly Schools is a global network of future-forward schools designed to "nurture student voice, global citizenship and environmental stewardship through technology-rich and project-based learning". As an initiative of TakingITGlobal there are strong links with community development and professional learning. Participation is through school membership and entry to a supportive online community that showcases teacher achievement and supports school vision for student engagement.

Connect with TakingITGlobal

Website: **www.futurefriendlyschools.org/**

Read more about this initiative in Case Study 2.7 with Michael Furdyk, co-founder of TakingITGlobal.

Center for Interactive Learning and Collaboration (CILC)

The Center for Interactive Learning and Collaboration has been around for over 20 years and is a clearinghouse for all things around video conferencing in education. CILC offers content programs from over 200 museums, science centers, and art galleries, as well as professional development and collaborative projects for all ages. Think of it as a "Match.com" between learners and world-class content providers. CILC specializes in the use of video conferencing solutions for live, interactive content, and provides consulting expertise in video conferencing integration and effective techniques for the delivery and development of quality programs.

Jan Zanetis is the Managing Director of CILC. She is also an ISTE Board member and founded the ISTE Interactive Video Conferencing PLN about 10 years ago.

Connect with Jan Zanetis

Twitter: **@janzan**

LinkedIn: **www.linkedin.com/pub/jan-zanetis/1/a5/498**

Current Activities

CILC is an online site and currently has over 40,000 educators members registered. It matches schools with virtual field trips and organises a booking system for this. It also provides a service for educators to connect with each other for global projects. Collaborations are posted on the CILC site where classroom matches are made by educators contacting the project proposer. Quite often relationships between teachers that last for years develop after one project is completed. CILC works hard to make valuable connections for learning and also provides links with professional development providers who run synchronous online sessions in a range of topics.

Connect with the Center for Interactive Learning and Collaboration

Twitter: **@cilcorg**

Website: **http://cilc.org/**

Facebook: **www.facebook.com/TheCILC**

Future Goals

CILC is undergoing a website transformation and is linking with new relevant partners.

Jan says this is a momentous time in video conferencing history as schools can make direct connections without buying expensive VC equipment. Schools can do Skype, Google Hangouts, Zoom—so the question is why are they not doing it more? CILC provides the bridge for educators across the world to learn from each other and to join their students.

Center for International Virtual Schooling (IVECA)

The Center for International Virtual Schooling started in 2009 and connects schools in different countries for cross-cultural virtual exchange and to develop intercultural competence. IVECA stands for Intercultural/International Virtual Exchange program of Classroom Activities and has become the name of the organization as well. The Executive Director and Founder of IVECA is Eunhee Jung.

Connect with Eunhee Jung and IVECA

Twitter: **@ejung_iveca**

LinkedIN: **www.linkedin.com/in/eunheejung**

Website: **http://website.iveca.org/**

IVECA Virtual Classroom: **http://class1.iveca.org/**

The main goal of IVECA is to promote interculturally competent global citizenship by providing global virtual learning opportunities for students throughout the education system. As Eunhee explained to me recently, it requires a lot of work to initiate and keep implementing programs that provide a global experience. The practicality of global learning is important in enabling any teachers to globalize teaching and learning on a daily basis. Therefore, IVECA offers professional development, global curriculum design framework, instructional consultation, and virtual collaboration platforms, and coordinates intercultural exchange partnerships of schools in different countries.

The focus of the global interactions is on paired partnerships. Eunhee discussed the disadvantage of putting too many countries and students together because some may not respond and some drop out of the collaboration altogether. IVECA paired partnerships work best as they try to be inclusive of all students, are semester-based and utilize Web 2.0 commonly shared tools. Teacher professional development includes intercultural, technological and pedagogical components at different levels and hours. The IVECA Virtual Classroom is based on a Moodle platform and provides programs for K–12 and university levels.

Eunhee shares that teachers' pedagogical capacity and foundation is influential in making a global project work more effectively. In addition, although they may be capable in curriculum design, classroom management and pedagogy, without intercultural competence it can go wrong. She describes that intercultural competence is an ability to communicate *appropriately* and work *effectively* together with people from different countries, based on understanding and respect towards cultural diversity. Some of the highly accomplished teachers sometimes tend to lead projects as they want, without being mindful of the school environment and culture of the partner country. When anything doesn't go as planned, those teachers show impatience and fail to communicate with respect, and eventually it affects students' learning experience. Eunhee emphasizes the importance of teacher professional development for 21st century global teaching and learning.

The strength of IVECA is that the program is designed and orchestrated based on in-depth doctoral research and pilot projects. The main focuses of Eunhee's first pilot study conducted in 2006 was to prove the effects of the program, the feasibility of the implementation model, and the framework of integrating global virtual learning with regular school curricula. She comments that many projects introduced international online exchange activities to schools, but few studies focused on discovering practical ways to run global learning sustainably through school systems. In her paper, she describes how the following two assumptions guided the design of the study, "First, that public schools need to prepare students to become capable global citizens equipped with intercultural competence and, second, that experiencing different cultures through direct interaction with people in other countries can help prepare students to become competent global citizens." (O'Neill, 2007, p. 207)

Eunhee's doctoral research completed the practical model of implementing global virtual learning into public schools having different curriculum systems and proved the effect of the program. Collaborative teaching and learning models for the ICT integration in IVECA and instructional strategies for teachers were demonstrated as well (O'Neill, 2008, p. 235–253). To promote adaptability of global virtual learning, she recommends each country set up education policies for making ICT available at all schools. Also, pre-service teacher programs need to be connected globally through virtual exchange activities (O'Neill, 2010).

Over the years, Eunhee has been striving to introduce IVECA to schools all around the world as part of her educational belief, "In today's global society, individuals with an understanding of different cultures that have the ability to apply this understanding to real world problem solving are more likely to become leaders. Preparing students for a global society is becoming a significant part of education." (O'Neill, 2007, p. 207)

Face to Faith

The Face to Faith organization is part of the Tony Blair Foundation. It is an education program working across the world to help prevent religious conflict and extremism. Facilitators bring students from different parts of the world together virtually for dialogue about issues and to support enhanced understanding about similarities and differences.

Face to Faith website: **www.facetofaithonline.org/**

Twitter: **@Face_to_Faith**

Flat Connections "Learning about the World, with the World"

Flat Connections shares a cutting edge approach to "flatten" the walls of learning by using digital and online technologies to connect learners globally for meaningful collaborations that build bridges between students our future can walk across. Educators will find access to a series of online global collaborative projects for K–12 that are fully supported and managed by Flat Connections Project Managers. This means there is less isolation in the global collaborative process. Regular online educator meetings, support with new tools, and input as to the project timeline and outcomes helps all global learners successfully come together and learn.

The Flat Connections Global Educator (10 week accredited course) and other online courses provide further professional learning support for educators and education leaders who are serious about taking their learning environment global.

Flat Connections website: **http://flatconnections.com**

Twitter: **@flatconnections** Hashtag: **#flatconnections**

Global Innokas

The Innokas network is a "collaboration of forward-looking schools, universities and companies focusing on children who are today learning their 21st century knowledge and skills." It is coordinated by the Department of Teacher Education, University of Helsinki, under the leadership of Tiina Korhonen. Tiina works to support teachers across Finland in building the innovative school. The goal is to make creativity, innovation and technology part of everyday learning. The "Innovative School" model developed has teachers, parents, students and other partners as innovators. It focuses on learning, teachership, leadership and partnership and is one way to help schools understand how they can develop their own system. Even if the school is from China or the USA there is the idea that they can start to develop schools that are innovative. There is a cultural background pertinent to each school and country, but the main idea is that students themselves are innovators, and an important aspect here is that this is global. Tiina says, "We believe that innovation must be at an operational level and also at the student level—how to support students from early childhood—and engage learning."

Connect with Tiina Korhonen, Head of Innokas Network, Department of Teacher Education, University of Helsinki: **@TiinaKorhone**

Global Innokas blog and information: **http://globalinnokas.com/**

Bridges Global Education Community: **http://ibridgelearn.net/**

Innokas aims to plan collaborations, and in a few years to develop a global curriculum, and a sustainable plan for this. One part is building global teams for learning challenges around a theme. Not just project teams that last for one year, but a longer lasting collaboration. For example, looking at common themes between curriculum in participating countries and developing teams and partnerships as well as supporting a step-by-step approach to collaboration—and sharing the use of technology. In addition, looking for a global understanding about how teachers can be supported for global collaboration.

Bridges Global Education Community is based in the USA (Wisconsin). It connects educators from the USA with China and provides a platform for global collaboration. It has also run conferences in China where global educators come together to discuss and plan future collaborations by learning more about each country and their educational needs, the most recent one being in Beijing that attracted educators from China, USA, Canada, Australia and Finland.

Tiina shared her observations about global collaboration saying short sessions (four weeks for example) are not always successful. One goal is to find teachers who will collaborate globally and build online global curriculum and design learning over 4-5 years—even if the teachers change schools—the aim is for them to continue in the "circle" of collaboration.

Professional development for teachers in Finland to go global is supported through a Global Innokas pilot. Educators were invited to participate and about 15 responded. Since then meetings to plan and build innovators as part of the pilot phase have been held. The Finnish global citizen and global collaboration national curriculum should also be starting in 2016.

Future plans for Innokas is to continue to develop teachers who will be part of the innovative rollout. They are also conducting an exploratory study on teacher attitudes to project-based learning including how it supports global collaboration. This is in conjunction with Chinese universities and Stanford University.

Professional Learning

Asia Society

The Asia Society is a non-profit organization that focuses on educating the world about Asia. The education division of the US based society provide excellent resources online and professional learning opportunities through conferences and online courses. There is a focus on developing global competence in addition to downloadable resources and "how to" guides on the website the society partnered with World Savvy and Columbia University to offer a Global Competence Certificate for K–12 educators.

Asia Society Website (education): **http://asiasociety.org/education**

Twitter: **@asiasociety**

Global Competence Certificate: **http://globalcompetencecertificate.org/**

Asia Education Foundation, Australia

The Asia Education Foundation (AEF) supports educators and school communities to develop Asia-capable young Australians. It has many curriculum and professional learning resources on the website including pathways to become and an Asia-capable leader or an Asia-capable teacher and a variety of toolkits, including a "Global Collaboration Toolkit" that I co-authored recently. The BRIDGE School Partnerships program brings educators together from Australia and other Asian countries (e.g., Indonesia) for joint learning, school visits and family homestays. The program encourages educators from both countries to design and build collaborative learning opportunities using emerging technologies.

Connect with the Asia Education Foundation

Twitter: **@AsiaEducation**

Website: **www.asiaeducation.edu.au/**

Global Collaboration Toolkit: **www.asiaeducation.edu.au/professional-learning/ toolkits/global-collaboration**

"Over the past seven years I've been part of a team designing and delivering an international school partnership and professional learning program that supports the development of these global competencies in educators and students. **B**uilding **R**elationships through **I**ntercultural-understanding and **G**rowing **E**ngagement, or BRIDGE, is a program that establishes partnerships between schools in Australia and the countries of Asia. It is a blended model that incorporates face-to-face and virtual teacher professional learning. Teachers break-down cultural and geographic barriers to make connections, foster intercultural understanding and to engage students in collaborative learning" (Bonnie Hermawan, @BonnieHermawan).

WISE Initiative

Qatar Foundation, under the leadership of its Chairperson, Her Highness Sheikha Moza bint Nasser established the World Innovation Summit for Education (WISE) in 2009. Originally designed as an international conference including a global competition for learning excellence, it has grown and expanded into many new and exciting areas always with the focus on creative thinking, debate and purposeful action. There is an annual summit and ongoing programs that support educational initiatives and innovation.

Connect with WISE

Twitter: **@WISE_Tweets**

Website: **www.wise-qatar.org**

Institute for Global and Online Education

The Institute for Global and Online Education is situated in the College of Education, University of Oregon. Yong Zhao, USA, currently serves as the Presidential Chair and Director.

This is an interesting potential resource for educators. Brian Flannery, the Coordinator for Global and Online Education says, "Training we do is geared towards globalization. Yong is the primary academic leading the department and teaching content in this area. Developing global leaders in education is a primary focus of the visiting scholar program."

The Institute works with educational institutions and leaders to help them become globally oriented, connected and competent. They run seminars, global exchanges and leadership institutes. What is also interesting is the online learning platform, ObaWorld, developed by Dane Ramshaw, CTO and his team. This is designed for collaboration and learning and the HigherEd version, ObaVerse, has been adopted by the UO as its learning portal. The technology empowers people and makes interesting connections, even if they are not global in the true sense of the word. They are looking at how OBA can be harnessed to support cognitive study while people are learning in an online environment because of the richness of the data collection possible. Current users of OBA can choose to use it just for their own learning community or they can use it to create a global community for a particular purpose. From the beginning the cost of OBA has been $1 per student.

Connect with the Institute for Global and Online Education

Twitter: **@ObaLearning**

Website: **https://globaleducation.uoregon.edu/** and **www.obaworld.net/**

Connect with Yong Zhao

Twitter: **@YongZhaoUO**

Brainwaves video: World Class Learners: **https://youtu.be/Wk--J3E8yqc**

EdCamp Global

As the lead global program developer for Calliope Global, Jennifer Williams, USA works with schools, universities, and organizations from around the world. Jennifer is the co-founder of EdCamp Tampa Bay and is part of the planning team for EdCamp Global along with Jaime Donally, Debra Atchison, Cassie Reeder, Nancy Watson, Leah Pendleton, Clara Alaniz, and Sean Gaillard. She is inspired every day by teachers and students that are catalysts for making the world a better place.

EdCamp Global website: **http://edcampglobal.wix.com/edcamp**

Twitter: **@jenwilliamsedu** and **@edCampGlobal**

Jennifer tells us, "As a globally focused educator, I am constantly looking for opportunities that will allow me to connect, learn, and share with teachers from around the world. In my search for networked collaboration, I was thrilled to discover the world of EdCamps, "unconference" events that empower and celebrate the voice of the teacher. Built on a model of participatory learning, EdCamps are specially designed for teachers to share their passions and explore their questions in education today. At an EdCamp, the schedule of sessions is determined organically as teachers indicate topics that they want to learn and ideas that they want to share. Following, groups come together at sessions in discussions that allow for actionable steps for the future and developing relationships that can continue and flourish. With EdCamps, I found that my learning was ignited and my world as an educator was connected and inspired.

EdCamp Global is a unique EdCamp experience that allows educators from around the world to come together in virtual conversations. Following in the EdCamp mission of allowing sessions to be guided by educator interest, EdCamp Global offers a system where sessions are determined over the course of several months as individuals register for the event online and indicate areas for exploration and discussion. The participant-driven process culminates with an extraordinary 24-hour event held at the end of July. Innovative sessions are offered via Twitter chats, Google Hangouts, Skype, Periscope, and Voxer. Session facilitators engage participants in topics of educational significance, such as Global Learning, Google in the Classroom, Digital Citizenship, Apps for Learning, and BYOD initiatives. In the inaugural year in the summer of 2015, over 1,200 educators representing 28 different countries from around the world registered to attend. Over the 24-hour period, global participants created their own session schedules by selecting from the 145 virtual sessions that were facilitated by international educators. For more information on EdCamp Global and to register for the next global event as a participant or facilitator, please visit the website. Learning in EdCamp Global is personalized and powerful, and always in the hands of the individual educator. And the great part is you can do it all in your jammies!" (Jennifer Williams, @jenwilliamsedu).

Take Learning Global Case Studies

In the final collection of case studies we explore opportunities for professional learning and collaboration. These include online and virtual courses and conferences as well as face-to-face events. The selection shared here is as diverse as it is exciting. In addition thought leaders and activators share their thoughts about higher education, community of practice development, and global learning across the curriculum.

Case Study 4.1 – Lucy Gray and Steve Hargadon: The Global Education Conference

The Global Education Conference, created by Steve Hargadon and Lucy Gray, both in the USA, is a collaborative, inclusive, worldwide community initiative involving students, educators, and organizations at all levels. It is designed to significantly increase opportunities for connecting classrooms while supporting cultural awareness and recognition of diversity and educational access for all.

As an education technology leader working in international schools I discovered a major push coming from the USA around 2006—with new initiatives and partnerships revolving around the ISTE conference (or NECC as it was called then) that spun out across the globe. Edubloggercon, a 1-day pre-NECC conference 2007 event in Atlanta, became a focal point for a small, and then growing number of educators hungry for the peer interaction, participant-led style and "flattened" learning opportunities that an "unconference" gathering provided. Educators together discussing emerging pedagogies for learning included David Warlick, Jeff Utecht, Scott McLeod, Chris Lehmann, Sheryl Nussbaum-Beach, Will Richardson, Peggy George....and many more. We sat as comrades around tables or in chair formations based on our interests for that hour and talked, and talked, and shared and discussed and together constructed a new paradigm for learning using emerging educational technologies.

Steve Hargadon was our inspiration and organisational guru for this and subsequent events. I particularly remember this 2007 event as I had flown from Bangladesh (in fact had just left Bangladesh for the last time, where I had been teaching at International School Dhaka as the E-Learning Coordinator for four years), knowing I "had to get to Edubloggercon" and arriving after midnight in Atlanta the night before to a hotel that was less than accommodating and a credit card that was not working!

As online technologies continued to develop there came a need to provide similar interactive and connected experiences for a global audience, to share global objectives for teaching and learning. Out of the excitement of peer-to-peer and face-to-face events was born, amongst other ideas, the motivation for a global online event.

Read about the vision, development, organization, achievements and future of this truly global event in the ebook case study.

A Declaration of the Value of Global Education, compiled by GEC participants and presented at the 2013 Global Education Conference

/www.GlobalEducationDeclaration.com

Lucy Gray: **@elemenous**

Website: **http://lucygrayconsulting.com/**

Steve Hargadon: **@stevehargadon**

Websites: **www.stevehargadon.com** and **www.learningrevolution.com**

The Global Education Conference: **@globaledcon** Hashtag: **#globaled**

Website: **http://globaleducationconference.com**

Global EdCon on YouTube: **www.youtube.com/user/globaledcon/**

Case Study 4.2 – The "Learning2" Conference

Learning2 is an innovative, engaging and constantly evolving face-to-face conference with a focus on leveraging technology to support learning globally. It is considered to be one of the leading annual technology conferences in the Asia region. For 2016, Learning2 conferences will be held in over four continents.

The story of Learning2 is one of hard work by a few dedicated leaders and is an inspiration to any professional learning organiser anywhere in the world. The vision that Jeff Utecht has shared and propelled through the years for social, relevant and participant led learning to emulations of the original Learning 2.0 format is now in different continents and still expanding through the new non-profit organization status. This statement within this Learning2 case study resonates with the themes discussed, "The glocalization of Learning2 will be, by far, our biggest challenge, as we continually evolve the global Learning2 'brand' and meet the needs of our participants locally."

International educators in Asia, and specifically China, will remember the flurry of excitement when the first few Learning2 conferences were held. I did not make it to Learning 2.0 (as it was called then) in 2007 as I had just started working in Qatar, however I did come across to Shanghai in 2008 as a presenter and discovered an amazing event, made lots of friends and extended my network considerably. The 2008 event had David Warlick (who I already knew), Alan Levine, Jabiz Raisdana, Clarence Fisher, Chrissy Hellyer, Jenny Luca … just too many to mention! It was while in Shanghai on that trip that I bought my daughter a tenor saxophone, as you do as a global educator, because we could not get one in Doha at the time!

This case study was written by Learning2 Advisors Madeleine Brookes (@mbrookes), Kim Cofino (@mscofino), Simon May (@samay99) & Jeff Utecht (@jutecht). It shares the mission, development, scope and future of one of the most innovative face-to-face professional learning events globally.

Connect with Learning2

Twitter: **@learning2** and **#learning2**

Website: **http://learning2.org/**

Board: **http://learning2.org/board-and-staff/**

Case Study 4.3 – THINK Global School: Learning to Be Global While Living Globally

THINK Global School (TGS) moves around the world and implements place-based learning to its fullest extent. The school of about 12 teachers and 60 students from Grades 9–12 literally moves each semester, relocating in a new environment and re-developing curriculum objectives and learning outcomes based largely on that location. In addition the school is very technology focused and from the outset in

2010 implemented a 3:1 mobile program where each learner (student and teacher) has a Macbook, iPad and iPhone.

My first reaction when learning about THINK Global School (TGS) was typical of most people....what? they do what? travel the world as a school? how does that work? I remember reading the website and thinking how exciting, and how ambitious. As it turned out in 2010 TGS spent a trimester based at the international school in Beijing where I was IT Director and I got to know the teachers and students very well. It was in its first year then so only about 16 Grade 9 students were in the school. Together with the TGS Head of School at the time, Brad Ovenell-Carter (@ braddo), we designed collaborative learning joining TGS students with my students, including a unit we called "Brand of Me" that focused on digital profiles and online branding (digital citizenship). In 2012-14 I worked for TGS as a consultant helping to build connected and collaborative learning and embed global collaborative practices into the curriculum.

TGS has spent a lot of time as a school contemplating what global learning and learning globally means. Interaction with host country schools and students physically is important, as is online interaction with other learners across the world. It should be noted here however that although the school is global in concept and practice it is not necessarily any more advanced than other schools across the world in the ability to connect, collaborate and co-create with others. They may have had more opportunities and better access to technology tools, but in many respects the playing field is level, or flat.

Read more in the case study about approaches to connected learning and making global connections while global!

Connect with THINK Global School

Website: **http://thinkglobalschool.org/**

Explore SPOT: **https://spot.thinkglobalschool.com/**

Twitter: **@tgsthinkglobal**

Case Study 4.4 – Peggy George and Wesley Fryer: The K12 Online Conference

The K12 Online Conference is a free, online, annual event and is run totally by volunteer educators. Two of these are Wesley Fryer (@wfryer) and Peggy George (@pgeorge) who team with others to provide a successful experience for all participants.

For many years, from 2006 onward, I created and co-created presentations in the form of self-contained videos for the K12 Online Conference. It was the first event I can remember that really brought people together with a single purpose—to share ideas and new modes of learning virtually. The archived videos, created as presentations for the virtual conference, became a rich store of readily available top quality professional learning. In the past I have used these presentations to kick start teacher meetings, and as inspiration for discussion in different scenarios. Peggy and Wesley share further insights about the history, benefits and future goals of this global online, asynchronous event in the ebook case study.

Connect with the K12 Online Conference

Website: **http://k12onlineconference.org/**

Twitter: **@K12online**

YouTube channel: **www.youtube.com/user/k12online/videos**

Case Study 4.5 – Our Global Friendships

Our Global Friendships is a small virtual community of global collaborative educators. It is a community of practice for the purpose of learning with and from each other. In many respects it is unique in its creation, and futuristic in its ability to bring together a disparate group of educators who, through their passion and vision, design and implement global projects that often include many other educators and classrooms.

Professional learning for educators has changed significantly in the past ten years. Gone are the days when I spent hours in university libraries pouring through magazines (especially the educational technology ones of the mid-1990s) photocopying articles and borrowing books, but never really feeling like I had the latest and best up-to-date information. Or when living in the Middle East just after the turn of the 21st century I downloaded and printed off just about every NECC (the previous name for the ISTE Conference) handout from presenters—such a diverse and joyous set of resources for an information starved educator who had nobody else in her school to talk to or learn from about digital and global collaborations!

Material for this case study came largely from a 1.5 hour Skype call in which about 10 of the "Our Global Friendships" group were present. They talked doggedly about the positive advantages, the personal commitment and global realities of their association. This story should inspire readers to take action and do this themselves. There is much to learn from "Our Global Friendships" in this case study!

Connect with Our Global Friendships

Wiki: **http://ourglobalfriendships.wikispaces.com/**

Case Study 4.6 – Judy O'Connell: Leadership for Global Learning– A reflection on Higher Education Experiences in Australia

Judy O'Connell, Australia, is a senior lecturer and Program Director for the School of Information Studies in the Faculty of Education at Charles Sturt University (CSU), Australia. She has responsibility for a number of undergraduate and postgraduate programs in education and information studies. Her professional leadership experience spans primary school, secondary school and tertiary education. Her work focuses on open education, social media, digital innovation, learning frameworks, and new directions for knowledge networks in digitally enriched environments.

This case study shares Judy's journey as a global educator, global connected learning at all levels, challenges, and focuses especially on teacher education in Australia including the new Master of Education (Knowledge Networks and Digital Innovation) at CSU.

Judy O'Connell's blog: **http://judyoconnell.com**

Twitter: **@heyjudeonline**

Case Study 4.7 – Leigh Zeitz: Integrating the Global Learning Experience into Teacher Education

Leigh Zeitz, University of Northern Iowa, USA, has been in teacher education for over 20 years and a firm believer in creating situations where students are engaged in actually working with others across the globe so that they can experience the immediacy of the process. He believes that when they realize that the connections between people are just a click away, it becomes part of their lives and part of their pedagogical options in the classroom.

Leigh has involved his pre-service teacher students in many globally collaborative opportunities, including escorting a large group to China to attend the Flat Classroom Conference in 2011. Read more in the ebook case study about how Leigh is bringing global learning opportunities to his pre-service student teachers.

Connect with Leigh Zeitz @zeitz
Blog: **http://drzreflects.com/**

Case Study 4.8: VIF International Education and VIF Learning Center

For over 25 years VIF International Education has advocated for global education. They do this through bringing international teachers into schools in the USA and also by creating global education programs. VIF leaders, David Young (CEO) and Mark Otter (COO) share what VIF has to offer educators who want a global and intercultural experience and who want to shift their learning into a global mode. VIF supports global-ready teachers through many programs and provision of facilities for further connections and learning.

The ebook case study captures some of the exciting work VIF International Education and the VIF Learning Center platform provide and includes stories from global teachers.

VIF International Education website: **www.vifprogram.com**
Twitter: **@VIFprogram**
VIF Learning Center website: **www.viflearn.com/**
Twitter: **@VIFLearn**

Case Study 4.9 – Terry Godwaldt: The Centre for Global Education

The Centre for Global Education (CGE), a Canadian-based organization, develops and delivers virtual projects to engage and empower youth as agents of change, through connecting them to the people and places they are learning about. The mission of (CGE) is to educate 21st century students for a 21st century world by providing global learning opportunities, enhanced through technology, informed by sound research and innovative teaching. Through a series of strategic relationships, The Centre has uniquely placed itself as an international hub of technology innovation, higher learning and global education. Founder and Director of Programming for CGE, Canadian Terry Godwaldt, Canada, shares more about CGE programs and initiatives in this case study.

Terry Godwaldt's website: **www.tcge.ca**

Twitter: **@tgodwaldt**

Centre for Global Education website: **www.tcge.ca/**

Twitter: **@cgeducation**

Case Study 4.10 – Larisa Schelkin: Global STEM Education Center

The Global STEM Education Centre was founded by Larisa Schelkin with the purpose of increasing participation in STEM disciplines by all students to meet the needs of an innovation-driven globally competitive workforce and to enable the next generation to be effective in and with other countries/cultures in solving the problems urgently confronting the world's populations.

Conversations with Larisa opened my eyes to the global possibilities of this type of learning, where strong collaborations are built not only across the world but also between industry and education. Larisa has an astute sense of where the gaps are in education and works hard to build global understanding and success.

Website: **www.globalstemclassroom.com**

Twitter: **@Larisa_Schelkin**

Global STEM Education Center website: **www.globalSTEMcenter.org**

Twitter: **@GlobalSTEMClass**

Conclusion:
The Imperative of Becoming Global

It is imperative that educators become global! This final chapter brings together the essential ideas and examples throughout the book and shares further actions for all educators to consider in order to embrace global learning.

"Engagement with the world will be a part of everyone's life. The countries where global outlook is integrated into their education are now excelling, however those that are continuing to be introspective and narrow-minded are going to be left behind. Ultimately the widespread integration of the globe into classrooms through technology will play a key role in ensuring international understanding and world peace. There is no more important aspect than the value of knowing and engaging with the world to a student's future life" (Ed Gragert, USA, @egragert).

Think Globally, Celebrate Locally

I was discussing the imperative of global learning with a colleague recently in light of a recent New South Wales Department of Education (Australia) initiative to bring "History" into the elementary levels as a distinct (rather than interdisciplinary) discipline. The challenge is to move away from the memorization of facts and make learning authentically challenge-based, problem-based and project-based—yes, we all know the drill—but how to do this in today's education climate? The answer, as I see it, is to become global! I do not say this flippantly.

There are two main aspects when planning for this. The first is maximizing use of online technologies to support and enhance learning approaches (such as the use of a social bookmarking tool like Diigo, and collaborative platforms like Google

Apps). The second is to connect teachers and students with the world with a view to understanding and sharing intercultural perspectives on history (through the use of Twitter, blogs and other tools). These two objectives together can be transformative for learning.

Striving for Glocalization

In Chapter 10 we discussed "glocalization" as a combination of the words "globalization" and "localization" used to describe products and services that are both developed and sold to global customers but designed so that they suit the needs of local markets. A glocalized curriculum supports global collaborative practices whereby learners are encouraged to think globally, make authentic global connections and collaborate and co-create with others at a distance while at the same time maintaining and in fact celebrating their own local identity. Becoming global must include adopting a glocalized approach.

> "Our future is going to be affected by other people in the world and not only by the people who live in our community. Part of this global education should be tied to young people working together to create the preferable future" (Yvonne Marie Andres, USA, @YvonneMarieA).

Often educators ask me how they can connect with African countries and/or third world countries—they want to provide real life examples for their students that go beyond the textbook. Of course! Although I lived in Zambia for 3 years, I have struggled for many years to make connections with local (and even international schools) on the African continent due to their lack of reliable internet access and therefore ability to engage learners in ongoing meaningful ways. However, times are changing quickly. My usual response to educators now is: Well, many countries in Africa and other parts of the world are opening up because they are leap-frogging over what we in "the west" or developed parts of the world have been through to implement educational technology.

Today students across Africa, India and China (to mention a few areas) have access to mobile phones and also to networks that provide a bridge to the rest of the world. As things change it will be much "easier" to connect with diverse learners—*but*, (and this is what I continue to say to global educators and global education leaders), will *you* be ready? Will you be ready for when students in an African village are online and wanting to learn *together*? Will you be ready when there are opportunities for joint curriculum and global project design and richer learning experiences to be had for all participants? Will you be ready and knowledgeable about how to implement and facilitate online global collaborations? Will *you* be able to lead the way?"

"We live in a Global Society and our 21st century students need to feel comfortable when connecting with peers of different cultures and countries. While social and cultural diversity can be found in many of our own communities, it is not until we connect with people in different countries that we can appreciate our similarities and differences" (Leigh E. Zeitz, PhD, @zeitz). **Read more about Zeitz in Case Study 4.7 in the ebook.**

Are You Designing a Global Learning Environment?

So, what are you and your school or institution doing to prepare to become global? What is the master plan for this? Is something like a Google Apps implementation a step along the road, or a diversion without real focus—it certainly cannot be an end in itself!? Are "coding" and "makerspaces" merely trendy flavors of the month or are these being implemented within the vision to globalize and glocalize learning for all?

I already mentioned I have yet to find a truly global learning environment/school—despite working with many educators and schools in the past two decades.

In my view, a truly global learning environment:

1. Shares a vision that at EVERY grade level students will have a variety of interdisciplinary online global learning experiences with others beyond their immediate learning environment

2. Understands how to "flatten" the learning so that EVERY DAY there is encouragement and opportunity to learn beyond the immediate. As students get older—upper elementary, moving into middle school and high school—these learning experiences will be more personal, more one-to-one, and more socially collaborative

3. Understands digital scholarship, peer review, peer learning, co-creation of solutions to global problems, sharing of local resources to build a global database, social entrepreneurship as a global collaborative objective for learning….and much more

Why Aren't More Modern Learning Environments Becoming Global?

Lack of Understanding

Yes, lack of understanding about how to connect, communicate and collaborate is a large barrier, and this book (I hope)—with it's contributions from 100+ educators—should move toward supporting better understanding. We need to see a "change in mindset" across education—the breaking down of stereotypical approaches to learning that inhibit and enslave free-range learners. If the teacher is the barrier to becoming global, the student must be allowed to take initiative otherwise they are missing out. Ask yourself, how can a K–12 learning environment allow students to complete 12 or 13 years of schooling today without providing a RANGE of online global collaborative experiences? How can teacher education courses provide graduates with no idea how to collaborate online locally and globally?

> "How often do our teachers as students have the opportunity to share their learning achievements with the world? Sharing, not marks, is surely the foundation of global postgraduate education" (Judy O'Connell, Australia, @heyjudeonline).

Unwillingness to Harness Online Technologies, and Policy Issues

Examine your learning environment carefully—do a digital audit if needed—what are the main obstacles between your learners and being able to fully connect and converse with the world? Maybe school policies need updating, maybe parent and community awareness meetings need to be held so that there is shared understanding of how *you* as a global educator have done your homework, done the research. Maybe the learning community needs reassurance, through policies and new curriculum designs that *you* have set up the learning experiences so that becoming global is possible, safe and therefore imperative to a modern learning outcome.

Gone are the days when the IT Manager (non-education) and IT Department dictated what educators could do in their classrooms. Do not put up with the situation where learning is blocked because of IT dominance and ignorance (as a colleague in Australia had to recently—told by her IT support that the use of Skype was against government regulations she was blocked at every corner until in desperation she facilitated life-changing global experiences for students through her own personal laptop that bypassed the school network!). Of course the way forward is not by stubbornness and obtuseness—it is by open communication and round table teamwork—*talk* with all stakeholders until there is a satisfactory outcome, remembering that there is always more than one way to do something. As someone who has worked in a country like China, finding alternative ways to connect globally is a daily practice and challenge!

> "Global cannot just be for the elite few. If we use technology effectively we can train teachers to infuse global content into any subject at any level through digital resources, and we can recognize teachers through digital badging" (David Young, CEO VIF International Education). **Read more about VIF in Case Study 4.8 in the ebook.**

Student Autonomy: Creation of the "Flat Student"

This is one of my favorite topics! In order to become global we need to develop student autonomy to build learning networks and communities of practice for collaboration, both local and global. Students need to be learning "flat"—including freedom to communicate across rather than up or down. We talk about the teacher as a connected and collaborative global learner, but we need to redesign the learning paradigm further to connect students (particularly at the middle and high school levels) more independently with others. The role of the teacher as activator or "learning concierge" for student network building is crucial. Knowledge construction via a non-hierarchical approach means the student must also learn to take responsibility for adopting independent and professional learning modes and not be reliant on the teacher as the conduit.

In *Next Generation Learning* Steve Wheeler (2012) shares ideas about Learning 2.0, where learning based on social constructivist ideals, is participatory, relies on interaction with other learners (I say, at a distance), and is not about what you know, but who you know. Learning 3.0, a semantic-based architecture of webs supports new ways of thinking and learning that are networked, multi-modal, based on connectivist theory and support the "collaborative" web (I say, online global collaboration).

How do we promote the networked student? How do we encourage learning autonomy so that students are not relying on an outdated, "unflat" learning system to launch them into their adult lives, or into their professional lives? What does student autonomy in learning look like? Some thoughts:

- Giving students choices within their learning environment for subject matter, approach and pace
- Project-based learning and authentic assessment
- Experiential or project-based learning modes
- Mastery-based learning
- Peer-review and peer interaction
- Alternative and agile approaches to digital scholarship
- Personalized learning
- Online global collaborative independence to learn with anyone, anytime, anywhere

If "normal" school is not supporting student autonomy for global connections, what alternatives exist now? Virtual school, home schooling, blended learning, distance education...What has this got to do with becoming global?

Student autonomy in learning: The level of control, autonomy and power a student experiences in an educational situation.

Global Educators and Social Change

Social change in this discussion refers to a paradigm shift to constructivist and connectivist teaching modes infused with online technologies that supports global and collaborative practices and student autonomy in learning. Before we consider social change we need to focus on pedagogical change—what is it global educators are doing well that is changing the learning paradigm for better outcomes? We know many educators at all levels are becoming more connected and even more collaborative, and many are now starting to consider what "global" looks like for them and their students. The practice of cosmogogy, learning while connected to the world using online technologies whereby the context of learning is "with" rather than "about", is starting to get traction. With digital technologies in the hands of learners, coupled with confident online global project and learning design capabilities, educators *will* effect change in the way they teach and learn, and *will* achieve the social changes we want to see in education.

"With the advancement of technology there is no other pathway except to go global. For those who do not believe this they will fall behind. Those who do not believe in "flat" connections—if they are not on the wagon they are off the wagon" (Larisa Schelkin, USA, @Larisa_Schelkin).

Get Involved in Becoming Global Today!

My final message is, get involved! Be an advocate for all things global and embed global collaborative learning across the curriculum—not just in isolated pockets. The K–12 online conference and the Global Education Conference, for example, are always looking for volunteers . . . get yourself in there! Be a communicator and a reliable contributor. Design effective learning opportunities that connect students with each other and see how through these collaborations better understanding about the world and how to solve its problems will be one important result.

Advocate for a pro-active and balanced online learning environment where students are able to freely connect, share and collaborate—and in fact encouraged to do so.

A Vision for the future....

"There has to be a shift in the way we teach at all grade levels to competency-based…... not age-based, and there should be more options for students and non-compulsory activities, and teamwork. It needs to be more student-led in collaboration with teachers to build understanding of why learners come to school. School needs to be a place where people come together to ask the right questions and generate solutions" (Ann S. Michaelsen, @annmic).

"There is nothing going to stop this! Young people need it and want to engage collaboratively. We cannot imagine the changes in technology over the next 10 years, but whatever comes will make interaction and collaboration easier" (Ed Gragert, USA, @egragert).

Stay strong, be resolute, and commit to becoming global. Good luck!

REFERENCES

Adichie, C. (2009). The Danger of a Single Story, Retrieved from http://www.ted.com/talks/chimamanda_adichie_the_danger_of_a_single_story.html

An, Y.-J., & Reigeluth, C. (2011). Creating technology-enhanced, learner-centered classrooms: K-12 teachers' beliefs, perceptions, barriers, and support needs. *Journal of Digital Learning in Teacher Education, 28*(2), 54-62. doi: 10.1080/21532974.2011.10784681

Arteaga, S. (2012). Self-directed and transforming outlier classroom teachers as global connectors in experiential learning. (Doctoral Dissertation, Walden University).

Arthur, C. (2006, July 20). What is the 1% rule? Retrieved from http://www.theguardian.com/technology/2006/jul/20/guardianweeklytechnologysection2

Berry, B. (2010). The Teachers of 2030: Creating a student-centered profession for the 21st century. *Center for Teaching Quality*. Retrieved from http://files.eric.ed.gov/fulltext/ED509721.pdf

Berry, B., Byrd, A., & Wieder, A. (2013). *Teacherpreneurs: innovative teachers who lead but don't leave.* San Francisco: John Wiley & Sons.

Bonk, C. (2007, October 5). USA today leads to tomorrow: Teachers as online concierges and can Facebook pioneer save face? [Blog post]. Retrieved from http://travelinedman.blogspot.com.au/2007/10/usa-today-leads-to-tomorrow-teachers-as.html

Boss, S. (2015, June 3). How teacherpreneurs spread good ideas [Blog post]. Retrieved from http://www.edutopia.org/blog/how-teacherpreneurs-spread-good-ideas-suzie-boss

Brown, J. S. (1999). Learning, working, and playing in the digital age. Paper presented at the American Association for Higher Education Conference on Higher Education.

Caples, Y., Casey, L., Cherian, G., & Espejo-Vadillo, X. (n.d.). Teacherpreneurs. Retrieved from https://docs.google.com/document/pub?id=13_zB_wki4A6mnYk0C8RdYUYS5h8JNw1N_p5jS5x2wkQ

Collaborative Society. (2013). Collaboration - on the edge of a new paradigm [video file]. Retrieved from https://vimeo.com/77240879

Corneli, J., & Danoff, C. J. (2011). Paragogy. In: *Proceedings of the 6th Open Knowledge Conference,* Berlin, Germany. Retrieved from http://metameso.org/~joe/docs/Paragogy-talk-PDF.pdf

Crowther, F., Ferguson, M., & Hann, L. (2009). *Developing teacher leaders: How teacher leadership enhances school success* (2nd ed.). Thousand Oaks, CA: Corwin Press.

Crowther, F. (2010). Parallel leadership: The key to successful school capacity-building. *Leading and Managing,* 16(1), 16-39.

Downes, S. (2005). An introduction to connective knowledge. Stephen's Web, 22, 2005.

Downes, S. (2006). Learning networks and connective knowledge. *Collective intelligence and elearning, 20,* 1-26.

Downes, S. (2008). Places to go: Connectivism & connective knowledge. *Innovate: Journal of Online Education, 5*(1). Retrieved from http://bsili.3csn.org/files/2010/06/Places_to_Go-__Connectivism__Connective_Knowledge.pdf

Edmondson, A. (2012). *Teaming: How organizations learn, innovate, and compete in the knowledge economy.* San Francisco, CA: Jossey-Bass.

Ertmer, P. A., Ottenbreit-Leftwich, A. T., Sadik, O., Sendurur, E., & Sendurur, P. (2012). Teacher beliefs and technology integration practices: A critical relationship. *Computers & Education, 59*(2), 423-435. doi: 10.1016/j.compedu.2012.02.001

Esterman, M. (2013, September 16). You own #teachmeet [Blog post]. Retrieved from https://mesterman.wordpress.com/2013/09/16/you-own-teachmeet/

Friedman, T. (2007). *The world is flat 3.0: A brief history of the XXI century.* New York, NY: Picador.

Fullan, M., Langworthy, M., & Barber, M. (2014). *A rich seam: How new pedagogies find deep learning.* London, UK: Pearson.

Gladwell, M. (2008). *Outliers: The story of success.* London, UK: Hachette.

Gore, A. (2013). *The future.* New York, NY: Random House.

Hanvey, R. G. (1982). An attainable global perspective. *Theory into practice, 21*(3), 162-167.

Hase, S., & Kenyon, C. (2000). From andragogy to heutagogy. *Ultibase Articles, 5*(3), 1-10.

Hett, E. J. (1993). *The development of an instrument to measure global-mindedness* (Doctoral dissertation, University of San Diego).

Kemp, C. (2014, July 29). From lone wolf to hunting with the pack - becoming a globally connected educator [Blog post]. Retrieved from http://mrkempnz.com/2014/07/from-lone-wolf-to-hunting-with-the-pack-becoming-a-globally-connected-educator.html

Kemp, C. (2015, February 20). 5 tips for managing a fast-paced Twitter chat [Blog post]. Retrieved from http://mrkempnz.com/2015/02/5-tips-for-managing-a-fast-paced-twitter-chat.html

Kotter, J. P. (1992). *What leaders really do.* Oxford, UK: Blackwell.

Krechevsky, M., Mardell, B., Rivard, M., & Wilson, D. (2013). *Visible learners: Promoting Reggio-inspired approaches in all schools.* San Francisco, CA: Jossey-Bass.

Kruse, S., Louis, K. S., & Bryk, A. (1994). Building professional community in schools. *Issues in Restructuring Schools*(6), 3-6.

Lee, M., & Ward, L. (2013). *Collaboration in learning: transcending the classroom walls.* Camberwell, Victoria: ACER Press.

Lemelson-MIT. (2009, January 7). Teens prepared for math, science careers, yet lack mentors [Blog post]. Retrieved from http://newsoffice.mit.edu/2009/lemelson-teens-0107

Lieberman, A., & Mace, D. P. (2010). Making practice public: Teacher learning in the 21st century. *Journal of Teacher Education, 61*(1-2), 77–88. doi:10.1177/0022487109347319

Limerick, D., Cunningham, B. (1993). *Collaborative individualism and the end of the corporate citizen: Managing the new organisation.* Chatswood: Business and Professional Publishing.

Limerick, D., & Cunnington, B., & Crowther, F. (2002). *Managing the new organisation: Collaboration and sustainability in the postcorporate world* (2nd ed.). St Leonards, NSW: Allen and Unwin.

Lindsay, J., & Davis, V. (2012). *Flattening classrooms, engaging minds: Move to global collaboration one step at a time.* New York, NY: Allyn and Bacon.

Lindsay, J. (2007, November 2). The straw, the camel and the ning [Blog post]. Retrieved from http://www.julielindsay.net/2007/11/straw-camel-and-ning.html

Lindsay, J. (2009, October 11). V-BISS day: Virtual, visible, vocal [Blog post]. Retrieved from http://www.julielindsay.net/2009/09/v-biss-day-virtual-visible-and-vocal.html

Lindsay, J. (2014, June 16). New world students crossing global borders. [Online presentation]. Retrieved from https://docs.google.com/presentation/d/1O8fiKfqHd5QulkMD0N8NqU7dF19_LS4W-zNKgx27Q0c/edit#slide=id.g34f3bc35c_2_75

Lindsay, J. (2014, December 5). Applause for student presenters: Global Education Conference 2014 [Blog post]. Retrieved from http://www.julielindsay.net/2014/12/applause-for-student-presenters-global.html

Lucier, R. (2012, June 5). Seven degrees of connectedness [Blog post]. Retrieved from http://thecleversheep.blogspot.ca/2012/06/seven-degrees-of-connectedness.html

Martin, J. (2011, September 20). Creating innovators with "Outlier teachers": A sneak peek at Tony Wagner's new book [Blog post]. Retrieved from http://connectedprincipals.com/archives/4588

McLoughlin, C., & Lee, M. J. (2010). Personalised and self regulated learning in the Web 2.0 era: International exemplars of innovative pedagogy using social software. *Australasian Journal of Educational Technology, 26*(1), 28-43.

Meister, J. (2012, August 14). Job Hopping Is the 'New Normal' for Millennials: Three Ways to Prevent a Human Resource Nightmare. *Forbes.*

Mills, K. A. (2010). A review of the "digital turn" in the new literacy studies. *Review of Educational Research, 80*(2), 246-271.

New Zealand Ministry of Education (2014, December 1). Connecting to share professional learning. Retrieved from http://future-focused.tki.org.nz/Schools/Newmarket-School/Connecting-to-share-professional-learning

November, A. (2012). *Who owns the learning?: Preparing students for success in the digital age.* Bloomington, IN: Solution Tree Press.

O'Neill, E. J. (2010). Integrated cross-cultural virtual classroom exchange program: How adaptable public schools are in Korea and the USA? S. Mukerji & P. Tripathi (Eds.). *Cases on Technological Adaptability and Transnational Learning: Issues and Challenges,* (pp. 284-310). Hershey, PA: IGI Global.

O'Neill, E. J. (2008). *Intercultural competence development: Implementing international virtual elementary classroom activities into public schools in the U.S. and Korea,* University of Virginia. Charlottesville, VA.

O'Neill, E. J. (2007). Implementing International Virtual Elementary Classroom Activities for Public School Students in the U.S. and Korea. *Electronic Journal on E-Learning (EJEL), 5*(3), 207-218.

Osler, A., & Starkey, H. (2010). *Teachers and human rights education.* London, UK: Trentham Books. ISBN 978-1858563848

Papa, R. (2011). *Technology leadership for school improvement.* Thousand Oaks, CA: Sage Publications.

Price, D. (2013). Open: How we'll work, live and learn in the future. United Kingdom: Crux Publishing.

Puentedura, R. (2013). SAMR and TPCK: An introduction [Slide show]. Retrieved from http://www.hippasus.com/rrpweblog/archives/2013/03/28/SAMRandTPCK_AnIntroduction.pdf

Rheingold, H. (2012). Toward peeragogy. *DML Central, 23.* Retrieved from http://dmlcentral.net/blog/howard-rheingold/toward-peeragogy

Rheingold, H. (Ed.). (2014). *The peeragogy handbook*. Retrieved from http://peeragogy .org

Rienties, B., & Kinchin, I. (2014). Understanding (in)formal learning in an academic development programme: A social network perspective. *Teaching and Teacher Education, 39*, 123–135.

Robinson, K. (2013). How to escape education's death valley [TED transcript]. Retrieved from http://www.ted.com/talks/ken_robinson_how_to_escape_ education_s_death_valley/transcript?language=en

Rooney, Ann. (2014, October 2). Fostering global digital citizenship [Blog post]. Retrieved from http://annrooney.edublogs.org/2014/10/02/fostering-global -digital-citizenship/

Rorabaugh, P. (2012, August 6). Occupy the digital: Critical pedagogy and new media [Blog post]. Retreived from http://www.hybridpedagogy.com/journal/occupy-the -digital-critical-pedagogy-and-new-media/

Salopek, P. (2013). Out of Eden Walk, *National Geographic*, Retrieved from http:// outofedenwalk.nationalgeographic.com/

Schmidt, T. (2015, February 14). Playing the mystery Skype game [Blog post]. Retrieved from http://corkboardconnections.blogspot.com.au/2015/02/mystery -skype-game.html

Siemens, G. (2005). Connectivism: A learning theory for the digital age. Retrieved from elearnspace website: http://www.elearnspace.org/Articles/connectivism.htm

Siemens, G. (2006). Knowing knowledge: Lulu.com.

Shareski, D. (2011, October 24). Stop saying "Rigor" [Blog post]. Retrieved from http://ideasandthoughts.org/2011/10/24/stop-saying-rigor/

Stommel, J. (2014, November 18). Critical digital pedagogy: A definition [Blogpost]. Hybrid Pedagogy. Retrieved from http://www.hybridpedagogy.com/journal/ critical-digital-pedagogy-definition/.

The Lemelson Foundation (2011, January 19). The Lemelson-MIT program releases its 2011 Invention Index [Blog post]. Retrieved from http://www.lemelson.org/ resources/news/lemelson-mit-program-releases-its-2011-invention-index

Thomas, D., & Brown, J. S. (2011). *A new culture of learning: Cultivating the imagina- tion for a world of constant change* (Vol. 219). Lexington, KY: CreateSpace.

Tolisano, S. (2012, June 7). Seven degrees of connectedness [Blog post]. Retrieved from http://langwitches.org/blog/2012/06/07/seven-degrees-of-connectedness/

Tolisano, S. (2012). Seven degrees of connectedness [Infographic]. Retrieved from http://langwitches.org/blog/wp-content/uploads/2012/06/7degreesofconnected ness.png.

Tolisano, S. (2014, December 21). 3 reasons why you should share and 3 things you can do to start sharing [Blog post]. Retrieved from http://langwitches.org/blog/2014/12/21/3-reasons-why-you-should-share-and-3-things-what-you-can-do-to-share/.

Tolisano, S. (2014, July 1). Taxonomy of a Skype conversation [Blog post]. Retrieved from http://aroundtheworldwith80schools.net/blog/taxonomy-of-a-skype-conversation/

Van Schaijik, S. (2014, October 5). Global digital citizenship [Blog post]. Retrieved from http://www.svanschaijik.blogspot.co.nz/2014/10/global-digital-citizenship.html

Van Schaijik, S. (2014, October 26). Beyond global connectedness, What's next?? [Video file]. Retrieved from https://youtu.be/caLJr1OmwTk

Van Schaijik, S. (2014, October 18). TeachMeetNZ running a session [Blog post]. Retrieved from http://sonyavanschaijik.com/2014/10/18/teachmeetnz-running-a-session/

Van Schaijik, S. (2015, March 20). TeachMeetNZ meets science [Video file]. Retrieved from https://youtu.be/A4wimf6NXtw

vitalsteve (2011, June 1). Ewan McIntosh TMNE11 TM5 talk [Video file]. Retrieved from https://youtu.be/N2nLmK_dTkQ

Veletsianos, G., & Kimmons, R. (2012). Networked participatory scholarship: Emergent techno-cultural pressures toward open and digital scholarship in online networks. *Computers & Education, 58*(2), 766-774.

Wagner, T. (2012). *Creating innovators: The making of young people who will change the world*. New York, NY: Simon and Schuster.

Wenger, E. (2000). Communities of practice and social learning systems. *Organization, 7*(2), 225-246. doi: 10.1177/135050840072002

Wenger, E., McDermott, R., & Snyder, W. M. (2002). Seven principles for cultivating communities of practice. In *Cultivating communities of practice: a guide to managing knowledge* (pp. 49-64). Boston, MA: Harvard Business School Press.

Wheeler, S. (2012, November 1). Theories for the digital age: Paragogy [Blog post]. Retrieved from http://steve-wheeler.blogspot.com.au/2012/11/theories-for-digital-age-paragogy.html

Wheeler, S. (2012, November 11). Next generation learning [Blog post]. Retrieved from http://steve-wheeler.blogspot.co.uk/2012/11/next-generation-learning.html

Whitby, T. (2012, August 6). How does #EdChat connect educators? [Blog post]. Retrieved from http://smartblogs.com/education/2012/08/06/how-edchat-connect-educators-2/

Whitby, T. (2015, February 16). What's a Twitter chat? [Blog post]. Retreived from https://tomwhitby.wordpress.com/2015/02/16/whats-a-twitter-chat/

Wiggins, G. (2012, January 7). What works in education - Hattie's list of the greatest effects and why it matters [Blog post]. Retrieved from https://grantwiggins.word press.com/2012/01/07/what-works-in-education-hatties-list-of-the-greatest-effects -and-why-it-matters/

Wolfer, D., & Harrison-Lever, B. (2007). *Photographs in the mud*. Fremantle, WA: Freemantle Press.

Wylie, J. (2015, July 17). Free mystery Skype curriculum for schools [Blog post]. Retrieved from http://jonathanwylie.com/2015/07/17/free-mystery-skype -curriculum-for-schools/

INDEX